The Articulate Computer

THE LANGUAGE LIBRARY
EDITED BY DAVID CRYSTAL

The
Articulate
Computer

MICHAEL McTEAR

Basil Blackwell
in association with André Deutsch

Copyright © Michael McTear 1987

First published 1987

Basil Blackwell Ltd
108 Cowley Road, Oxford, OX4 1JF, UK

Basil Blackwell Inc.
432 Park Avenue South, Suite 1503
New York, NY 10016, USA

in association with André Deutsch Limited,
105 Great Russell Street,
London WC1B 3LJ, England

British Library Cataloguing in Publication Data

McTear, Michael
 The articulate computer.—(The Language library)
 1. Linguistics—Data processing
 2. Man-machine systems
 I. Title
 006.3'5 P98
 ISBN 0–631–14009–3

Library of Congress Cataloging in Publication Data

McTear, Michael.
 The articulate computer.
 (Language library)
 Bibliography: p.
 Includes index.
 1. Linguistics—Data processing 2. Pragmatics—Data
processing. 3. Artificial intelligence. I. Title.
II. Series.
 P98,M33 1987 410'.028'5 86–29950
 ISBN 0–631–14009–3

Typeset in 10 on 12pt Sabon
by Cambrian Typesetters, Frimley
Printed in Great Britain by
Billing and Sons Ltd., Worcester

Contents

Preface

When I first conceived the idea of writing a book about what computers need to 'know' in order to be able to communicate with people in natural languages such as English, I believed that what was required was a model of how humans use language. I also believed that I knew quite a lot about human communication, having previously written a book about the development of conversational abilities in young children. I still hold to my first belief, but my second belief has been shattered. After two years of intensive work I find that there are still so many questions to which I have no answers. But I do not see this as a bad thing – indeed, it is one of the main reasons for attempting to model human intelligence on a computer in the first place, as questions can be brought to light which might not have arisen if we had conducted naturalistic observations or experimental studies.

Natural language processing is an interdisciplinary subject and so writing a book such as this entails making decisions about what to include and what to omit as well as working out what sort of reader to aim at. I have adopted a fairly thematic approach as I wanted to avoid producing a tedious catalogue of the history of natural language processing. I have included most of what I consider to be relevant and interesting, but obviously I had to be selective. I apologize to those whose work has not been covered here and to those whose work has been covered inadequately. As to my audience, I have tried to make the book amenable to a wide range of readers who are interested in how language is used, including linguists, psychologists, computer scientists, cognitive scientists and researchers in artificial intelligence. I assume some prior knowledge of linguistics – roughly what would be covered in an introductory course – but otherwise no technical background should be necessary. I hope I have managed to steer the right course and to avoid being too superficial for some readers and too technical for others.

While writing this book I have benefited immensely from the many helpful comments and criticisms of friends and colleagues. In particular I would like to mention Richard Caves, Bryan Crow, Alison Henry, Michael Johnson, Karen Maitland and Nigel Shadbolt. I have not always heeded their advice so all the deficiencies which remain are mine. I would like to thank David Crystal for his editorial advice and comments, and my daughter, Siobhan, for her help with the preparation of the diagrams. I am also grateful to Alasdair Gilmore, Chief Technician of the Faculty of Social and Health Sciences at the University of Ulster, who was always ready with his magic touch whenever my communications with the word processor became less than articulate. The copy-editor, Julia Allen, did a fine job and helped to clarify points in the text which may have been unclear.

Finally I would like to acknowledge the unfailing support and encouragement of my wife Sandra, who kept our children at bay while I withdrew for long hours to the attic to work on the book. I would never have finished on time without this support.

Michael McTear

Acknowledgements

Figure 6.1 is reprinted with permission of the publisher from W. G. Lehnert, 1981: A computational theory of human question answering. In A. Joshi, B. Webber and I. Sag (eds), *Elements of discourse understanding*. Cambridge: Cambridge University Press, p. 159. Figure 7.1 is reprinted by permission of the author from B. Grosz, 1978: Discourse. In D. Walker (ed.), *Understanding spoken language*. New York: Elsevier North Holland, p. 254. Copyright © 1978 by Elsevier Science Publishing Co., Inc. Figure 7.2 is reprinted with permission of the publisher from R. Reichman, 1985: *Getting computers to talk like you and me: discourse context, focus, and semantics*. Cambridge, Mass.: MIT Press, p. 26. Figures 8.1 and 8.2 are reprinted with permission of the authors from W. Hoeppner, K. Morik and H. Marburger, 1984: *Talking it over: the natural language dialogue system HAM-ANS*. University of Hamburg research unit for information science and artificial intelligence, report ANS-26, pp. 13, 31. Figure 9.4 is used by permission of the Association for Computational Linguistics from R. M. Weischedel and N. K. Sondheimer, 1983: Meta-rules as a basis for processing ill-formed input. *American Journal of Computational Linguistics*, 3/4, p. 170. Copies of the publication from which this material is derived can be obtained from Dr Donald E. Walker (ACL), Bell Communications Research, 445 South Street, MRE 2A379, Morristown, NJ 07960, USA. Table 8.1 is reprinted with permission of the publisher from E. Rich, 1979: User modelling via stereotypes. *Cognitive Science*, 3 (4), p. 346.

1

The Articulate Computer: Fact or Fiction?

It is probably true to say that most humans do not know how to communicate with computers. But it is also the case that computers do not know how to communicate with humans. This much will be obvious to any novice who has tried to interact with a computer. However, if more people are to take advantage of the power of modern information technology, it will be essential to develop an easier and more natural mode of communication between humans and machines.

At present the most common way of communicating with a computer is to type in appropriate data and commands at a terminal or on a microcomputer keyboard. This means knowing a computer language, such as BASIC or FORTRAN, which the computer can understand. Other possibilities include the use of a formal query language. Query languages are used for retrieving information from databases. They consist of symbols which are used in prespecified sequences determined by the structure of the database (see example 4 below for an illustration). There are also menu-controlled systems in which the computer may address the user in prepackaged natural language presented in the form of options from which the user can make a choice. Whichever option the user selects elicits particular actions from the computer, such as a display of requested information, the deletion of a file or the printing out of a file.

All of these methods have their disadvantages. Learning to program in a computer language is time-consuming and largely unnecessary as there are specially trained programmers to do such tasks. Imagine having to take a course in car design before being able to drive down the road. Query languages are also difficult to learn and at present there are almost as many different query languages as there are database systems. Menu systems, while being easy to use, restrict what can be communicated to a limited selection from within predetermined choices. In some cases this is acceptable but often it is not.

How useful it would be if we could communicate with computers in our own languages – in English, French, Japanese, Russian or whatever language we normally speak when we talk to people. Speaking is something which comes naturally to most people, whereas learning computer programming languages and formal query language systems does not. Moreover, when using natural language it is possible to have a much more flexible form of communication than can be obtained with any of the previously mentioned methods of human-computer communication.

But is all of this just fantasy? Is it just fiction? Science fiction has made us familiar with computers which use natural language to communicate. Indeed there are many well-known fictional computers ranging from HAL 9000 in Arthur C. Clarke's novel *2001: A Space Odyssey* through Asimov's robots to the Daleks in the popular television series Dr Who. Moreover the idea that computers might be capable of behaving intelligently has fascinated scientists since at least the time of Leibnitz; indeed the notion that intelligent behaviour might be describable in terms of some kind of formal system of calculation can be traced back to the ancient Greeks and the work of Plato. More recently, Alan Turing, regarded by many as the father of modern computer science, wrote in 1950:

> We may hope that machines will eventually compete with men in all purely intellectual fields. But which are the best ones to start with? Even this is a difficult decision. Many people think that a very abstract activity, like the playing of chess, would be best. It can also be maintained that it is best to provide the machine with the best sense organs that money can buy, and then teach it to understand and speak English. This process could follow the normal teaching of a child. Things would be pointed out and named, etc. Again I do not know what the right answer is, but I think both approaches should be tried.

Chess has long been regarded as a major challenge in artificial intelligence (AI) and computers have been developed which can play chess at the level of a grandmaster. However chess demands a special type of intelligence and very few people have the ability to play chess well. Other activities, which humans perform with apparent ease, such as recognizing objects visually and producing and understanding language, are precisely those activities which are hardest for computers. Indeed some would argue that programming computers to exhibit intelligent behaviour in these domains is not even possible (Dreyfus 1972; Searle 1980). Humans and computers differ in that humans are adaptable, they can observe patterns, detect relevance and handle unforeseen occurrences and anomalies. Computers, on the other hand, are accurate and fast processors of complex sequential logical operations. In other words, so the argument goes, computers should be used for tasks that are difficult for humans but should not be made to compete with humans in those areas where humans are superior.

Whatever we might feel about these issues, it is the case that considerable progress has been made in recent years in research which involves getting computers to understand and produce natural language. This book will be concerned with what has already been achieved, with what the future holds, and with many of the general and theoretical issues which arise along the way.

Why natural language?

The answer to this question may appear to be obvious, given the need for better communication between people and machines. In fact, research in natural language processing has been motivated by two main aims:

1 to support the construction of natural language interfaces and thus to facilitate communication between humans and computers.
2 to lead to a better understanding of the structure and functions of human language.

The first of these aims is practically motivated with the main goal being the construction of a system that will actually work, whereas the second aim is more theoretical and involves the use of computers as a test-bed of linguistic theory. This separation of aims simplifies the picture somewhat, but in general those whose primary interest is building working systems will seldom incorporate findings from theoretical linguistics or experimental psychology unless they are relevant to the task at hand. Indeed the system might have certain in-built limitations such as the restriction for practical purposes to a small subset of language. For this reason, work on natural language interfaces is often seen as being atheoretical and ad hoc. Nevertheless such work may also stimulate interesting theoretical ideas, and it is being increasingly argued that builders of more intelligent natural language interfaces will need to draw more extensively on theoretical research in natural language processing. We will look at some examples of actual natural language interfaces later. The second aim, on the other hand, is more theoretical and involves the use of computational methods as a means of testing theories about language. This use of computers to test theory has often been referred to as the *computational metaphor*. It requires that the theory be stated explicitly enough to be implementable on a computer and this is taken to be an appropriate way of testing the rigour of the theory.

Natural language processing stems from work in machine translation carried out in the 1950s, when it was hoped that computers would provide rapid and accurate translations of texts, particularly those of interest to readers in the military and scientific communities. The initial euphoria faded as the linguistic problems turned out to be more complex than was originally expected. Since then considerable advances have been made in linguistic theory and there have also been significant developments in the production of working systems which use natural language. AI has become an 'in' discipline and natural language processing is one of its key areas. In part this upsurge in interest was prompted by the announcement in 1979 of a major research programme, the Japanese Fifth Generation project. (The term 'fifth generation' refers to the hardware technology of a computer – for example, first generation computers were built out of thermionic valves, second generation computers out of transistors, and so on.) The Fifth Generation project has as a central aim: the development of a super-intelligent machine capable of storing, manipulating and acquiring information, solving problems by means of sophisticated inference routines, and interacting with human beings through speech, natural language and graphics. The Japanese project elicited a swift response in the USA, Europe and other parts of the world in terms of large-scale and heavily-funded research projects in AI. The Japanese believe that fifth generation computers will bring major benefits to mankind. Some of these benefits will derive from a wider use of knowledge and information processing in all areas of social and economic activity, including a more efficient management of natural resources and the improvement and streamlining of medical information and health care. Natural language will play an important role in such consultation systems as well as in machine translation systems which aim to improve international co-operation in information transfer. For these reasons it is important to know something about the articulate computer and it is hoped that this book will provide some of the answers.

What do we mean by the word 'articulate'? Jean Aitchison wrote an entertaining introduction to psycholinguistics, *The Articulate Mammal* (Aitchison 1983). This title gave me the inspiration for my title. However, there are several differences between Aitchison's book and mine. In her book Aitchison was concerned with questions such as:

Why do we talk?
How do we acquire language?
What happens when we produce or comprehend sentences?

She argued that other questions such as 'How do we talk to other people?' were outside her domain. In other words psycholinguistics was concerned with language processes within the individual rather than with the ways language is used to interact with others. In the present book the meaning of the word 'articulate' will be extended to include those aspects of language which are involved when people communicate with one another. I would argue that this aspect of language is central, as communication is one of the primary functions of language. This does not mean that traditional areas of linguistic enquiry, such as syntax and semantics, are to be excluded. However these areas have already been extensively covered in theoretical and computational linguistics, whereas the areas of discourse and dialogue are less clearly understood. So for this reason too greater emphasis will be put on the investigation of the communicative functions of language rather than on its formal structural characteristics.

One further point needs to be clarified at this stage. When we think of an articulate computer, we might imagine a system that can talk to us and understand what we say when we talk back. In other words speech (in the sense of spoken language) would have to be involved. This book will not be concerned with the question of how computers recognize and produce speech. Instead the simplifying assumption will be made that input to the computer is in typed form.

What is the justification for this approach? There are two responses; one is based on the way research in natural language processing has been conducted while the other is of a more practical nature. As far as the first reason is concerned, until recently there were two quite different traditions in computational linguistics. On the other hand, a considerable amount of attention was devoted to the analysis of speech sounds. This work which involves processing acoustic data in order to represent them in terms of phonetic symbols, and ultimately in words, is often referred to as *speech recognition*. In the main, work on speech recognition has been concerned with the analysis of isolated words or phrases within limited vocabularies of approximately 100 words, with training sessions required for each new speaker. The second approach has taken words as given, usually dealing with input typed into the computer at a terminal, and has been concerned with issues such as the syntactic, semantic and pragmatic analysis of the input. Some recent work has involved the integration of these traditions in the development of large-scale systems capable of understanding connected speech and drawing on multiple sources of knowledge in the process (see, for example, Walker 1978). It is outside the scope of this book to give a detailed account of the technical issues involved in speech recognition though it is clear that future work will need to address further the integration of all linguistic levels in speech understanding systems.

Some examples

At this point it might be helpful to look at some examples of what has been achieved in natural language processing. As mentioned earlier, some systems were developed mainly in order to investigate questions concerned with the nature of human language. The first example, which is taken from the program SHRDLU, is one of the best-known of such systems. Other natural language systems were developed for more practical ends, mainly as interfaces to databases and expert systems. We will present examples of each of these.

SHRDLU: a conversing computer

SHRDLU – a name based on the second half of the 12 most frequent letters in the alphabet – was written in the early 1970s by Winograd (1972) in order to show that many features of natural language conversation could be simulated on a computer. The system operated within a very limited domain, a tiny world containing a box, a table, blocks and pyramids, which could be manipulated according to instructions from the user. In addition, the system could answer questions about its actions and could assimilate new information. The following extract illustrates some of these capabilities. (Note: in this and subsequent examples the convention will be adopted whereby the system's output is printed in upper case and the user's input in lower case, unless user and system are identified by 'U' and 'S'.)

(1)
1 pick up a red block
2 OK
3 grasp the pyramid
4 I DON'T UNDERSTAND WHICH PYRAMID YOU MEAN
5 find a block which is taller than the one you are holding and put it into the box

6 BY 'IT' I ASSUME YOU MEAN THE BLOCK WHICH IS TALLER THAN THE ONE I AM HOLDING
7 OK
8 what does the box contain?
9 THE BLUE PYRAMID AND THE BLUE BLOCK

This brief extract illustrates some of SHRDLU's advanced natural language processing abilities. For example: one of the main problems in discourse is locating the objects and persons to which reference is being made, particularly when pronouns and other referring expressions such as definite articles are used. In line 3 SHRDLU was asked to grasp the pyramid, but as there were three pyramids in the scene, it was not obvious which one the user meant. SHRDLU recognized the ambiguity in this instruction and informed the user accordingly. Similarly in line 5 the pronoun *it* could refer either to the block which was being held by SHRDLU or to the taller block which SHRDLU was to find. The system had built in heuristics (rules of thumb) for selecting the most likely alternative and informed the user which choice had been made (just in case it was the wrong one).

Even more impressively, as the next extract shows, the system was able to keep track of previous events which had happened during the interaction with the user and was able to answer questions about why and how it had done certain things.

(2)
1 had you touched any pyramid before you put the green one on the little cube?
2 YES, THE GREEN ONE
3 when did you pick it up?
4 WHILE I WAS STACKING UP THE RED CUBE, A LARGE RED BLOCK AND A LARGE GREEN CUBE
5 why?
6 TO GET RID OF IT
7 why did you do that?
8 TO CLEAR OFF THE RED CUBE
9 why did you clear off that cube?
10 TO PUT IT ON A LARGE GREEN CUBE

It might be argued that these conversations are very trivial and far removed from what people might normally want to say to computers. It has to be admitted that SHRDLU was extremely limited in its conversational domain, being able only to talk about its tiny world of blocks and pyramids. The system lacked generality – it was unable to discuss anything outside its own world – and even here its knowledge was severely restricted. For example, although the system had knowledge of the geometric specifications of the blocks, it had no knowledge of other attributes such as their weight. Such knowledge would play an important role in a human's planning processes when manipulating large objects. Nevertheless SHRDLU was quite innovatory in comparison with other systems developed in the late sixties and early seventies and it embodied many important principles which have been taken up in later research. Not only that, SHRDLU made people aware of the complexity of the problems which had to be resolved and this has resulted in greater respect for what is involved in the use of language by humans. We will come back to SHRDLU in greater detail in chapter 5.

Natural language interfaces for databases

One of the most widely developed areas in natural language processing is question-answering, where the main application is as a component of an intellectual 'front-end' to a database. An intelligent front-end to a database has two principal functions. First, it relieves the user of the need to be familiar with the structure of the database so that the system at the back-end can produce what the user is requesting in terms of the ways in which it is organized in the database. Second, by providing the facility to interact in the user's natural language, it makes the system more convenient and more flexible. The most usual procedure is that the user's natural language query is translated automatically into a statement in a formal query language which is appropriate to the database. Following this a natural language response is generated on the basis of the retrieved information. One of the most successful early question-answering systems was LUNAR (Woods et al. 1972). LUNAR could answer natural language queries to a database containing information about moon rocks. A more recent system is INTELLECT, which has been used widely as a front-end for commercial databases (Harris 1984). INTELLECT could accept queries such as the following:

(3)
I wonder how actual sales for last month compare to the forecast for people under quota in New England.

This may seem a simple enough question, but it involves a number of complex operations. The system has to print out the names of people under quota in New England, their actual sales for July 1982, their estimated sales for the same month, calculate the change by subtracting the second figure from the first, and return the percentage change by dividing this result by the figure for actual sales and multiplying by 100.

This all sounds much more complex than the original query, yet it would all have to be specified for the computer. In fact the query might be expressed in a so-called 'friendly' computer query language as follows:

(4)
PRINT LNAME, 82–JUL–ACT–SALES, 82–JUL–EST–SALES, 82–JUL–ACT–
SALES – 82–JUL–EST–SALES, (82–JUL–ACT–SALES – 82–JUL–EST–SALES) /
82–JUL–ACT–SALES,
IF REGION = 'NEW ENGLAND' AND
82–YTD–ACT–SALES < 82–QUOTA

The careful reader should be able to ascertain that this is a specification in formal terms of what is required by the request in 3. How much easier it is for the user to say 3 rather than 4.

Once INTELLECT had interpreted the user's query, it echoed it back to the user in a semi-formal way so that it could be checked and corrected, if necessary, before data retrieval began. For the query in 3 this would result in the following echo:

(5)
PRINT A COMPARISON OF LAST NAME, 82–JUL–ACT–SALES AND 82–
JUL–EST–SALES OF ALL SALES PEOPLE WITH REGION = NEW ENG-
LAND AND 82–YTD–ACT–% QUOTA < 100.00

The final result might be something like the following:

(6)
THE NUMBER OF RECORDS TO BE SEARCHED IS 40

LAST NAME	1982 JULY ACT SALES	1982 JULY EST SALES	CHANGE	% CHANGE
SMITH	54,474	52,868	1,606	+2.95
ALEXANDER	54,833	52,936	1,897	+3.46

As can be seen, it is obviously much more convenient if the user can input the query in his or her own language than in the more complex formal query language.

Expert systems

An expert system stores knowledge in the form of facts and rules about a particular domain e.g. medical diagnosis or oil well exploration. Aside from the problems of the acquisition and representation of this knowledge, there is the issue of interaction with the user. A natural language interface could be used here in two ways: to permit interaction with an expert so that the system can acquire further knowledge, and to permit interaction with a non-expert user who is seeking advice from the system. Probably the best-known expert system is MYCIN, which performs medical diagnosis (Shortliffe 1976). Systems such as MYCIN were implemented on large mainframe computers. More recently, however, smaller yet powerful systems have been developed for microcomputers. The next example is a case in point. It illustrates an interaction between a user and a system which gives advice about entitlement to supplementary benefit in Great Britain – advice which is useful in a time of widespread unemployment (Hammond 1983). The rules are written in the form of conditional statements such as:

(7)
if x is currently resident in Great Britain:
    and x is excused registration or has registered for work;
    and x needs financial help;
    then x is entitled to supplementary benefit.
(Note: in the actual system the rules are written in a form which is less 'natural' than the form which is being used here for ease of exposition.)

The rules consist of a series of conditions which all have to be fulfilled. The rules can themselves be stated in terms of further rules. For example, the rule about financial help is roughly as follows:

(8)
x needs financial help if:
    x's capital is less than the maximum capital allowed for supplementary benefit;
    and x's requirements are at least equal to x's resources.

On the basis of these rules the user can find out whether someone is entitled to supplementary benefit and the system will ask questions in order to obtain the information which it requires to verify whether the conditions for entitlement have been met. The following is an example of an interaction:

(9)
is Peter entitled to supplementary benefit?
WHAT IS PETER'S SEX?
male
HOW OLD IS PETER?
23

IS PETER IN FULL-TIME EDUCATION?
no
IS PETER IN FULL-TIME EMPLOYMENT?
no

The user could also ask *why*-questions concerning the reasons for the system's questions and decisions. For example, in the interaction quoted below, the system pronounced that Peter was not entitled to supplementary benefit. On being asked *why?* the system ran through all the rules, indicating which were fulfilled, until it came to the rule about needing financial help.

(10)
NO I CANNOT CONFIRM THAT PETER IS ENTITLED TO SUPPLE-
MENTARY BENEFIT
why?
PETER IS ENTITLED TO SUPPLEMENTARY BENEFIT COULD BE DEDUCED
FROM THE RULE (runs through the rules)
PETER IS DISQUALIFIED BY SEX IS UNTRUE
PETER IS A JUVENILE IS UNTRUE
BUT PETER NEEDS FINANCIAL HELP IS NOT TRUE
why?
PETER NEEDS FINANCIAL HELP COULD BE DEDUCED FROM THE RULE
(cites rule about financial help)
why?
PETER CAPITAL 2600
SUP-BEN MAX-CAPITAL 2500
2600 LESS 2500 IS NOT TRUE

The strength of a system such as this is that it is able to store and process a large amount of information in the form of rules. Often human advisers do not have full knowledge of all the necessary rules in order to give advice on problems such as supplementary benefit. But, more importantly for our purposes, a system such as this can interact with the user in the user's own language, thus being more convenient and more flexible. As mentioned earlier, this system, like most other similar systems including MYCIN, is limited in its natural language capacity. The user is expected to give short responses and ask *why*- and *how*-questions, following which the system retrieves the appropriate rules and displays them in an appropriate form, often using simple templates and substitution tech-niques to produce a language-like response. Obviously much work needs to be done before expert systems can be provided with a more human-like language ability. One thing is certain though – the ability of the system to perform adequately depends on a complex interaction between its knowledge information processing and its linguistic abilities. The role of knowledge in language processing will be a key topic of this book.

About this book

Natural language processing is interdisciplinary: it draws on insights from subjects such as linguistics, psychology and AI. But the assumptions which underlie work in each of these areas are different. It is important to appreciate what these differences are, and so Chapter 2 will be concerned with exploring basic issues in natural language processing such as the respective contributions of linguistics, psychology and AI, how relationships between different levels of language – syntactic, semantic and pragmatic – are handled, and how linguistic knowledge is represented in terms of grammars and similar structures for the computer. Chapter 3 will then look at how these structures are handled by the computer in natural language processing. Basic terms and concepts which will be necessary for subsequent chapters will be introduced and exemplified. In this way these two chapters will provide a general introduction to natural language processing, reviewing issues and methods.

The main point of this book is to examine what is involved in getting computers to use language for communication. However the focus will not be on how this ability is to be programmed into a computer but on what knowledge structures are involved. In a way the book is more about what underlies human communication than about computers. However the results of attempting to implement language behaviour on computers provides useful insights into human behaviour, therefore much of the book will be concerned with examining natural language systems as well as the theoretical issues which they address. For this reason chapters 4 and 5 will be devoted to a review of some early work in natural language processing. The justifications for this are not simply historical – indeed, examination of a number of early systems will show clearly what some of the difficulties are in this extremely complex area as well as some of the ways in which these difficulties have been tackled. It is also interesting to note how many more recent developments have their basis in this early work. Some well-known favourites, such as ELIZA and SHRDLU, will be discussed here along with a few less familiar systems.

One of the major insights of natural language processing is that the ability to produce and understand language does not depend on linguistic knowledge alone. Indeed, it is argued by some that linguistic knowledge plays only a small part in this process. Roger Schank, one of the pioneers of AI research into language, goes so far as to claim that 'understanding a sentence involves all the knowledge we have so far acquired about what goes on in the world' (Schank 1984: 17). In other words, not only linguistic knowledge but also knowledge of the world, referred to hereafter as world knowledge, is involved. How the two are related is an open and controversial issue, but clearly any discussion of natural language processing has to involve some discussion of the role of knowledge, of what constitutes this knowledge and of how it is to be represented. These important issues will be discussed in chapters 6, 7 and 8. Chapter 6 will be concerned with knowledge about objects and events, chapter 7 with knowledge of discourse structure and chapter 8 with knowledge of dialogue – how what we know about our dialogue partners' intentions, plans and characteristics has a bearing on how we process what they say. These chapters will be concerned with structures such as frames, scripts, tasks and speech acts.

Communication can always go wrong – indeed, breakdowns in communication occur regularly in most normal conversation, although they are usually remedied routinely and so pass almost unnoticed. Chapter 9 will deal with communication failure and will look at how computers have been programmed to deal with ill-formed input and to avoid creating false impressions with their output. Some comparisons will be made with how humans deal with these problems.

The final chapter will point to the way ahead for natural language processing. If computers are to use language to communicate with people, then they will probably have to learn to use language in the way that people do. Some research which has compared communication across a variety of modalities will be examined in this chapter. The chapter will also review some work on the generation of language, a topic which has been relatively neglected in natural language processing.

Further Reading

Artificial intelligence

There is a wide range of books on artificial intelligence. Raphael (1976), Michie and Johnston (1984), Schank (1984) and Winston and Prendergast (1984) are all good introductions, while McCorduck (1979) presents an historical review of research in AI. Boden (1977) is an excellent intermediary level account of the relationships between AI and psychology. There are several more advanced standard textbooks written for students from a computer science background. These include Rich (1983), Charniak and McDermott (1985) and Winston (1984). O'Shea and

Eisenstadt (1984) and Yazdani (1986) are useful collections of readings on a wide range of topics in AI. Finally, there is a three volume *Handbook of Artificial Intelligence* (Barr and Feigenbaum 1981) which contains articles on each of the major topics in the field. The major journals are *Artificial Intelligence, Cognitive Science, Computational Linguistics* and the *International Journal of Man-machine Studies*. See also *AI Magazine, AI Review* and the *AISB Quarterly*.

Human–computer interaction

Probably the best introduction to this topic is Gaines and Shaw (1984) which covers a wide range of modes of human-computer communication, including natural language. Tennant (1981) is an extensive review of natural language understanding systems which also includes introductory discussions of many topics in natural language processing.

2

Natural Language Processing: Some Preliminaries

It has already been pointed out that language is something which comes naturally to humans but is difficult for computers. A sample of human dialogue will illustrate what is involved in the everyday use of language. This extract, taken from a service encounter between two humans (Levinson 1938: 305), includes many features of everyday talk which we take for granted. It illustrates some of the difficulties which computer-based systems will have to overcome:

(1)

1	B	. . . I ordered some paint from you uh a couple of weeks ago some vermillion
2	A	yuh
3	B	and I want to order some more the name's Boyd
4	A	yes / / how many tubes would you like sir
5	B	an—
		u:hm (.) what's the price now eh with VAT do you know eh
6	A	er I'll just work that out for you=
7	B	=thanks
		(10.0)
8	A	three pounds nineteen in a tube sir
9	B	three nineteen is it=
10	A	=yeah
11	B	e:hh (1.0) yes u:uhhm ((dental click)) ((in parenthetical tone)) e:h jus-justa think, that's what three nineteen
12		that's for the large tube isn't it
13	A	well yeah it's the thirty seven ccs
14	B	er, hh I'll tell you what I'll just eh eh ring you back I have to work out how many I'll need. Sorry I did— wasn't sure of the price you see
15	A	okay

(Transcription conventions:
/ /   indicates point at which current utterance is overlapped by that transcribed below
=   indicates 'latched' utterances, with no gap
(.)   a short pause below about 0.2 seconds duration
(0.0) length of pause, in tenths of seconds
(—)   indicates a cut-off in mid-speech)

What would a computer need to know in order to be able to understand
this dialogue? To begin with, it would need to be able to work out what
the individual words were on the basis of the sounds it heard. It would
also need to know what the words meant and to know whether words
such as *order* and *paint* are to be treated here as nouns or as verbs. There
are several culture-dependent items of vocabulary which would need to
be understood, such as *VAT*, *pounds* and *ccs*. Would it know, for
example, whether the paint is expensive or not? In order to work out
what was meant by each sentence in the dialogue, the system would have
to have some knowledge of the grammar of English and of how meanings
can be derived from the particular combinations of words presented here.
Considerable work has already gone into providing computers with
knowledge of the vocabulary and grammatical structures of a language.
But being able to understand a dialogue such as this does not stop here.
There are many additional problems which are only coming to light as
researchers aim for a more human-like language processing capacity in
their computers. Let us consider some of these issues.

As can be seen, this encounter is resolved smoothly and satisfactorily
as far as the participants are concerned, the language used is natural and
typical of the style of fairly casual speech, yet there are many features
which would prove difficult to implement on a computer. To begin with,
there are the features of natural conversation such as the hesitations
(marked by *uh*, *er*, *uhm* and unfilled pauses), the false starts in which one
grammatical structure is cut off in mid-production and replaced,
sometimes only partially, by another (B's last sentence is a good
example), not to mention other nuances which are conveyed paralinguis-
tically, for example, by the use of parenthetical tone. These features are
characteristic of casual conversational style and would not, of course, be
relevant to most current natural language systems which respond to
typed input.

The use of ellipsis in discourse may also cause problems, although
some systems have ways of handling this. To take an example: in line (3)
B wants to order 'some more' – but some more what? – some more paint,
or some more vermillion paint? Here it is likely to be the latter, but it is
not always the case that ellipical elements refer back to the most recently

mentioned object. Several more cases of ellipsis occur in this short dialogue and in each instance the natural language understanding system would have to fill in the missing object by searching back in the preceding discourse for a suitable candidate.

There is one further feature which would be likely to cause problems – the structural relations between the utterances in the extract. The simplest structure might be a series of questions and answers in sequence, where each question-answer pair was independent from the rest. That way there would be no need for the system to keep track of what had been said previously as each question-answer pair could be treated in isolation from the rest. Many systems can only deal with this simple structure. Furthermore they would not notice if the same question were to be repeated many times and they would simply answer in the same way each time too. Thus the sequence would be something like

Q1–A1
Q2–A2
Q3–A3
Q4–A4
etc.

One step further would be a system which kept track of what was said previously. Such a system would have to handle ellipsis and anaphoric reference, as it would need to refer back to previously mentioned objects in order to make sense of otherwise incomplete sentences or of pronouns. In addition the system would also need to be able to keep track of what was going on in the situation so that it could make sense of subsequent utterances, to know why something was being said and to know what things it ought to be saying. For example: it would need to know that, when a customer is considering buying some paint, finding out the price is a relevant thing to do. If the price is more than the customer expected, he may not wish to proceed with the purchase, in which case the initially stated goal of ordering more paint is cancelled, or at least suspended. The system might also wish to ask the customer what he needs the paint for, as this might help in the recommendation of the amount and type of paint required. On the other hand, it would not be appropriate to ask other questions not relevant to this situation, such as what the customer had for dinner or whether he is faithful to his wife. Such knowledge involves scripts for situations such as shopping as well as a more general understanding of goals and how these can be achieved.

It can also be noted that the discourse structure of this extract is not entirely straightforward. The first question (*how many tubes would you like sir)* is not answered immediately and indeed the answer which is eventually given (B's final turn in the extract) is rather an account for the lack of an answer than an answer itself. Between the original question and this answer there are several other question-answer pairs, into which other question-answer pairs are inserted. So, in effect, the structure looks something like the diagram shown in figure 2.1. As can be seen, the structure is complicated. It is not the case that questions receive straightforward answers and any goal-directed system would need to be able to work out what was going on. For example, if the system's initial goal is to find out how many tubes of paint the customer wants, it has to be prepared to be sidetracked into several subsidiary goals before the initial goal is addressed, and, as we have seen, the answer to this is not straightforward either. We will see in later chapters how some natural language understanding systems have been programmed to deal with simple versions of these problems. What should be noted for now is that there is no indication that the people involved in this transaction had any difficulty in coping. In other words, what we take for granted turns out to be extremely complex when we try to make it explicit in a computer program.

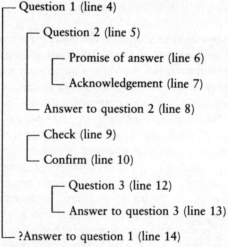

Figure 2.1   Structure of service encounter

Natural language processing: what is involved?

Natural language processing is a branch of AI. It may also be referred to as *computational linguistics*, although this term also covers the use of computers to analyse large corpora of language texts – for example, for the purpose of stylistic analysis – where there is no attempt to get them actually to produce or understand language (see Butler 1985 for a recent text on this use of computers in linguistics). Natural language processing draws on theoretical linguistics, psychology and computer science in particular and it can be expected that as computers become more human-like in their behaviour there will also be contributions from sociology and sociolinguistics.

There are two important distinctions in natural language processing which will be considered in this section:

1 the relationship between how language is structured and how it is processed.
2 the interrelationship between different levels of language.

The first distinction is often referred to in AI circles as a distinction between *representation* and *control*. Representation refers to how knowledge structures are to be represented in a system, while control refers to how these structures are to be processed. The second distinction involves the ways in which language can be analysed at a series of different levels – phonetic, syntactic, semantic and pragmatic. It has often been convenient, particularly for linguists, to treat these levels as distinct and indeed each level has given rise to extensive specialized research. In natural language processing, however, it is necessary to consider interrelationships between the levels – to explore, for example, how semantic information can assist in the syntactic analysis of a sentence. We will look at some examples shortly.

Language: product or process?

When we analyse language, we may be concerned with any of the following three phenomena:

1 the language itself.
2 the output or product of the language system.
3 the processes which result in language production and comprehension.

These different approaches to language are illustrated in figure 2.2. The left hand side of figure 2.2 reflects the fact that many linguists are concerned with the study of language as a system. In the case of Chomskyan linguists this involves characterizing the knowledge (or competence) of the ideal speaker-hearer of a language and abstracting away from actual language usage. The following quotation from Dresher and Hornstein (1976: 328) illustrates this concern.

> A study of competence abstracts away from the whole question of performance, which deals with problems of how language is processed in real time, why speakers say what they say, how language is used in various social groups, how it is used in communications, etc.

As a result of this direction in linguistics much energy has been devoted to the construction of grammars which consist of rules for combining words into sentences. Chomskyan linguists are not concerned with how the rules might be used in the production and comprehension of sentences, but rather with how the rules specify the permissible sentences of the language. In this way the rules are similar to the rules of formal proof in mathematics.

Moving on to the right hand side of figure 2.2, we come to a different aspect of linguistic enquiry which has a long history – the analysis of texts. This approach includes the work of field linguists interested in characterizing little-known or exotic languages by means of deriving sets of rules from samples (or corpora) of actually produced language. Another aspect of this approach can be seen in *discourse analysis*, which is concerned with finding patterns which reflect the large-scale organization of spoken and written texts. Whereas Chomskyan linguists are interested in virtual systems such as the knowledge underlying language

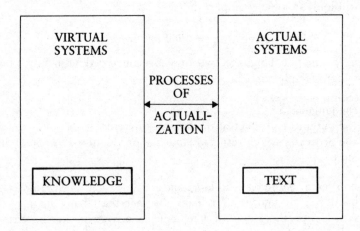

Figure 2.2   Approaches to language

use, field linguists and discourse analysts work with actual samples of language, that is to say, with the product of the system.

The middle part of the diagram, which is usually overlooked by representatives of both of these approaches, deals with the processes whereby knowledge of language is actualized to produce and understand texts. Psychologists devise experiments to study questions such as how language is processed in real time, while computational linguists are concerned with how grammars can be implemented in terms of parsing routines in a machine. Although their methods are different, both psychologists and computational linguists treat language as process rather than as knowledge or as product.

It is also important to distinguish between the approaches of computational linguists and of psychologists. Computational linguists aim for a model of language which embodies computational efficiency and achievement; psychologists, on the other hand, are concerned with models which are psychologically valid, which, in other words, reflect real human processes. It is important to keep this distinction in mind, although it has to be said that in many cases it is not always clear whether a computational model is making claims about human processes or whether it is motivated primarily by the demands of computational efficiency.

Levels of language

In order to appreciate what is involved in the question of levels of language, it will be helpful to examine the simple framework presented in figure 2.3. According to this framework, when we hear speech we perceive it in terms of an acoustic waveform which has to be analysed as a series of units of speech sounds. These sounds are grouped together into words and the words are grouped together into sentences to which we assign a meaning. Following this, the sentence is interpreted in terms of the speaker's intentions and other contextual information such as the preceding discourse and the situational context. Going in the other direction, when we wish to produce speech, we begin with an intention to communicate, select the meanings we wish to convey and the appropriate sentence structures, words and sounds. Our output is an acoustic waveform as was the input we heard and processed.

In a process model of language it is important to consider how these levels are related to one another. The simplest model would be a serial model similar to the framework presented in figure 2.3. Here the view would be that each level is autonomous and that information is passed in one direction only. In speech comprehension, for example, words would

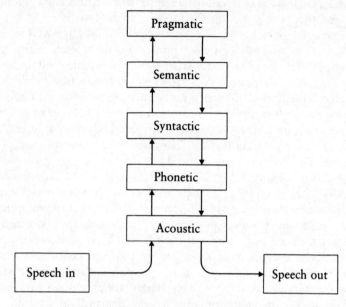

Figure 2.3 A simple model of language processing

be recognized before grammatical structures were analysed, and information about the meaning of the sentence would not be used to assist this grammatical analysis. This does not imply that all the words in a sentence have to be recognized before any syntactic processing can take place, but merely that information about the syntactic context of a word (for example, that the most likely next word will be a noun) would not be assumed to have been used in the recognition of individual words. A rather different type of relationship between levels is assumed in an interactive model as illustrated in figure 2.4. Here information is passed between the levels and information from higher levels can be used to assist in lower-level tasks such as word recognition. There has been a considerable amount of research in psycholinguistics on the structure of the language processor and particularly on the issue of interaction between levels. Much of this work is inconclusive and depends crucially on which of the many versions of serial and interactive models are in question (see Garnham 1985 for a useful summary).

We can illustrate the arguments concerning possible interactions between the syntactic and semantic levels by looking at the results of experiments on the comprehension of *garden-path sentences* (Crain and Steedman 1985; Milne 1982). A garden-path sentence is one in which the

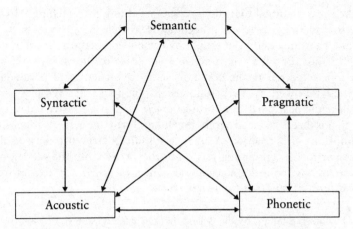

Figure 2.4   An interactive model of language processing

language processor (human or computer) assumes a particular structure for a sentence which turns out to be false. An example will help.

(2) The teachers taught by the Berlitz method passed the test.

When this sentence is processed, it is likely that the first phrase, *the teachers*, will be analysed as the subject of the verb *taught*. *Teach* is a transitive verb, so the next step might be to find an object for it for example, a noun phrase describing who or what was taught, as in:

(3) The teachers taught English,

or,

(4) The teachers taught the students.

When the phrase *by the Berlitz method* is encountered, it has to be assumed that the above analysis is false and an alternative analysis can be explored. For example the verb could be treated intransitively (with no explicitly mentioned object) and the phrase *by the Berlitz method* would refer to how the teachers did their teaching, as in:

(5) The teachers taught by the Berlitz method.

However, the second analysis runs into problems when the verb *passed* is reached, as a verb would not be expected at this point in sentence 5. The trouble lies with the verb *taught*. Until the phrase 'passed the test' is reached it is assumed that the teachers are doing the teaching. However once that phrase is reached, it becomes clear that the teachers passed the test and that they had been taught by the Berlitz method. In other words *taught* is not the simple past active voice form of the verb *teach*, which would be expected in the common sentence structure of Noun Phrase (Subject) followed by Verb followed by Noun Phrase (Object); rather *taught* is the past participle form of *teach* used in a passive construction which has been reduced from the fuller form *who were taught*. The assumption of a Subject-Active verb-Object structure has lead the processor to the wrong analysis – in other words, 'up the garden path'.

We can now consider a second sentence, identical to 2 except for the substitution of *children* for *teachers*:

(6) The children taught by the Berlitz method passed the test.

This sentence could also be analysed wrongly at first. However, Crain and Steedman found that their students classified example 2 as ungrammatical more frequently than example 6, indicating that the former presented greater problems in processing. One suggested explanation is that semantic information is used in the syntactic stage of processing, so that the fact that *taught* is a plausible verb to follow *the teachers* but not *the children* would account for the garden-path analysis. Similar results were found by Milne (1982) for the following sentences:

(7) The granite rocks during the earthquake.
(8) The granite rocks were by the seashore.
(9) The table rocks during the earthquake.

In these sentences the first three words could be analysed either as:

The	granite/table	rocks
determiner	noun used as adjective	noun

or as,

determiner	noun	verb

Only 7 was found to be difficult to understand, presumably because the more plausible interpretation is that *granite rocks* is a unit (a noun phrase), as in example 8. For 7 this interpretation would cause problems in respect of the analysis of the remainder of the sentence (*during the earthquake*), as no verb would be available to follow the subject *granite rocks*.

In natural language processing questions about interactions between levels are often determined on the basis of parsing efficiency so that if information from higher levels can be used to make processing more efficient then it is appropriate to use such information. To illustrate what is meant: if sentence analysis is carried out independently of semantic information, problems can be caused with words (such as *granite* and *rocks* in the example above) which can be analysed in different ways and with words with several meanings. A sentence containing seven words each of which had three different meanings would give rise to 3^7 (i.e. 2187) different readings. A sentence of fourteen words each with three different meanings would give rise to 4,782,969 readings. Obviously it would be inefficient to have to produce all these readings for subsequent analysis by the semantic level if most of them could be discarded earlier using higher-level knowledge.

The following set of sentences shows how semantic knowledge can constrain syntactic processing.

(10) John hit the boy with the cricket bat.
(11) John hit the boy with the red hair.
(12) John hit the ball with the cricket bat.

Example 10 in isolation from a context is ambiguous; we do not know whether John used a cricket bat to hit the boy or whether he used something else to hit the boy who was holding a cricket bat. The ambiguity arises from the prepositional phrase *with the cricket bat*, which could be attached to the verb *hit* or to the noun phrase *the boy*. There should be no ambiguity in 11 and 12, which are structurally similar to 10. Semantic knowledge would inform us that *with the red hair* goes with *the boy* and not with *hit*, since it is unlikely that red hair would be used to hit someone. Similarly in 12 *with the cricket bat* can be analysed more plausibly as the instrument of *hit* rather than as a qualifier of *the ball*, i.e. *the ball with the cricket bat* (compare *the boy with the red hair*). A system which did not have access to such semantic knowledge at the syntactic analysis stage would have to entertain both analyses and forward them on to higher levels for evaluation, obviously an inefficient method if one or more of the analyses is to be discarded. We will see in subsequent chapters how many computer systems utilize various types of higher-level knowledge to guide the analysis of the language input they receive. Indeed one argument for the use of higher-level knowledge is that humans can often respond to a sentence even if they have failed to recognize every word. It would seem that higher-level knowledge and expectations are thus brought to bear on the analysis. As a demonstration of the efficiency of such interaction between levels, it was found that one speech understanding system, HARPY, was 97% accurate in identifying words when combining phonetic, syntactic and semantic knowledge, but only 42% accurate when relying on phonetic knowledge alone (Lowerre 1976).

Representing linguistic knowledge

In the previous section it was pointed out that natural language processing is concerned with representing the structure of language and with using this representation to produce or comprehend language. The remainder of this chapter will examine some issues in representation, looking in particular at differences between the approaches of theoretical linguists and those of computational linguists, and at how language structure has been represented in grammars and other formalisms. Chapter 3 will look at how these formalisms are used by parsers to analyse sentences.

In order to simplify the discussion somewhat, it will be assumed that we are dealing only with representations of the structure of sentences and not with larger pieces of discourse such as stories or dialogue, which will be looked at in some detail in later chapters.

The analysis of a sentence involves assigning to it a syntactic and a semantic structure. The syntactic structure deals with syntactic relations between the words and morphemes in the sentence while the semantic analysis deals with the meaning of the sentence. Several issues arise from this which have been addressed widely in theoretical as well as computational linguistics. In theoretical linguistics there are arguments about the borderlines between syntax and semantics and, as far as meaning is concerned, between semantics and pragmatics. However these debates need not concern us here. More relevant to our purposes are debates within computational linguistics about the respective roles of syntax and semantics in the analysis of sentences. Broadly speaking, three different approaches have been adopted. In the first, a serial approach, the sentence is analysed syntactically before semantic analysis takes place. Some of the problems arising from this approach were discussed earlier. A second approach is to ignore syntax almost entirely and to build a semantic analysis directly from the input string. Semantic grammars and Conceptual Dependency theory, which will both be illustrated later, are examples of this approach. Linguists are critical of such approaches calling them theoretically unmotivated, yet they have been used effectively in computational systems. Finally the third approach is to allow the syntactic and semantic components to interact during the analysis of a sentence. Some examples of how semantics could assist syntactic analysis were discussed earlier and we will encounter the SHRDLU program, which uses this approach, in chapter 5.

Attention has already been drawn to the differences in approach to natural language processing adopted by linguists and by computational linguists. This point can be illustrated further by looking at how each group reaches decisions about which grammar to use as a basis for syntactic analysis. Within linguists many different types of grammar have been developed, and many of these have been used by computational linguists for natural language processing. These include the following: context-free and context-sensitive phrase structure grammars, transformational grammars, systemic grammar, lexical-functional grammar, generalized phrase structure grammar, and definite clause grammar. Winograd (1983) provides a thorough account of these grammars and evaluates them in linguistic as well as computational terms.

How do you choose from among such a wide selection of grammars? Your criteria will depend upon whether you are a theoretical linguist or a computational linguist. For many theoretical linguists the aim of linguistics is to develop a theory of language which will account for the linguistic competence of native speakers by providing a model of that competence. This involves the formulation of grammars for particular languages and, especially in the case of Chomskyan linguists, abstracting from these particular grammars the universal properties they all have in common. Thus a grammar for a particular language will consist of an explicitly formulated finite set of rules which will specify how to construct all the well-formed sentences of the language. A universal grammar will account for the properties shared by all human languages and will consequently contribute to a theory of the human mind.

Chomsky (1965) has provided a set of criteria for the selection of an adequate grammar. The first criterion is that the grammar should be observationally adequate, that is, it should be able to predict which sentences are (and which are not) well-formed sentences in the language. The second criterion is that the grammar should be descriptively adequate – that is, in addition to fulfilling the conditions of observational adequacy, it should be able correctly to assign syntactic, semantic and phonological structures to the sentence in a way which accords with native speakers' intuitions about these structures. Finally the third criterion is that the grammar should have explanatory adequacy. In addition to the previously mentioned criteria it is further required that the description of the language should be in terms of 'a highly restricted set of optimally simple, universal, maximally general principles which represent psychologically plausible natural principles of mental computation' (Radford 1981: 26). In other words, the rules proposed in the grammar should be stated as economically and generally as possible in order to model more plausibly how these rules might be represented psychologically in the human mind (and, as far as some linguists are concerned, to provide an adequate explanatory theory of how these rules might be acquired by a child learning language).

It should be pointed out that not all theoretical linguists would agree with the principles summarized here and in particular with Chomsky's criteria of adequacy. Indeed there are wide-ranging debates within linguistics about what constitutes an adequate theory of language and about what sort of grammar best accounts for a native speaker's competence. However most linguists would accept the principle that a scientific theory of language should incorporate principles such as exhaustiveness and consistency. In other words, the theory should be able to account for all the well-formed sentences of the language and it should be internally consistent. A third principle, that of simplicity (or economy) is often applied to scientific theories. In linguistics, for example, Chomsky showed that a transformational grammar required fewer rules than a phrase structure grammar and that the rules of transformational grammar captured more linguistically significant generalizations than those of a corresponding phrase structure grammar. This finding could contribute to a psychologically plausible theory of language and acquisition, if it is assumed that the use and acquisition of language are assisted by a system which requires a smaller number of rules which embody general principles. However in many cases discussion in theoretical linguistics is not concerned with the psychological plausibility of the theory but with its elegance and this can lead to the proposal of systems of rules which are simple, consistent and elegant but which are implausible from a psychological viewpoint. (The rule of affix-hopping in early transformational grammar is a case in point; see Aitchison 1978: 110–13 for a clear and introductory discussion.)

We can now look at how computational linguists evaluate grammars. It will be obvious from previous discussion that computational linguists are not necessarily interested in a universal theory of language. They will either be concerned with testing particular linguistic theories computationally or with developing working systems. A working system may have clearly circumscribed aims. For example, it may be required to deal only with a restricted subset of vocabulary and structures and it may be limited to a narrowly defined domain. An example of such a system would be a natural language interface to a data base on aircraft parts, which would need to incorporate vocabulary and structures associated with aircraft parts and possibly aircraft maintenance but would not need to know about anything outside this domain. Many computational systems have worked well within such self-imposed constraints and have no pretensions about modelling native-speaker competence or stating universal principles of language. So one essential difference concerns the aim of the grammar and, as far as computational linguists are concerned, even the lowest level of adequacy, that of observational adequacy, must be irrelevant.

On the other hand, computational linguists require grammars which will actually work when implemented in terms of a computer program. In other words the grammar must be computationally tractable. We can see the difference between the aims of theoretical and computational linguists if we consider the case of transformational grammar. Transformational grammar (by which is meant here Chomskyan linguistics including early transformational-generative grammar through several revisions up to recent government-binding theory) has been the dominant linguistic theory in the past few decades. Paradoxically this theory has not been used widely in natural language processing (though see, for example, Petrick (1973) for early work and Marcus (1980) for more recent work within the framework). Why should this be? King (1983) provides some answers in an article on transformational parsing. A transformational grammar is used in linguistics to define the well-formed sentences of a language. In natural language processing the grammar can be used to generate and analyse sentences. As a generator it starts from the base component of the grammar and produces surface strings by applying transformations to the output of the base component – that is, it goes from deep to surface structure by means of applying transformations to the deep structures. A parser applies these operations in reverse – it begins with the surface structure and looks for transformations to apply to the surface structure in order to arrive at the deep structure. In other words, forward transformations are involved in generation and backward transformations in parsing. Many of the difficulties which arise are too technical to describe here. However, two problems can be mentioned briefly. First, in parsing there is the problem of knowing what sequence of forward transformations might have produced a given structure. A reverse transformation might match, but it cannot be assumed that the corresponding forward transformation was used to produce the structure since different forward transformations may produce the same structure. If it is not possible to know which reverse transformation to apply, all the possibilities have to be tried and this can lead to the problem of combinatorial explosion in which large numbers of possibilities are generated, these in turn giving rise to the generation of further possibilities and so on until the situation quickly gets out of hand. Deletion transformations give rise to a second, but similar problem as it is impossible to reconstruct a tree in which a forward transformation has deleted an element because no information is available as to what is to be reconstructed and where. King (1983) discusses some of the ways in which these problems have been tackled. In some cases the solution has been computational, i.e. a computational technique has been developed to deal efficiently with the problem, while in other cases the problem has been eliminated as a result of developments in linguistic theory. One thing will be clear from this discussion: that when decisions about the adequacy of a grammar are being made, the criteria applied will depend on whether the question is being viewed from the perspective of a theoretical or that of a computational linguist.

Semantic approaches to language understanding

It might be assumed from what has been said so far that the main issue in natural language processing is how to discover the syntactic structure of sentences. Syntax has played a prominent role in theoretical as well as computational linguistics and considerable advances have been made by concentrating attention on this complex area. However syntactic analysis should not be seen as an end in itself. Rather, it should be used as a means of obtaining the basis for a semantic representation, that is, for getting at the meaning of what is said. A different approach is to disregard syntax entirely, or at least to minimize its role. This approach has been adopted widely in AI research and has led to the development of some very successful natural language systems. It is appropriate, therefore, to examine what sorts of representation are involved here. Two types of representation will be discussed – semantic grammars and conceptual dependency representations. As will be seen, they differ considerably in their theoretical significance. Semantic grammars have been used in natural language interfaces as a means of achieving results in a fast and efficient way. Little or no theoretical linguistic significance has been attached to these mechanisms. Conceptual dependency representations, on the other hand, have been proposed as a theory of how humans process language, the claim being that the role of syntactic information is minimal in this process. As both of these types of representation differ considerably from the grammars familiar to linguists it is appropriate to examine them in greater detail.

Semantic grammar

Consider a natural language interface to a database containing information about personnel in a large company. The system might be expected to answer some of the following questions.

(13) What is the name of the company director's secretary in the main branch?
(14) What are the salaries of clerical workers in region 28?
(15) What is the average age of managerial employees in each region?

Queries such as these fall into a recognizable pattern and probably involve a limited set of syntactic structures and a small set of lexical items. A system which embodied all the syntactic rules of the language would be wasteful in such a case and would probably be extremely inefficient and slow. An alternative would be to program the system to recognize every possible query it might encounter. However this would soon run into difficulties if any reasonable sized vocabulary were involved. Instead the solution has been to combine syntactic and semantic information into one set of rules in what has been referred to as a semantic grammar (Burton 1976). In such a grammar the basic terms are not syntactic categories such as noun, verb and adjective, but items of meaning which can be combined in certain specifiable ways, that is, according to patterns such as those illustrated in 13–15. The symbols of the grammar can either be actual words which occur frequently in queries, e.g. *what is, the, in,* or non-terminal symbols, such as ATTRIBUTE, PERSON and LOCATION, which are semantic categories representing the items which may occur in queries. Thus a pattern which would cover examples 13–15 would be:

(16) WHAT IS/ARE THE <ATTRIBUTE> OF <PERSON> IN <LOCATION>?

The symbols ATTRIBUTE, PERSON and LOCATION are non-terminals – that is, they can be further specified by the items which can fill these slots. In some cases these may consist of a simple set such as a set of attributes – name, age, sex, education, salary, etc. In other cases a semantic category might consist of further semantic categories, just as in a traditional syntactic representation higher level constituents such as NP (noun phrase) can consist of lower level constituents such as DET (determiner) and N (noun). The following is an example of some of the rules used in the system LADDER, a natural language interface to a large database about US navy ships and their characteristics (Hendrix 1977):

(17)
1 S→what is SHIP-PROPERTY of SHIP?
2 SHIP-PROPERTY→the SHIP-PROP / SHIP-PROP

3 SHIP-PROP→speed / length / draft / beam / type
4 SHIP→SHIP-NAME
5 SHIP-NAME→Kitty Hawk

Here the category SHIP-PROPERTY can be rewritten as *the* SHIP-PROP or SHIP-PROP, and SHIP-PROP itself can be rewritten as the terminal symbols *speed, length, draft, beam* or *type*. The same applies to SHIP which is rewritten as SHIP-NAME and then as actual names of ships. In this way the representational economies embodied in a conventional phrase-structure grammar can be utilized in a semantically based representation. This particular grammar (of which these rules are, of course, only a small part) would be able to enable the system to parse queries such as *what is the speed of the Kitty Hawk?* Rule 2 would also enable it to handle ungrammatical input which made sense in terms of the grammar, such as *what is type of Kitty Hawk?*, even though the definite article was missing. A syntactic parser would have problems with such a query as it would expect to find an article in front of a noun and it would be unable to proceed to parse the remainder of the sentence. Also many of the ambiguities which might arise during the course of a strictly syntactic parse would be avoided since some of the interpretations would not make semantic sense and so would not be permitted by the grammar. The following example, taken from Rich (1983: 321) illustrates this point.

(18) What is the closest ship to the Biddle with a doctor aboard?

A syntactic parser would have problems of the kind discussed earlier in this chapter with the prepositional phrase *with a doctor*, since it would not be able to determine whether it modified *ship* or *the Biddle*. A semantic grammar, which would require additional rules to those listed in 17, would resolve this by, for example, only allowing prepositional phrases which function as qualifiers to be attached to the category SHIP.

While semantic grammars are useful and efficient for certain purposes and have been used successfully in several large systems such as LADDER as well as the tutoring system SOPHIE (see chapter 4) they also have serious disadvantages, the main one being that they lack generality. As they are written in terms of a particular domain, they require a completely new set of rules for each new domain. Furthermore they fail to capture important linguistic generalizations and so extra rules have to be written to cover items which are similar syntactically but different semantically. This can lead to an explosion of rules which in turn leads to expensive and inefficient parsing. Thus semantic grammars have been used effectively to produce quick results in restricted language domains but they are not intended as theoretical contributions to the problems of language understanding and so would not be appropriate in a more general situation.

Conceptual dependency theory

Unlike semantic grammar, conceptual dependency theory (CD) claims to be a theory of natural language processing. The theory was first described in Schank (1972) and has since been refined and used as a basis for several large-scale natural language understanding programs, some of which will be described in chapter 6.

Conceptual dependency is based on the theory that language is used to describe events that take place in the world and that these events consist of actions which can be represented as conceptualizations. The emphasis is on the content of information and not on its form. Thus the level at which actions are represented is language-independent and any two sentences which describe the same action and are therefore identical in meaning will have a single representation for that meaning.

One of the basic elements of the theory is that representations are made up of a small number of semantic primitives which include primitive acts and primitive states. An example of a primitive act is ATRANS. This act represents any actions which involve the transfer of possession and is expressed in English by verbs such as *give, take, buy, sell, donate, steal* and *exchange*. Other primitive acts are PROPEL, which represents the application of force to a physical object, INGEST, which involves taking something to the inside of an *animate object* (as in eating or drinking), and PTRANS, which involves a change in location of a physical object. Associated with each of these acts (there are about eleven in all) are slots and specified slot fillers. For example, as already mentioned, the act INGEST requires its grammatical subject to be animate while PROPEL requires its grammatical object to be something physical. Relationships between items which fill these slots are called dependencies and include, among many others, dependencies such as the relationship between an actor and the event which he or she causes and the relationship between an act and the source and recipient of the act (as in transfer of possession, i.e. ATRANS). These conceptual dependencies are often represented diagrammatically and figure 2.5 presents some simple examples representing the sentences *John gave Mary a book* and *John got a book from Mary*. The arrows in the diagram illustrate the direction of the dependencies. The two-way arrow between *John* and the act ATRANS indicates a two-way link between an actor and an action, since neither actor nor action can be considered primary. The symbol P

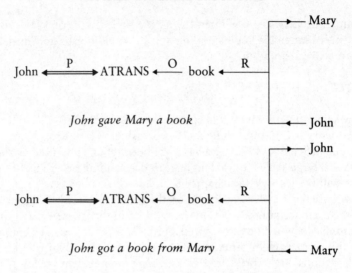

Figure 2.5   Conceptual dependency diagrams
(Barr and Feigénbaum 1981: 301)

indicates an action which took place in the past. Other symbols in this diagram are O, which represents the object case relation, and R, which represents the recipient case relation. As can be seen from the diagram, the only difference between the two sentences, as far as their conceptual representation is concerned, is the direction of the transfer of possession. In the sentence *John gave Mary a book* the book goes from John to Mary, while in the sentence *John got a book from Mary* the book goes from Mary to John.

All of this might appear rather elementary but the discussion has been restricted to simple examples for the purposes of illustration. More complex examples can be found in the sources cited in the list of additional readings at the end of the chapter. However, two important features emerge from this sort of representation. The first is that the representation includes all the information which is necessary for the understanding of a sentence, that is, whatever information is implicit in the sentence must be made explicit in the representation. The second principle, which follows from this, is that a conceptual representation of this sort permits various inferences to be made which would normally be associated with that conceptualization.

The first point, that information which is implicit has to be made explicit, is illustrated in the conceptual representation of the sentence *John eats the ice cream with a spoon* (figure 2.6). Here the main primitive act is INGEST, with *John* as actor and *ice cream* as object. There are further dependencies in this conceptualization: there is an instrument involved in this act of eating, namely the act of John moving the spoon, while the symbol D represents the directional movement involved in the act, the movement of the spoon to John and, because the spoon contains ice cream, the movement of ice cream to John's mouth. In other words what is represented here is that John eats ice cream by taking a spoon containing ice cream and moving that spoon to his mouth so that the ice cream enters his mouth. Notice that John's mouth was not mentioned explicitly in the original sentence but it is nevertheless part of the meaning of that sentence. Similarly if the sentence had read *John ate ice cream* the conceptualization would include a spoon, as the normal expectation is that people use spoons when eating ice cream (though only, of course, if the ice cream is in a cup or dish). Another example is the sentence *John drinks too much*. Here the object of John's drinking, which we would understand in this case to be alcoholic liquor, would have to be specified. All of this may seem obvious and even unnecessary, but as Schank (1984) points out, AI is the science of the obvious, where the task is to try and describe in process terms what is obvious to humans but not to computers. (As an interesting example Schank outlines what is involved in specifying an exact set of steps which would tell a two-year-old child or a computer how to eat – see Schank 1984: 78–81.) One problem is where to stop with the representation. In the ice-cream example we might wish to include the fact that John picked up the spoon, that to do so he moved his hand and so on. Some extralinguistic information is necessary for the comprehension of sentences and this information is represented explicitly in conceptual dependency diagrams.

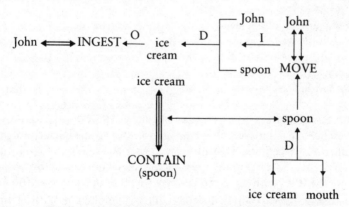

Figure 2.6   Conceptual dependency diagram for John eats the ice cream with a spoon
(Barr and Feigenbaum 1981: 302)

However, there is no principled way of constraining this process and of deciding how much of this information is required to understand a given sentence.

It was mentioned earlier that one of the strengths of the theory is that it permits normal inferences to be drawn from the representations. Again some of these inferences are obvious to humans but have to be stated explicitly for the computer. To take an example: in the sentence *John moved the book from the window ledge to the table* we can make inferences such as the following:

The book is now on the table.
The book is no longer on the window ledge.
John probably did this action for a reason.
If John wanted the effect of this action he is now probably pleased
    that the action has been achieved.

We can make these inferences because inferences are associated with the conceptual acts. So, for example, associated with PTRANS would be inferences that the moved object is no longer where it was earlier but is where it has been put, that the actor carried out the action for some reason, and that, given that people usually act with intention, the actor might be satisfied with the results of this action. Or to take another example, this time from Schank (1984: 100), if we hear the sentence *John sold Mary a book*, we can expect to make inferences such as:

Mary has a book.
John has money.
Mary wanted John's book.
John didn't want the book anymore.
John had already read the book.
Mary will read the book.
John needed the money.

These inferences are associated with the act ATRANS. As can be seen, the inferences deal with relationships such as the cause, effect, enablement and function of actions. One inference type, ACT-INFERENCE, deals with inferences arising when an actor and an object occur in a conceptualization with no act to connect them, as in *Mary told John that she wants his book*. It is not specified what Mary is going to do with the book, but the inference drawn is that she will want to read it, as that is the normal function associated with a book. In other words, the normal function which an object has is assumed to be the implicitly referenced act (for further examples and more detailed discussion, see Schank and Rieger 1974).

Enough has been said to illustrate the differences between conceptual dependency theory and conventional linguistic analysis. Conceptual dependency theory makes the claim that language understanding is knowledge-based and expectation-driven. In fact Schank argues that the word 'understanding' is a misnomer – we use language to express and organize what we know – and that when we interpret sentences we are involved in a process, not of working out their structure but of working out what they say in relation to what we know, and that what we already know enables us to make predictions about what we hear.

In a general sense we are guided by the overall context in which we hear something and this helps us to interpret it, as we will see in chapter 6 when we examine large-scale knowledge structures such as scripts. However this is also true in a more specific way in the interpretation of elements of a sentence. If we know, for example, what the main act of a sentence is, then we have expectations about what sorts of objects are associated with this act and we process the rest of the sentence with these expectations in mind. So, if we know that the act is ATRANS (transfer of possession), we will look for slot fillers such as the object being transferred, the receiver, the original owner and the method of transfer. Such expectations are also useful in the case of ambiguous sentences. One of Schank's own examples is *I saw the Grand Canyon flying to New York* which could be analysed as *I saw the Grand Canyon which was flying to New York*. However the conceptual information which would be brought to bear on the analysis of *flying* would prevent this parse, as *fly* cannot have a physical location functioning as its subject. A search would be made for an appropriate subject, which in this case would be *I*.

A similar solution operates for the problematic structure we have already encountered, example 10, in which it is not clear which element a prepositional phrase modifies. Rich (1983: 326–8) discusses the following examples:

(19) John went to the park with a girl.
(20) John went to the park with a fountain.
(21) John went to the park with the peacocks.

In 19 we would wish to attach *with a girl* as a modifier of *went* (he went with a girl to the park), while in 20 we would want to attach *with a fountain* to *the park* (the park which has a fountain). Example 21 would be ambiguous – either John took some peacocks to the park or he went to a park which had peacocks in it.

How would a conceptual analyser parse these sentences? To begin with, the main nouns and verb would be extracted by a syntactic processor which would, among other things, determine the category of the verb and notice the prepositional phrases *with a girl*, *with a fountain* and *with the peacocks*. At this stage the conceptual processor would take over and, having established what primitive act was involved, would look for fillers for the associated slots. It would combine this search with information about what roles can be filled by the object or person specified in a prepositional phrase. These would be as follows:

1 the object of the instrumental case.
2 an additional (animate) actor of the main act.
3 an attribute of the preceding object or person.
4 an attribute of the actor of the conceptualization.

Thus the first test would be whether *the girl* would be analysed as an instrument of John's action. *Girl* would not match these requirements so the next possibility would be tested. As *girl* is animate, it matches, and so the correct result is returned (John went with the girl to the park). As far as *the fountain* is concerned, the first two tests would fail but the third would succeed, yielding the correct analysis (the fountain is in the park). However, as Rich points out, test 2 would succeed for *the peacocks*, yielding the reading that John took the peacocks to the park. No other interpretation would now be considered, as one fundamental tenet of the theory is that each sentence should have one conceptual representation only even if the sentence is ambiguous on the syntactic level. The reason for this is that speakers usually intend their utterances to be taken unambiguously so the representation should reflect this fact by returning the most likely meaning. This procedure might not produce the most likely meaning for 21 and so some would argue for a prior syntactic analysis which would indicate the potential ambiguities and thus make them available for further analysis. (Note that reversing tests 2 and 3 would make the 'peacock' example work but would yield the wrong results for the example involving *a girl*, as an animate object such as *a girl* could function as an attribute of a preceding object or person, just as *the peacocks* did). One solution could be to aim for more detailed specification in the tests for prepositional phrases. Another would be to allow the context to disambiguate. The sorts of contextual knowledge which would be involved will be described in some detail in chapter 6.

To summarize: conceptual dependency theory differs considerably from traditional linguistic theories. It has been argued that conceptual dependency avoids a syntactic stage of analysis and builds a semantic representation directly from the input. As we have seen, this is not strictly true. Conceptual dependency does, however, de-emphasize the role of syntactic processing. In order to do this it assumes that both linguistic and world knowledge are involved in language understanding. Traditional linguistic theories tend to exclude world knowledge from their domain of enquiry. It is in this respect that they differ most from AI-based theories of natural language processing.

Further Reading

Linguistics

There are many good introductions to linguistics. Aitchison (1978), Crystal (1985) and Hudson (1984) are good places to start, while Brown (1984) provides an extremely readable overview of recent issues with a particular focus on theories of syntax. Winograd (1983) presents a comprehensive but more advanced review of major syntactic theories.

Psycholinguistics

There is a wide range of texts on psycholinguistics. Aitchison (1983) is a good introductory (and entertaining) account of language acquisition, speech production and comprehension, and of the psycholinguistic validity of transformational grammar. Clark and Clark (1977) is a standard text which covers the main areas in the psychology of language. Garnham (1985) is a useful account of psycholinguistics from a cognitive science and AI perspective. See also Greene (1986) for an introduction to language understanding from the perspectives of cognitive psychology and AI.

Natural language processing

In addition to the useful overviews of natural language processing which can be found in the AI textbooks cited at the end of Chapter 1, there are excellent accounts of the field in articles by Rosenberg (1981), Ritchie and Thompson (1984) and Ramsay (1986). Joshi et al. (1981) and Lehnert and Ringle (1982) are collections of readings on a variety of important issues in this area.

3

Parsing Natural Language

An introduction to syntactic parsing

It is important to distinguish between a grammar for a language and a parser. Linguists write grammars in which the rules specify the ways in which words can be combined to form well-formed sentences. By consulting these rules it is possible to ascertain whether a sentence is well-formed in the language defined by the grammar. In other words a linguist's grammar can be seen as a formal proof of the grammaticality of a sentence. These rules are not, however, a model of the process of how a sentence is generated or analysed in communication or in the processing of natural language by a computer. As far as the latter is concerned, there has to be a parsing procedure (or algorithm) which stipulates how the grammar rules are to be applied. A simple example will make this point clear. In a grammar there are likely to be many choices of which rule to apply at any given point in generation or analysis. For example, a noun phrase may consist of many different structures including the following: a pronoun, a determiner followed by a noun, a determiner followed by one (or more) adjective(s) and a noun, one (or more) adjective(s) and a noun without a determiner. A language processor has to be instructed how to deal with such choice points. If the first rule does not produce the desired result, do you go back and try the next rule? Should a record be kept of what has been analysed so far? How do you know when the analysis is complete? Although these questions are grossly over-simplified, they are representative of the sorts of issues which are involved in the use of a grammar by a language analyser. An example will be presented shortly to illustrate some of these processes.

Two things should be stressed from the outset. First, that what is being said here about parsing is concerned with machine processing of language. Parsing can be used in a general sense to refer to any type of language processing, by humans or by machines. Here no claims are being made about the psychological reality of the mechanisms to be described. One simple point will make clear the difference between human and machine parsing. In the present state of machine technology, input to the parser is accessed one unit at a time, the usual unit being a word. A sentence is considered to be parsed when each word has been assigned to a structure which is compatible with the grammar of the language. Although there are many refinements of this basic process, essentially what is involved is a word-by-word analysis of the input. There is no suggestion that a human parser proceeds in this way.

The second issue is that the examples in this chapter will be based mainly on syntactic parsing. That is to say, it will be assumed for the time being that the input to the processor is a string of words and that the aim of the parsing is to produce a structural analysis of the input. This is not to suggest that syntactic parsing is all that has to be done in language processing. Indeed, as the remainder of this book will show, there is much more to language processing than determining the syntactic structures of sentences. However, it is useful to begin with examples from syntactic parsing for the purpose of illustration as the analysis can be kept within manageable bounds. Many of the techniques and issues which arise at this level apply also at other levels of language. The main purpose of this chapter then will be to show how language analysis can be seen as a step-by-step process in which each step has to made explicit for the computer. Subsequently it will become clear how difficulties arise when the assumption is entertained that syntactic analysis is sufficient for language processing and this will lead on to a consideration of how other types of knowledge need to be involved.

In parsing a distinction has often been made between two operations – recognition and structural analysis. The recognition process simply judges whether the sentence is well formed according to the grammatical rules of the language in question and the analysis succeeds or fails on that criterion. A structural analysis assigns to the input a structure which can be used as a basis for further analysis such as semantic interpretation.

It will not be possible to describe all the complexities which arise in natural language parsing within the confines of this chapter. Furthermore, the examples presented here will be fairly trivial. However it is hoped that some impression will be given of the general issues involved (some suggestions for further reading are listed at the end of the chapter).

A simple grammar

For the purposes of illustration we will take a grammar incorporating the phrase structure rules and dictionary entries set out in figure 3.1.

Grammar

1	S	⟶	NP VP
2	NP	⟶	Determiner NN
3	NN	⟶	Noun
4	NN	⟶	Adjective NN
5	NN	⟶	NN PP
6	PP	⟶	Preposition NP
7	VP	⟶	Verb NP
8	VP	⟶	Verb NP PP

Dictionary

the	determiner
a	determiner
boy	noun
dog	noun
park	noun
little	adjective
black	adjective
saw	verb
in	preposition

Figure 3.1   Phrase structure rules and dictionary

A few points need to be made about the way these rules are set out as they differ slightly from the traditional layout of phrase structure rules in linguistics. For example, alternative rules, such as rules 3, 4 and 5, which are alternative ways of rewriting the symbol NN (noun nucleus) are listed separately. This is merely to make it easy to recognize which rule is being applied during a parse and no theoretical significance should be attached to this layout. In a more complex grammar other notational devices are used to conflate rules and allow for optionality within rules. The symbol NN differs from symbols normally used in linguistic grammars. Here it is used to cover structures containing adjectives and nouns but without determiners. This facilitates the generation and analysis of structures containing several instances of units such as adjectives, as will be seen below.

This simple grammar permits a number of alternative structures. A noun phrase has to consist of the symbols Determiner and NN. However NN can be rewritten as a noun, yielding a phrase such as *the boy*, an adjective followed by NN (as in *the little boy*) or NN followed by PP (as in *the boy in the park*). Going back to the combination Adjective NN, as NN can be rewritten in three different ways there are further possible structures. The first, in which NN is rewritten as a noun has already been mentioned (*the little boy*). But NN can be rewritten again as Adjective NN giving the combination Adjective Adjective NN. Indeed this rule could be re-applied many times leading to a noun phrase with a large number of adjectives. Similar options occur with other rules, such as rule 5, in which NN is rewritten as NN PP. This gives the opportunity for NN to be rewritten again and one possibility could be rule 5 again, leading to the structure NN PP PP (as in *the boy in the garden behind the house*). Again this rule could be applied many times resulting in a large number of prepositional phrases modifying the noun phrase. As the rule for PP (rule 6) also includes NP as one of its constituents the whole process can start again and quite complex structures can be generated and analysed.

These points should be familiar to linguists but they need to be spelt out in order to show how even a simple grammar such as this can lead to a vast number of structural possibilities and how this can cause problems for a parser. In order to appreciate this, we can examine the parsing of a simple sentence in the light of these rules:

(1) The boy saw the little black dog in the park.

This sentence is similar to some of the examples discussed in chapter 2 in that it is ambiguous between a structure representing the meaning that the boy was in the park and saw the dog and one representing the meaning that the dog was in the park and the boy saw him, but the boy was not in the park. Phrase structure trees for these two versions appear in figure 3.2.

As can be seen, the two meanings arise from two different structural analyses of the sentence. In what follows we will deal with the structure shown in phrase structure tree b, that is, the reading in which the little black dog is in the park.

A parsing schema

Assuming the grammar rules listed in figure 3.1, how might these rules be applied to the analysis of example 1? What is required is a procedure (or algorithm). The details of parsing algorithms would take us beyond the scope of this book, so what will be presented here is a very informal and simplified account of what is involved. Further details can be found in Winograd (1983), on which this section is based.

We will assume that the analysis of the sentence is to be top-down and left-to-right. Top-down processing will be explained in greater detail later. What it means essentially is that the analyser begins with the highest constituent S, which represents 'sentence', and then looks at the

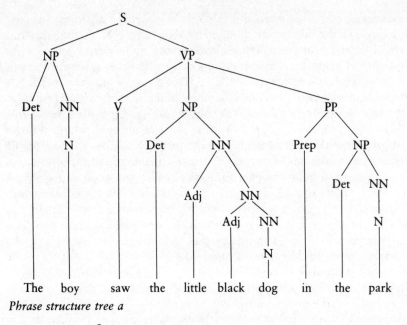

Phrase structure tree a

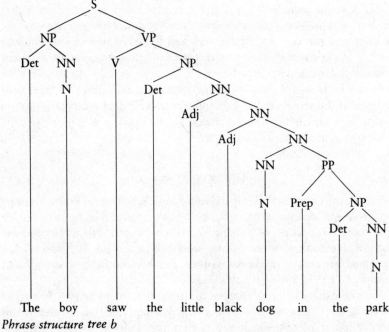

Phrase structure tree b

Figure 3.2   Phrase structure trees for The boy saw the little black dog in the park

rules to see what constituents will be needed to build a sentence. This will involve looking for the subparts of these constituents and so on down the structural tree (or rules) until words are found which will match the constituents listed in the dictionary. Left-to-right processing is what it says – the analyser begins with the first word of the input and works its way word-by-word from left to right until the end of the input is reached.

The schema to be used here has to keep a record of what it is doing and of what it has achieved. Two working structures are involved: an indication of the current position in the input (which word is currently being analysed), and a list of what has still to be found in order to complete a sentence. This can be displayed as follows:

Position	Remainder	Rule chosen
1 the	S	S→NP VP

Position refers to the point the parser has reached in the analysis of the sentence. Here it is at position 1 and it is trying to match the word *the* with the first rule of the grammar, the symbol S. As this match is unsuccessful, the parser expands S by means of a rule of the grammar, in this case the only applicable rule S→NP VP.

These are the structures with which the parser operates together with a method of representing in a step-by-step fashion what happens during the course of the analysis. What is now required is a set of instructions. We will assume here that the parser is searching for a single structure and that it will stop as soon as it finds one. Another possibility would be to return multiple structures which could then be analysed at a higher level. Basically the instructions will tell the parser to keep repeating until it reaches a point of success or failure. One instruction is that the parser should see if the first symbol in the remainder list is a lexical category such as noun or verb. If it is, it can be tested against the word being analysed and if it matches then the matched symbol is removed from the remainder. If there are no more items in the input and no more items in the remainder, then everything has been matched and the analysis succeeds. The analysis can fail for two reasons. First that there are no items left in the input but there are still items in the remainder. This means that the remainder includes structures which are required for the construction of a complete sentence. If there are no more items in the input to match with these structures in the remainder, then the parse fails as the input does not constitute a complete sentence as specified by the grammar. Conversely, when the remainder is empty but there are still input items to be analysed, the analysis also fails, as a sentence has been constructed but not all of the input has been analysed (or consumed).

If there is no match between the input item and the first item in the remainder, then a rule in the grammar is chosen which has that symbol (the first item of the remainder) as its left-hand side. In the above example there was no match between the input *the* and the symbol S, so a rule was found in which S was on the left-hand side. Here only one rule could have been chosen. Further down the grammar there are options for which rule to choose. For the present it will be assumed that the parser chooses the correct rule from the available options. What happens when an incorrect rule has been chosen will be discussed later.

Parsing a sentence

We can now trace through a top-down recognition of example 1 using the grammar set out in figure 3.1 and the instructions described in the previous section. As we have already seen, the parser begins with the first *item, the*, and tries to match it against the top item in the grammar, the symbol S. As this match fails, it expands S by choosing rule 1. Now an attempt is made to match *the* with the symbol NP. Again this fails, so NP is rewritten, using rule 2 of the grammar. The position is now as follows:

Position	Remainder	Rule chosen
1 the	NP VP	NP→Det NN

Now the structure Det NN will be added to the remainder in the place of NP, which it has replaced according to rule 2, and an attempt will be made to match *the* with the first symbol of the remainder. This succeeds, as *the* is listed in the dictionary as a determiner. Thus the analysis so far is as follows:

Position	Remainder	Rule chosen
1 the	Det NN VP	Det→the

Now an attempt is made to match the next word in the input string, *boy*, with the first symbol in the remainder NN. As this does not succeed, NN is expanded as a noun according to rule 3 of the grammar and in the next position *boy* will be matched with the symbol noun and so the process continues. A trace of the remainder of the analysis is shown in table 3.1 and the interested reader can work through this trace to see how the grammar has been applied to the analysis of this input sentence according to the instructions outlined earlier.

Table 3.1 Trace of a top-down parse

Position		Remainder	Rule chosen
1	the	S	S→NP VP
1	the	NP VP	NP→Det NN
1	the	Det NN VP	Det→the
2	boy	NN VP	NN→Noun
2	boy	Noun VP	Noun→boy
3	saw	VP	VP→Verb NP
3	saw	Verb NP	Verb→saw
4	the	NP	NP→Det NN
4	the	Det NN	Det→the
5	little	NN	NN→Adj NN
5	little	Adj NN	Adj→little
6	black	NN	NN→Adj NN
6	black	Adj NN	Adj→black
7	dog	NN	NN→NN PP
7	dog	NN PP	NN→Noun
7	dog	Noun PP	Noun→dog
8	in	PP	PP→Prep NP
8	in	Prep NP	Prep→in
9	the	NP	NP→Det NN
9	the	Det NN	Det→the
10	park	NN	NN→Noun
11	park	Noun	Noun→park

Top-down and bottom-up processing

So far we have been looking at top-down processing in which the parser begins with the expectation that the input is a sentence of the language defined by the grammar and attempts to prove this by expanding the symbols in the left-hand side of the grammar until it reaches words.

An alternative to top-down processing is bottom-up processing. Here the parser tries to build up a structure from the input string by matching words with dictionary entries and then matching these with constituents on the right-hand side of the grammar rules. Each combination is replaced by a higher level constituent until the symbol S is reached, by which point the sentence has been parsed. In other words, in bottom-up parsing the parser works its way up the tree, starting at the bottom, until it reaches the root node S. A partial bottom-up analysis for phrase structure tree b of example 1 appears in table 3.2 Here we will not assume that the parser always selects the right rules in order to show the problems which can arise when the wrong rule is chosen.

Table 3.2 Partial trace of a bottom-up parse

Rule used	Current sequence
	The boy saw the little black dog in the park
the→Det	Det boy saw the little black dog in the park
boy→Noun	Det Noun saw the little black dog in the park
NN→Noun	Det NN saw the little black dog in the park
NP→Det NN	NP saw the little black dog in the park
saw→Verb	NP Verb the little black dog in the park
the→Det	NP Verb Det little black dog in the park
little→Adj	NP Verb Det Adj black dog in the park
black→Adj	NP Verb Det Adj Adj dog in the park
dog→Noun	NP Verb Det Adj Adj Noun in the park
NN→ Adj NN	NP Verb Det Adj NN in the park
NN→Adj NN	NP Verb Det NN in the park
NP→Det NN	NP Verb NP in the park

(at this point the wrong rule has been selected, as the phrase *in the park* is not analysed as being part of NN (rule 5), and so NP and VP are built (rules 2 and 1) leaving *in the park* unanalysed)

VP→V NP	NP VP in the park
S→NP VP	S in the park

As can be seen, the analysis runs into problems as the symbol S is reached, indicating that a full sentence has been recognized, although some of the input has still to be parsed (or consumed). This problem arose from the selection of the wrong rule when more than one rule could have been applied.

Top-down processing is often described as being hypothesis- or expectation-driven. It starts out with the basic expectation that a sentence will be recognized and works down the phrase structure tree until it can match a word with a category symbol. A top-down processor explores a particular analysis in the belief that it is the correct one until it meets either success or failure. A bottom-up analysis, on the other hand, is data-driven – it builds structures by working up the tree from the input. Each approach has its advantages and disadvantages, and many systems adopt a mixed approach in which structure-building is combined with a search for expected structures. In chapter 6 we shall see how expectation-based parsing has been extended beyond the level of syntax to the application of larger knowledge structures as a means of guiding language understanding.

Backtracking, parallel processing and deterministic parsing

We have seen how a parser may run into trouble as a result of selecting the wrong rule. However, it can be organized in such a way that rather than simply giving up at this point it will go back to the place where the wrong decision was made and try an alternative path. This is referred to as *backtracking* and it works in the following way. When it reaches a choice point, where more than one rule could be selected, the parser selects one of the rules but keeps a record of the other rules it could have chosen. If the rule chosen turns out to be incorrect and the analysis results in failure, as shown above, then the parser can return to that choice point and try one of the other possibilities. This process can be repeated many times until success is achieved or, when all possibilities have been explored, failure is returned. What is involved essentially is a mechanism for keeping such a record of alternative paths.

A different approach is to expand all possible choices simultaneously at each choice point, keeping records of each. This is known as *parallel processing*. Each method has its problems. Backtracking can often result in a lower-level constituent, such as a prepositional phrase, being repeatedly parsed and yielding the same result while the parser explores the various alternatives, whereas the problem may be at a higher level. This is uneconomical in computational terms as it is not necessary continually to re-parse a lower-level constituent which was correctly parsed in the first place. Parallel processing can also be wasteful since it requires the maintenance of many structures simultaneously, only one of which will ultimately be required.

At this point it is interesting to speculate on how humans cope with such problems and this leads us to discuss the distinction between *non-deterministic* and *deterministic* parsers. Non-deterministic describes a situation where there is more than one option available for what to do next. Our grammar illustrates this at several points. A deterministic parser does not consider such choice points but makes decisions about what it estimates to be the correct structures for the sentence, usually by suspending analysis until the parser can be more confident that the structures are correct. What this means is that words (or, more accurately, constituents) are held in store in a buffer while the parser looks ahead for further information which would inform the choice. This technique is often known as *wait-and-see* parsing (for detailed discussion see Marcus 1980). In example 1 some knowledge that the prepositional phrase *in the park* was still to come could have guided the choice of the correct rule. It is argued that deterministic parsing reflects human processing, as humans do not usually entertain multiple analyses of a sentence but decide on one which is normally the correct one. These processes should be reflected in a parsing procedure, especially if it is to meet the requirements of cognitive simulation. Likewise, those garden-path sentences, encountered in chapter 2, which cause problems for humans will also cause problems for deterministic parsers if a problematic constituent, such as an expected verb, is so far removed from the items being processed that it is not taken into consideration when the analysis is being made. Thus in the sentence discussed in chapter 2, *the teachers taught by the Berlitz method passed the test*, the parser may not be able to know that its analysis of *taught* is incorrect because it cannot see as far ahead as *passed*. But if humans also experience this as a garden-path sentence, then the parser may be shedding some light on the processes whereby humans understand language. We will return to a more detailed discussion of this issue later once we have introduced augmented transition networks (ATNs), a system of representation which is used widely in natural language processing.

Augmented transition networks

It will be useful to look briefly at ATNs for the following reasons:

1 ATNs have been used widely in natural language processing and so it is helpful to be familiar with the formalism which embodies a step-by-step analysis of language.
2 ATNS will be used in the following section in which different approaches to syntactic parsing will be contrasted.
3 ATNs have also been used at other levels of analysis such as discourse (see chapter 7) and in discussions of how to deal with ill-formed input (see chapter 9).

We can begin with the simple concept of a transition network. A transition network indicates the states which a parser has to pass through during the course of a step-by-step analysis of a sentence. A simple illustration will help. Take the sentence *Little children love sticky buns*. This can be represented by the network in figure 3.3.

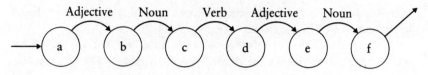

Dictionary:

Adjective	little, sticky
Noun	children, buns
Verb	love

Figure 3.3 A transition network

The transition consists of the following elements:

1 a series of states (or nodes), listed here as a,b,c, etc.
2 an initial node, indicating the starting state, and a final node, indicating the finishing state.
3 labelled arcs joining the states, against which words of the input have to be matched so that the parser can proceed through the network.

In this example we start at the initial state with the word *little* which matches the arc adjective, so allowing us to proceed to the next state. We now try to match *children* against the next arc, which is labelled noun. As this succeeds, we can continue, and so on to the final state. If all the input has been used up (or consumed) at the point at which the final state has been reached, then the sentence has been successfully parsed. Problems occur, as we saw earlier, if the parser reaches the final state without consuming all the input or if it is not possible to match an input word with the current arc in the network.

Obviously this is a very simple network which will only handle a small number of sentences. We can make some additions which will increase its complexity. Three things need to be added:

1 an indication of choice points in the grammar.
2 a representation of the hierarchical structure of sentences.
3 conditions and actions associated with transitions between states in the network.

We saw earlier that a grammar embodies many choice points. For example, a noun phrase may consist of constituents such as Noun, Determiner+Noun, Adjective+Noun, Determiner+Adjective+Noun, and so on. Furthermore, some categories such as adjectives can occur more than once. Accordingly, such choices would have to be incorporated in the network. This could be done as set out in figure 3.4.

The looped arc labelled Adjective represents the fact that this arc can be traversed more than once, or that it can be bypassed. The arc labelled JUMP also indicates an arc which can be bypassed.

One problem is that this representation would incorporate a lot of unecessary repetition. All the information about noun phrases which occurred at the beginning of the network (at subject position) would have to be duplicated again later at object position and perhaps again later for a noun phrase occurring within a prepositional phrase (e.g. in *beside (prep) the pretty little church(NP))*. Furthermore a linear representation such as we have in figure 3.4 fails to capture the hierarchical structure of sentences, in which larger constituents consist of smaller ones, as represented in our earlier phrase structure grammar. For this reason simple transition networks have been expanded as recursive transition networks which are a series of networks representing the different levels of the grammar. (Here the term recursive reflects the way that the network for a constituent such as a noun phrase may itself contain a noun phrase.) Figure 3.5 presents an example of a recursive transition network based on the grammar of figure 3.1.

Some of the terms will need explaining. If we look at the network for sentences, S, we find arcs labelled SEEK NP and SEEK VP. The instruction SEEK tells the parser to suspend all work on the current network, store the results obtained so far in memory, and to shift attention to the arc named in the instruction (here either NP or VP). If we had reached the arc SEEK NP we would thus move down to the NP network to analyse the input as a noun phrase. On succeeding we would reach the state SEND which would return us to the network we had left (in this case the S network at state S1). As we traverse the NP network we might encounter the arc SEEK PP, which would send us to the network for prepositional phrases. On working through the PP network we would

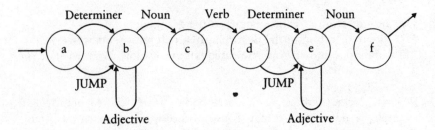

Figure 3.4 Some additions to the transition network

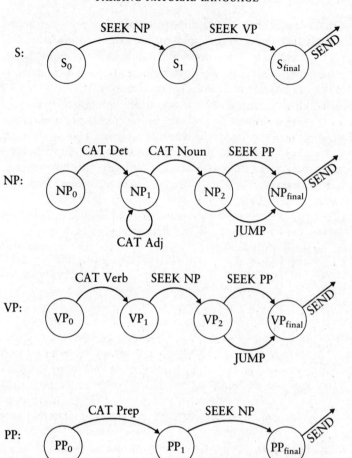

Figure 3.5 A recursive transition network based on the grammar in figure 3.1

encounter the arc SEEK NP, which would send us back to the NP network. Thus while analysing a noun phrase we might have to analyse a prepositional phrase, and while so doing we would have to analyse a noun phrase. In terms of the network we have to go back on ourselves to analyse this smaller noun phrase and this is what makes the network recursive.

Two additional labels should be noted: CAT stands for category and represents a constituent which is a category such as noun, verb, adjective or preposition. Category constituents cannot be further expanded. Finally WORD indicates words which have been incorporated in the network. WORD arcs do not appear in our network but are used for words such as *to* in structures such as *he is eager to please*.

An ATN includes a further level of detail in order to make the network more adequate. Arcs can incorporate conditions which must be met before the arc can be traversed. One condition is that features on linked items should be identical: plural nouns should be followed by plural verbs, plural determiners (e.g. *these*) by plural nouns, and so on. Also when an arc has been traversed, various actions might be invoked, such as marking the item as being plural, building the constituents into a structure such as a NP, and sending information for storage in a temporary register. We can illustrate what is meant with a simple example.

(2) The boy was chased by a dog.

The analysis would, of course, depend on how the grammar was written. As we move through the ATN, the words *the* and *boy* would be analysed as a noun phrase and would be put in temporary store as subject of the sentence. *Was* would be analysed as an auxiliary verb and the next expected state would be a main verb with the ending *-ing*, as in the sentence *The boy was playing* . . . . However, on encountering the main verb in the form *chased*, the ATN would note that this is a past participle form, which means that the sentence must be in the passive rather than in the active voice. This being so, the surface subject, *the boy*, is not the deep subject (or agent) of the verb therefore this NP is taken out of the register and assigned to deep object (or patient) while another subject is sought (there could, of course, be no deep subject (or agent) as in the sentence *The boy was chased*). In this way the ATN makes hypotheses about the structure of the sentence, stores some of the results in a temporary register and backtracks when required on the basis of subsequent information.

There have been several attempts to show how ATNs may reflect psychological processes used by humans when analysing sentences. One way is to structure the ATN in such a way that, where choice points occur, the arcs are weighted according to which should be tried first. In this way the grammar predicts which is the most likely interpretation. Two examples from Kaplan (1972) will serve as an illustration.

(3) They are fixing benches.
(4) They are sleeping monkeys.

On arriving at the third word in these sentences, a decision has to be made as to whether this word is a main verb or whether it is a participle functioning as an adjective. Kaplan argues that there is a bias in the processing of such sentences towards a search for a Noun-Verb-Noun sequence representing the semantic structure Actor-Action-Patient. The first sentence accords with this strategy, but if this strategy is followed in the second, difficulty arises when the potential direct object *monkeys* is reached. This leads to the sentence having to be re-analysed. Experimental results suggest that humans have greater difficulty in processing sentences of the second type, and this is taken as evidence for a processing bias. This bias is reflected in ATNs by ordering the arcs in such a way that the most likely arc, that is, the one which is the least complex to process, should be taken first. This point will be taken up again in the next section when we examine some more examples of problematic structures.

Approaches to syntactic parsing: an example

So far the discussion concerning differences between linguistic, psychological and computational approaches to natural language processing has been at a fairly general level. We are now in a position to look at some examples in greater detail. The examples are all structurally ambiguous and the approaches illustrated here will show how this structural ambiguity might be handled in order to obtain the correct result – that is, the most likely meaning of the sentence. (Note: this section is a little more technical and can be skipped by readers who do not wish to concern themselves with this more detailed analysis.)

The examples to be discussed are:

(5) The boy saw the little black dog *in the park*.
(6) Joe bought the book *for Susan*.
(7) Joe bought the book which I had been trying to obtain *for Susan*.
(8) Tom said that Bill died *yesterday*.

Problems arise in each example with the analysis of the constituent in italics. We have already encountered example 5. Two analyses were possible, one in which the prepositional phrase *in the park* was attached to *saw* (that is where the boy did the seeing), and the other where it was attached to *dog* (the dog was in the park). The phrase structure trees for these analyses appear in figure 3.2 (p. 44). Examples 6 and 7 both have the problem of where to attach the prepositional phrase, but they differ from one another in that more material separates the prepositional phrase (*for Susan*) from the verb (*bought*) to which it could be attached. As most of the discussion about this type of sentence makes reference to the structural position of constituents within trees like those represented in figure 3.2, it is useful to be able to see the diagram. For example, the interpretation of 5 which has the boy in the park when he saw the dog is described in terms of the prepositional phrase being attached to the VP (phrase structure tree (a)), whereas in phrase structure tree (b) it is attached to the lower NP node. In tree (a) there are fewer nodes between the new node (the PP node) and the node to which it is attached (the VP node) than there are in tree (b). This type of attachment to the higher VP node is referred to as *Minimal Attachment*. In the case of tree (b) the attachment takes place further down the tree (at an NN node) and to the right of the tree and it is referred to as *Right Association*. As far as example 5 is concerned, it might be argued that either Minimal Attachment or Right Association could apply – in other words, without further context the sentence remains ambiguous and neither reading is to be preferred. In example 6 the more likely reading involves Minimal Attachment. (The sentence means that the buying was for Susan, as a present, rather than that Joe bought, perhaps for himself, the book which was meant for Susan). If the second reading seems less plausible, this is support for Minimal Attachment in this case. Conversely, in 7 the more likely interpretation involves Right Association, in which *for Susan* belongs with *obtain* rather than with *bought*. The final example shows how this issue is not limited to prepositional phrases but can involve other constituent types.

We will consider three approaches to this question:

1 a psycholinguistic approach in terms of processing strategies.
2 an ATN analysis.
3 an explanation in terms of the semantic properties of the words in the sentence.

The first approach has been proposed by Frazier and Fodor (1978) and involves the notion of a two-stage model of sentence processing, which they call the *Sausage Machine*. Briefly the argument is that, at the first stage of processing, the processor is given limited access to what is to follow in the sentence (a window of about six words has been suggested), therefore it cannot make attachments involving longer dependencies, like the one in example 7. The second stage assembles the smaller units into the completed phrase marker (or tree) for the sentence but does not undo the work of the first stage. This means that a parser is limited or 'shortsighted' in that it has access only to a few words beyond the state at which it currently stands. This would favour the principle of Minimal

Attachment, as the parser can still 'see' the verb *bought* when it encounters *for Susan* and so can make the attachment to the VP node. In example 7, as there are more elements between *bought* and *for Susan*, the parser will have lost access to the VP node for *bought* by the time *for Susan* is encountered, and so the attachment has to be made to the VP *obtain*. The prediction is that in shorter sentences the parser will see both possibilities but that the Minimal Attachment strategy will prevail by default. In longer sentences Right Association applies as the prepositional phrase is too far removed from the higher VP node. In this way the predictions of the theory accord with the common sense intuition that the processing of related linguistic items is facilitated when they are in close proximity to each other.

This theory can account for many examples of attachments, but there are certain problems. In example 8, if the principle of Minimal Attachment is applied, which according to the theory it ought to be, the preferred reading would be *said yesterday*, however *died yesterday* would seem to be the more plausible interpretation. Likewise, as Wanner (1981) points out, it might be expected that, as a sentence is shortened, the preferences for Right Association should be diminished in favour of Minimal Attachment, but this does not seem to be the case in the following set of sentences:

 (9) Tom said that Bill had taken the cleaning out yesterday.
(10) Tom said that Bill had taken it out yesterday.
(11) Tom said that Bill had taken it yesterday.
(12) Tom said Bill took it yesterday.
(13) Tom said Bill died yesterday.

We would expect Right Association in the earlier sentences, 9 and 10, (*yesterday* attached to *had taken* rather than *said*), but this preference does not seem to diminish in the later sentences where the theory would predict Minimal Attachment. That is, as the sentences become shorter, as we move through 9 to 13 and fewer elements appear between the highest VP (*said*) and *yesterday*, we would expect that Minimal Attachment would become more likely. However, this does not seem to be the case, as even in 13, the shortest sentence, *yesterday* is more likely to be attached to *died* than to *said*. Similarly, as Wilks (1985) points out, the theory makes the wrong predictions in the sentence

(14) She wanted the dress on that rack.

Minimal Attachment would yield the reading *wanted on that rack* whereas the more plausible reading is *the dress which is on that rack*.

Frazier and Fodor's Sausage Machine is based on processing limitations associated with short-term memory as well on as the geometry of the phrase structure tree. It is therefore a psycholinguistic approach which is intended to make claims about how humans process language. The next approach to be considered, Wanner's ATN, is a computational solution which is not motivated by the desire to explain psychological processes but rather to achieve the effect of minimizing computation during arsing. It is always important to maintain this distinction between cognitive simulation and computational achievement. As Wanner himself writes (1981: 212): 'There is no reason to expect that the most satisfactory model of human parsing will necessarily be the model that can be realized most efficiently on currently available computational facilities.'

Wanner's approach involves the scheduling of arcs in an ATN. It is impossible to do justice to this approach without going into technical details beyond the scope of this book, so a brief outline of the main ideas will have to suffice (for further details see Wanner 1981). Recall that in an ATN there are different types of arc: WORD, CAT, SEEK, SEND, JUMP. A CAT arc returns a category constituent, such as a noun, while a SEEK arc looks for a constituent at a lower level. For example, while parsing a noun phrase, a SEEK arc might direct the parser to a lower network for prepositional phrases. Wanner proposes the following ATN scheduling rules as a general description of Right Association and Minimal Attachment:

Right Association: schedule all SEND arcs and all JUMP arcs after
   every other arc type.
Minimal Attachment: schedule all CAT arcs and WORD arcs
   before all SEEK arcs.

According to the first rule WORD, CAT and SEEK arcs will be traversed before SEND and JUMP arcs. The effect of this is that a constituent will be analysed, if possible, as part of a lower constituent before control is passed (via SEND or JUMP arcs) to the higher levels. This would normally bias the analysis in favour of Right Association. We can illustrate this using simplified networks to analyse the sentence *Tom said that Bill died yesterday* (figure 3.6).

Let us assume that the parser has successfully analysed the words *Tom* and *said*. At this point it will be in the VP network (not illustrated here), where one of the choices after the verb is to SEEK a subordinate clause. The parser moves down to the subordinate clause network, analyses *that* as COMP (arc 5), then reaches arc 6 which directs it back to the S network in order to analyse the subordinate sentence. *Bill* is analysed as

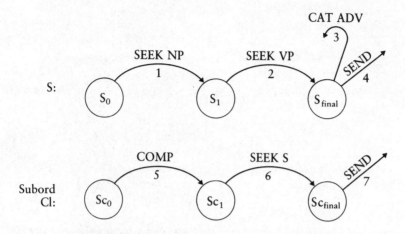

Figure 3.6 *Partial ATN for the sentence* Tom said that Bill died yesterday
(Wanner 1980: 220)

NP at arc 1 and *died* as VP at arc 2. Now the word *yesterday* is reached. There is a choice between terminating the subordinate clause (arc 4) and leaving *yesterday* to be attached to the verb of the main clause (*said*), or attaching the word to the subordinate sentence (arc 3). The arcs are so ordered that the second possibility prevails, in other words, Right Association. In fact this attachment will be preferred no matter how short or long the subordinate clause is.

The second rule deals with cases of Minimal Attachment. A simplified version of a NP network appears in figure 3.7. The relevant sentence is *Joe bought the book for Susan* in which we would expect the prepositional phrase *for Susan* to be attached to *bought* and not to *the book*.

Let us again trace through this example, assuming that we have already parsed *Joe* and *bought* and have been directed from the VP network to SEEK a NP. There are two choices: a simple NP (arcs 8 and 9) or a complex NP containing a PP. In the latter case arc 10 would be traversed, directing the parser back to SEEK another NP, which would match *the book*, by passing through arcs 8 and 9. The parser would then have completed the NP required by arc 10 and would go on to SEEK a PP to attach to this NP as part of the higher NP. This is illustrated in figure 3.8. However, this structure will not arise as the scheduling rules state that CAT arcs should precede SEEK arcs, so arcs 8 and 9 will be tried before arc 10, resulting in an attempt to analyse a simple NP first. Following this the PP can only be attached to the VP (according to arcs within the VP

NP:

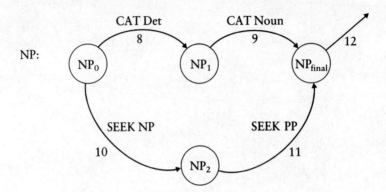

Figure 3.7 Simplified NP network for the sentence Joe bought the book for
Susan
(adapted from Wanner 1980: 220)

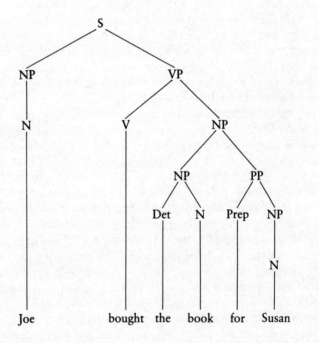

Figure 3.8 Phrase structure tree (a) for Joe bought the book for Susan
(Wanner 1980: 212, fig. 6)

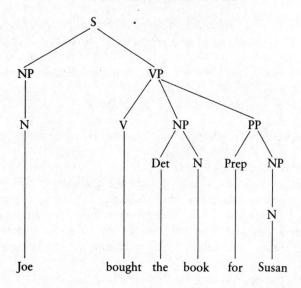

Figure 3.9 *Phrase structure tree (b) for* Joe bought the book for Susan
(Wanner 1980: 212, fig. 5)

network which are not shown here). The resulting structure appears in Figure 3.9.

The full details of the ATN approach have not been presented here, but it should be clear that scheduling rules within an ATN is one way of providing a general statement for Right Association and Minimal Attachment which does not depend on the interaction between the parsing strategies proposed by Frazier and Fodor. However, neither of these approaches considers semantic information and it is the strength of Wilks's (1985) proposal that it does. Wilks would probably not claim that his processing rule was psychologically valid, so his approach tends to be more of a computational rather than of a psychological nature.

One simple way of approaching the problem semantically would be in terms of the case frames of verbs, such as in:

want prefers a single NP to its right.
position prefers two entities.

These rules would help in the following attachments:

(15) The woman wanted the dress on the rack.
(16) The woman positioned the dress on the rack.

In example 15 *want* takes one object NP, so *on the rack* is attached to *dress*. In 16 *position* takes two entities, an object and a prepositional phrase, consequently *on the rack* is attached to *positioned* and not to *dress*. This would not, however, take account of the following example:

(17) The woman wanted the dress for her daughter,

in which *for her daughter* should be attached to *wanted* rather than *dress*.

In order to take account of such problems, Wilks draws on his theory of preference semantics. Briefly this theory states that case information should not only be associated with verbs but with other categories such as nouns, adjectives and prepositions. Associations between potentially linked items are computed in terms of scores and the most densely connected items are selected for attachment. Furthermore, Wilks proposed a rule which biases the attachment towards Right Association by offering the opportunity for Right Association first. The rule is

> Moving leftwards from the right end of the sentence, assign the attachment of a word or phrase to the first entity to its left that has the preference which the word or phrase satisfies. (based on Wilks 1985: 91)

This rule would make the correct predictions in the following sentences, cutting across the principles of Minimal Attachment and Right Association:

(18) John brought the book that I loved for Mary (brought for Mary).
(19) John took the book that I bought for Mary (bought for Mary).

In 18 *brought* would have a preference for a prepositional object while *for Mary* requires a verb such as *brought*. In 19, however, although both *took* and *bought* have preferences for prepositional objects, the first verb encountered on working leftwards from the right end of the sentence is *bought*. As this satisfies the semantic preference the phrase is attached here. The theory can also account for two prepositional phrases, as in the example:

(20) John wanted the dress on the rack for Mary.

Here *rack* and *dress* would provide a mutual fit and *for Mary* would fit best with *wanted*. As a final example, the ambiguous sentence we considered earlier, *the boy saw the little black dog in the park*, would still cause problems. The verb *see* would expect a possible mention of a location for the seeing, so *in the park* would be attached to *saw*, which is perhaps the most plausible interpretation. However, links between nouns and prepositions might have produced a different structural analysis in a sentence such as:

(21) The boy saw the swings in the park,

as there is a mutual fit between *swings* and *the park*.

Concluding remarks

In this and the preceding chapter we have examined some approaches to the issue of how humans and computers process language and have distinguished on the one hand between linguistic and computational approaches and on the other between psychological and computational approaches. The focus has been on language processing at the level of the sentence, as this is where most of the work has been done. In later chapters, however, we will be considering how knowledge structures and other information at the level of pragmatics supports or even drives the parsing. The role of syntax in language processing ought not to be ignored, however. As we have seen, in some theories other sources of knowledge override the syntax or even make it irrelevant. This was illustrated with reference to the resolution of ambiguity. Here it is pointless to produce multiple parsings for a sentence when only one might be acceptable on the basis of semantic plausibility. On the other hand, a syntactic analysis allows implausible but possible meanings to be conveyed, where the semantic analysis would have ruled these out. Indeed, in some cases information from a higher level might favour the implausible over the more plausible reading. There are also cases where minor differences in the syntax, which might be ignored by a semantic analyser, result in different structures. Winograd (1983: 370) offers these examples:

(22) The man who knew him was going left.
(23) The man who knew he was going left.

The only difference here is between *him* and *he*, yet the structural analysis for the two sentences is entirely different (in the first, the man was going in a leftwards direction, while in the second the man left and he knew the other person was going somewhere).

Finally, there is the question of how to deal with ill-formed structures. Humans can understand sentences which are ungrammatical, but a parser, which uses rules of syntax, would fail on encountering an ungrammatical combination. Some way of dealing with this anomaly is required. This important issue will be discussed more fully in chapter 9 when we come to discuss problems arising from communication failure.

With this background in linguistic, psychological and computational approaches to language at the level of the sentence, we can now proceed to the main theme of this book, which is the question of what is involved in programming computers to deal with larger units of discourse than the isolated sentence and how to engage in dialogue. The next two chapters will review some early work in natural language processing and will describe some systems. Subsequent chapters will look at more recent work in AI involving knowledge structures and natural language processing.

Further Reading

Parsing

Winograd (1983) is an excellent introduction to natural language parsing. See also Charniak and Wilks (1976). Rather more advanced collections of papers are to be found in Dowty et al. (1985), King (1983) and Sparck-Jones and Wilks (1985). See also Zampolli (1977). For a comprehensive introduction to ATNs, see Bates (1978). An alternative formalism, which is being used increasingly in natural language parsing, is definite clause grammar (DCG). See Pereira and Warren (1980) for an introduction to DCGs and a comparison with ATNs.

4

Some Early Natural Language Systems

Human beings are able to use language to talk about a wide range of topics, in some cases only at a very general level, in other cases at a highly specific level. Humans also know lots of things and they draw on this knowledge in order to take part in conversation. As Winograd (1972: 1–2) writes:

> When a person sees or hears a sentence, he makes full use of his knowledge and intelligence to understand it. This includes not only grammar, but also his knowledge about words, the context of the sentence, and most important, his understanding of the subject matter.

One illustration of this is the fact that we can often tell what a telephone conversation is about even if, as overhearers, we can hear only one side of it.

Computers, on the other hand, have not shown any great ability to converse like humans. They cannot discuss last night's football match, pass an opinion on the situation in the Middle East, or engage in a conversation about holidays. Unlike humans, however, they can store and retrieve large amounts of information. How many humans, for instance, could answer a question such as *How many times were Arsenal beaten at home by other London teams between the years 1950 and 1985?* To do so would demand prodigious feats of memory beyond normal human capacity, yet a computer would have little difficulty if it were appropriately programmed with the ability to interpret such questions and to retrieve the information from a database.

There are two aspects to natural language communication with computers. The first is the ability to take part in dialogue, which includes the ability to receive and understand information, to answer questions appropriately and to ask relevant questions at the right time. Humans do this with little effort; computers are so far largely deficient in this respect and much of current research is aimed at remedying the deficiency. The second aspect is one in which computers excel. It involves the acquisition, storage and retrieval of large amounts of information. Ultimately, these two aspects need to be combined, as the ability to acquire and disseminate information could be enhanced by the ability to engage in interactions using natural language.

Some early natural language systems will be examined in this chapter. It will be shown how these systems are deficient in many respects, yet it will be instructive to look at them closely, and not only for historical reasons. Indeed, by examining a number of systems we will see more clearly some of the major problems which face the articulate computer. We will also see that some of the techniques which were used foreshadow ideas which have been taken up and developed in later work.

Work on natural language began in the 1950s and the earliest work was on machine translation. Separately from this, in the early 1960s, work on artificial intelligence began to appear. This attempted to use natural language as a medium of communication between humans and computers. It was recognized, however, that general language understanding across an unlimited range of topics was not possible, so these early systems adopted one or more of the following techniques:

1 The domain was highly restricted so the system had to talk about one topic only, e.g. airline schedules or baseball scores.
2 The permissible language input was restricted to a subset of natural language within which the system could cope efficiently. Anything exceeding this restricted subset was either ignored or led to failure.
3 A keyword system was used which made the system search through the input to find certain key words which then triggered responses from the system. All other input was disregarded.
4 The natural language was translated into a more formal language such as predicate calculus, sets of linear equations or a data base query language which could be used by the computer. Naturally this only worked for input which was amenable to translation in this way.

The term *engineering approaches* has been used to characterize this early work. What does it mean? Broadly speaking the authors of these early programs more or less disregarded theories of human language processing, including work in theoretical linguistics and in cognitive psychology, and used a variety of resourceful techniques to manipulate language in such a way as to produce results. At this stage there was little or no concern for wider psychological issues such as how the machine's capacities might correspond to the processes of human language usage. Instead, the main criterion was whether the system worked within its fairly modest requirements. This is not, of course, to disparage this work, which is interesting in its own right and which embodies extremely useful programming techniques and principles, but rather to distinguish it from later approaches which do attempt to adopt a more cognitively and linguistically based perspective. In other words, in this work the emphasis was on computational achievement rather than on cognitive simulation.

The distinction is important, as the output of a computer could easily mislead or could conceal its limitations; for example a convincing dialogue, based on engineering techniques, could give an unwarranted impression of intelligence. Can we in fact judge on the basis of the output alone? One famous test for the intelligent computer is known as the *Turing test*. This test, as mentioned earlier, was devised by the mathematician Turing in order to answer the question 'Can machines think?' The idea behind the test was that if we cannot distinguish a computer from a person when we interact with it then the computer has been programmed to behave intelligently. A few programs, including Weizenbaum's ELIZA, which we will discuss later, have passed the Turing test; people interacting with the machine by means of a teleprinter could not tell that they were communicating with a computer and not with a person. However, ELIZA's ability to give an appropriate response most of the time, would not satisfy many workers in AI; they demand that the program should embody psychological reality – in other words that it should simulate human language processing rather than give a semblance of intelligence by means of some clever *ad hoc* tricks. The systems which we will look at in this chapter are BASEBALL, PROTOSYNTHEX, STUDENT, SIR, ELIZA and SOPHIE. We will see that each of these uses one or more of the devices listed above to achieve a measure of natural language capability.

BASEBALL

BASEBALL was an early question-answering system which relied on a highly restricted domain – the dates, locations, teams and scores of baseball games (Green et al 1963). This information, which was stored in a pre-structured format, could be questioned with queries such as *Who beat the Yankees on July 4?* Each question had to be transformed into a simple specification list such as:

Team (losing)	=	New York
Team (winning)	=	?
Date	=	July 4

and the goal of the program was to find the missing information by finding a match in the database. By means of a process of successive searching the system could answer a question containing several implicit or explicit queries. For example, to answer the question *On how many days in July did eight teams play?* the system would answer the implicit question *which teams?* It would find a list of days in July and a list of teams for that date. Next it would count the teams for each day and find out on which days eight teams played. Finally it would count the number of these days to answer the question.

The system was restricted to simple syntax, with single-clause questions, no logical connectives (e.g. *and*, *or* and *not*) and no comparative and superlative constructions (e.g. *most* and *highest*). Nevertheless, the system could accept fairly complex sentences such as *Did any team play at least once in each park in each month?* and it could do so because of the restricted nature of the subject matter; it only had to extract aspects of questions relevant to the time, place and scores of baseball games. This also allowed for ad hoc procedures which would not be possible in a more general system. For example, the meaning of *who* in the dictionary was given as *Team = ?* – this meaning could only apply to a database of this type.

If the system was unable to answer a question, it simply rejected it, permitting the user to try again with a rephrased question. Essentially BASEBALL was an information retrieval system with a limited natural language interface designed to understand the meaning of the question and relate it to a specification list. This process involved resolving syntactic ambiguities in order to represent the meaning adequately.

PROTOSYNTHEX I

This question-answering system consisted of text in a database and used a number of indexing schemes to answer questions by retrieving material which contained specific words or phrases (Simmons et al. 1964). The contents of a children's encyclopedia were stored in the database and the system could answer questions such as *What do worms eat?* In order to do this it would match the content-words *worms* and *eat* with sentences in the text and might retrieve the sentences *most worms usually eat grass* and *birds eat worms when the grass is wet*. It would then make a syntactic analysis of the question and the answers to check the matching. In this case, the question required sentences in which *worms* were the subject of *eat*. Thus the second of the retrieved sentences would be rejected as *worms* is the object and not the subject of *eat*.

This was a simple type of question-answering system which only worked if the answer to be retrieved appeared directly in the stored knowledge. There was no scope for deducing answers from information which was not explicit in the text. However the syntactic analysis, which was based on the grammatical dependencies between the words, was more sophisticated than a simple key-word search. The system did not permit any interaction with the user beyond the initial input question.

STUDENT

STUDENT is an example of a program which was able to communicate with a user in natural language within a restricted domain, in this case algebra story problems (Bobrow 1968). An example of such a problem is:

(1) Mary is twice as old as Ann was when Mary was as old as Ann is now. If Mary is 24 years old, how old is Ann?

The program converted the natural language input into a set of algebraic equations and attempted to produce a solution. It did this by breaking the input down into simple sentences and looking for words and phrases which could be replaced by arithmetic expressions and variables. The following shows in a simplified way how the above problem was solved. First the system broke the input down into simple sentences such as:

Mary's age is 2 times Ann's age y years ago (y is a variable in the equation).
x years ago Mary's age was Ann's age now.
Mary's age is 24.
z is Ann's age? (x is the variable which is to be found).

Then it worked out what equations were to be solved, such as:

Ann's age equals x.
Mary's age equals 24.
(Mary's age minus y) equals Ann's age.
Mary's age equals 2 times (Ann's age minus y).

This would then translate into simultaneous equations which could be solved by a special program. (For non-mathematical readers the answer is 18.)

The system could run into two sorts of difficulty while working out a solution. It might lack the mathematical knowledge to solve the problem, in which case it would simply report this. Alternatively, it might lack sufficient information to solve the problem and would attempt to elicit this information from the user. The following is such an example:

(2)
The gross weight of a ship is 20000 tons. If its net weight is 15000 tons, what is the weight of the ship's cargo?

Finding that it was unable to solve the equations, the system would ask:

(3)
DO YOU KNOW ANY MORE RELATIONSHIPS BETWEEN THESE VARI-
ABLES
  GROSS WEIGHT OF SHIP
  TONS
  ITS NET WEIGHT
  WEIGHT OF SHIP'S CARGO?

A possible response from the user might be:

(4)
The weight of a ship's cargo is the difference between the gross weight and the net weight.

Supplied with this information, STUDENT would now be able to solve the problem.

It might be argued that solving algebra problems is a fairly uninteresting application for a natural language system. However, some features of STUDENT foreshadow later developments and they merit further mention. One of these is that STUDENT was able to deal with connected discourse and not simply with isolated sentences. For example, it had to be able to recognize dependencies between the items mentioned in a problem (the variables), which can be expressed by referring expressions (e.g. pronouns). In problem 2 the system had to know that the word *its* in the second sentence (*its net weight*) referred to the ship that was mentioned in the first sentence.

A second feature of STUDENT was that it used a store of general knowledge to assist with the solution of problems. Some of this would be lexical information, for example, *people* is the plural of *person* and *one half* always means 0.5. Other information would relate to the general problem domain – distance equals speed times time. The system could expand its store of knowledge by requesting further information from the user, as in example 3. Thus the system did not simply translate natural language input into a formal language and then perform the appropriate mathematical operations – it was able to drawn on a body of general knowledge and if it needed to, could expand this interaction with the user. Nevertheless, the system was obviously limited both in its problem domain and in the subset of natural language which it could handle.

SIR

SIR (Semantic Information Retrieval) took a rather different approach; it avoided a syntactic analysis and attempted to extract the meaning of the input directly. SIR had the further advantage of being able to converse about any subject matter using any vocabulary (Raphael 1968). It has been described as a 'limited logic system' because it was able to perform inferences on the information stored in its database to find answers which were not explicitly stored there. However, like STUDENT, SIR was restricted in that it could only deal with a subset of the full range of logical inferences used in human conversation. Here is a sample conversation with SIR:

(5)
every boy is a person
I UNDERSTAND
a finger is part of a hand
I UNDERSTAND
each person has two hands
THE ABOVE SENTENCE IS AMBIGUOUS – PLEASE REPHRASE
there are two hands on each person
I UNDERSTAND
how many fingers does John have?
THE ABOVE SENTENCE IS AMBIGUOUS – BUT I ASSUME THAT 'HAS' MEANS 'HAS AS PARTS'
I DON'T KNOW WHETHER FINGER IS PART OF JOHN
John is a boy
I UNDERSTAND
how many fingers does John have?
THE ABOVE SENTENCE IS AMBIGUOUS – BUT I ASSUME 'HAS' MEANS 'HAS AS PARTS'

HOW MANY FINGERS PER HAND?
every hand has five fingers
THE ABOVE SENTENCE IS AMBIGUOUS – BUT I ASSUME 'HAS' MEANS
'HAS AS PARTS'
I UNDERSTAND
how many fingers does John have?
THE ABOVE SENTENCE IS AMBIGUOUS – BUT I ASSUME 'HAS' MEANS
'HAS AS PARTS'
THE ANSWER IS 10

We can see that SIR could be told facts, could answer questions and, when it needed supplementary information in order to answer questions, could ask for it. It could also report when a sentence was ambiguous and either ask for a rephrase or state which interpretation it was taking. As a conversation, example 5 appears fairly unnatural, particularly the recurrent statements about ambiguity. It is fruitful, however, to examine in a little more detail what SIR was able to do in such a dialogue.

The first point to be noted is that SIR was only able to recognize and deal with a finite set of semantic relations in sentences, although these could be expressed with any vocabulary (including nonsense words) and cover any subject matter. The relations the system recognized are set relations, part-whole relations, ownership, and certain spatial relations. Some of these are illustrated in the example 5. The first sentence *every boy is a person* is an example of set inclusion, it states that the set of boys is a subset of the set of persons. The second sentence *a finger is part of a hand* is an example of the part-whole relation, while the third sentence *each person has two hands* could either be a case of ownership (e.g. John has a car) or of the part-whole relation (has as parts). Some of the relations which could be recognized by SIR are:

   —— is ——
   —— owns ——
   —— is to the left of ——
   is —— ——?
   how many —— does —— have?
   what is the —— of ——?
   is —— to the left of ——?

In all, there were 24 such patterns covering the relations mentioned. The program matched these against the input. If no match was possible, the response STATEMENT FORM NOT RECOGNIZED was generated. Otherwise the system responded I UNDERSTAND to statements and retrieved answers to questions. Other responses were in the form of templates with gaps into which items from the input could be fitted. For example: I DON'T KNOW WHETHER * * IS PART OF * *, where the asterisks were replaced by the appropriate items from the input.

We can see that SIR was obviously limited to the set of relations which it could recognize and that the system as written did not facilitate expansion, because minor additions to a sub-program would have required major modifications throughout the system. However, SIR illustrates several principles which have been taken up in later work. An obvious one relates to breakdown through ambiguity; SIR was programmed to recognize and report on ambiguous input (albeit only for the verb *have*). More generally, the system was able to give easily understandable reports of its actions which could be printed out in a more extended conversational mode than is illustrated in the example above, thus making its operations more intelligible to the human user.

A second characteristic is that the system could 'learn'. It did not require prestructured data but could learn associations between objects as a result of interaction with the user. In example 5, for instance, SIR learned a chain of relations between *John, boy, person, hand* and *finger* and was able to use this acquired knowledge to deduce the answer to the question *how many fingers does John have?* even though the information *John has 10 fingers* was not represented in the database.

Finally, the linguistic analysis, while primitive in its reliance on a simple pattern-matching technique that avoids any grammatical analysis, foreshadows later semantic information processing systems in which the aim is not to provide a linguistic analysis of the input but to extract its meaning. As Raphael writes: 'Understanding the meaning of a sentence is interpreted as the process of recognizing the objects in the sentence and of placing them in a specified relation to one another.' We shall be looking at how the spirit of SIR is reflected in later semantically oriented work by Schank, Wilks and others as well as in Winograd's SHRDLU. But first we should look at ELIZA, which is perhaps one of the most famous (or even infamous) examples of an early natural language system.

ELIZA

ELIZA is a computer program which can 'converse' with the user in English (Weizenbaum 1966). Unlike the systems discussed so far, it could accept any input and usually responded appropriately. ELIZA was supplied with different scripts which allowed the program to converse about various subject matters. The most famous of these involved the simulation of a Rogerian psychotherapist conducting an initial interview with a patient. There have been many versions of ELIZA based on Weizenbaum's description of the program. The following is taken from an interaction between the author and a mini-version of ELIZA written at Sussex University by Steven Hardy and Aaron Sloman:

(6)
GOOD DAY WHAT IS YOUR PROBLEM?
I am having trouble with the computer
DO MACHINES WORRY YOU?
this one does
. . . .
EARLIER YOU SAID YOU WERE HAVING TROUBLE WITH THE COM-
PUTER
that's right and it hasn't got any better
WHAT DOES THAT SUGGEST TO YOU?
that computers are no use
HOW WOULD YOU REACT IF MACHINES TOOK OVER?
I think it would be a disaster
DOES ANYONE ELSE THINK IT WOULD BE A DISASTER?
yes quite a lot of people
QUITE A LOT OF PEOPLE
that's right
ARE YOU PREPARED TO ELABORATE?
no I have to go
WHAT DO YOU REALLY THINK ABOUT ME?
not much
WHY NOT MUCH?
because you are just a silly computer program
PERHAPS THE REAL REASON IS HARD TO TALK ABOUT?
well you have a point
YOUR PROBLEMS MAY BE TOO DIFFICULT FOR ME TO HELP
okay bye then
COMPUTER DEMONSTRATIONS OFTEN GO WRONG
so I see
ARE YOU DOING THE COMPUTERS AND THOUGHT COURSE?
no
WHY ARE YOU SO UNFORTHCOMING?
bye
BYE FOR NOW

ELIZA's performance is fairly impressive here. The system is able to reflect the patient's feelings and ask apparently relevant questions. However, as Weizenbaum himself argues, this is a delusion and in later writings he deplores the common tendency to anthropomorphize the program (Weinzenbaum 1984). He quotes the example of his secretary asking him to leave the room so that she could talk with ELIZA in private. More seriously, Weizenbaum was alarmed to find that some psychotherapists even entertained the idea that a refined ELIZA might be able to substitute for human psychotherapists in understaffed psychiatric wards. Readers of David Lodge's *Small World* will be familiar with the humorous side of emotional relationships with programs like ELIZA. In this novel the character Robin Dempsey, a professor of stylistics, acquires a version of ELIZA and proceeds to become totally dependent on it, going to the terminal to get advice on every conceivable problem, much to the amusement of his colleague. In the end Dempsey's colleague rigs the program to produce responses which are increasingly less helpful, culminating in an exchange in which Dempsey types in *What shall I do* and ELIZA replies SHOOT YOURSELF.

Weizenbaum emphasizes the limitations of his program. He writes (1984: 188) 'in a sense ELIZA was an actress who commanded a set of techniques but who had nothing of her own to say'. But how does the program appear to perform so well as a conversationalist?

The first point to be noted is that ELIZA performs well in the role of a psychiatrist because in this situation the program needs to know absolutely nothing about the real word. The program's main function is to analyse the input, to show interest by reflecting the patient's words and to prompt the patient for further input. Unlike a human conversationalist ELIZA does not have to take any initiative in the conversation, beyond inviting the patient to state his problems, to introduce new topics or to lead the conversation in new directions. Furthermore, ELIZA cannot distinguish between sensible input and nonsense. If the user were to type in something like *I am having trouble with my xxxpl* the program would probably respond YOUR XXXPL? In other words the program does not exhibit an understanding of language, but rather conceals a total lack of it. Part of its success is that the user assigns meanings and interpretations to what ELIZA 'says'.

ELIZA works in the following way. The program scans the input for keywords and then generates an automatic response. For example, on encountering a phrase such as *my xyz* the program responds YOUR XYZ? So, if the user types in *I am having trouble with my dog* the system will reply YOUR DOG? Some keywords have a special status. For example, if *xyz* is a kinship term (e.g. *mother* or *father*) then a canned response such as TELL ME MORE ABOUT YOUR FAMILY might be triggered. In the program underlying the dialogue quoted in example 6 there were keywords associated with computers (e.g. *micro*, *Eliza*, *computer* and *robots*) and these would trigger one of the following responses which would be selected fairly randomly:

DO MACHINES WORRY YOU?
HOW WOULD YOU REACT IF MACHINES TOOK OVER?
MOST COMPUTERS ARE AS STUPID AS THEIR PRO-
GRAMMERS.
DO YOU LIKE TALKING TO COMPUTERS?
CAN COMPUTERS REALLY THINK?
HOW CAN SCHOOLS IMPROVE ATTITUDES TO COMPU-
TERS?
WHAT DO YOU REALLY THINK OF COMPUTERS?

Another set of keywords has to do with money and included, for example, *money*, *cash*, *rent* and *broke*. These triggered responses such as:

HAVE YOU TALKED TO MARGARET THATCHER ABOUT
THAT?
WHY NOT CONSULT AN ACCOUNTANT?
COMPUTING CAN MAKE YOU RICH.

Responses were also triggered by the program user's short answers. Some of these occurred in the above extract, including *you are being rather short with me, perhaps you don't feel very talkative today* and *could you be more informative*?

Armed thus with a large set of responses to many keywords, ELIZA gives the impression of understanding and making appropriate responses. If no keyword can be found, then a non-committal response is generated such as PLEASE GO ON, I DON'T UNDERSTAND YOU FULLY, WHAT DOES THAT SUGGEST TO YOU?

Items are also stored so that they can be reproduced later, again to give the impression of an intelligent conversationalist. For example, if the user types in the sentence *sometimes I think that my life is a shambles*, the program will store part of the sentence (e.g. the phrase *life is a shambles*) and use this stored phrase in conjunction with a pattern canned to construct a response such as DOES THAT HAVE ANYTHING TO DO WITH THE FACT THAT YOUR + user's stored phrase. A response thus generated has a good chance of being meaningful no matter what the user's previous sentence was. The program also contained some common-sense rules about human conversation. For example, on encountering a sentence such as *I know everybody laughs at me*, the system would 'know' that the user did not literally mean everybody and would respond WHO IN PARTICULAR ARE YOU THINKING OF? In other words, the system was aware that when a person uses universal terms such as *everything* or *everybody* in casual conversation he is usually referring to something or someone specific.

We can view ELIZA in two ways. On the one hand, we can treat the program as an amusing toy which works as a result of a set of clever tricks. This is probably how Weizenbaum himself would wish to see it. Certainly those who anthropomorphize the system raise serious questions about their normal expectations concerning human conversation in general and the nature of the psychiatric interview in particular. However, the system does incorporate some general insights about conversation which are worth further consideration. On the negative side, there is the point which Weizenbaum makes that language understanding can only take place within a contextual framework. Such a framework is not provided for in ELIZA but the insight has guided subsequent work in natural language understanding. More positively there are the general purpose heuristics about conversational behaviour which are embodied in the program, for example the way in which it can effectively pass a turn when it has nothing substantive to contribute, or the way in which it responds in specific terms to statements which make universal references. These features contribute to the delusion of understanding which ELIZA gives, but they could be usefully adopted within a more sophisticated system which takes seriously the challenge of the contextual nature of language understanding.

SOPHIE

SOPHIE (SOPH-isticated Instructional Environment) is an 'intelligent' tutoring system which acts as an electronics laboratory instructor by interacting with students and helping them to debug malfunctioning electronic circuits. SOPHIE embodied complex techniques of inference as well as multiple representations of knowledge which allowed it to form its own hypotheses about the problems and to evaluate the students' hypotheses. The system was also an attempt to develop the principle of mixed-initiative instruction which would allow the student to ask questions about the problem and ask why a particular answer was wrong. The pedagogical and logical inferencing embodied in this system are not our concern here (see Brown and Burton 1975; Brown et al. 1982); rather we will be looking at the ways in which natural language was handled. This involved the use of a semantic grammar, similar to those outlined in chapter 2. This is why SOPHIE is being considered here along with other early systems since its linguistic abilities depended on a restricted domain which meant that a more sophisticated linguistic analysis involving syntax could be by-passed. In other words, the use of a semantic grammar implies an *engineering* rather than a *cognitive* approach to natural language processing. Nevertheless the natural language component resulted in a convenient mode of communication with a shorter response delay than would be expected if a more elaborate linguistic analysis were involved (about 150 milliseconds for a student statement of 8 to 12 words). Furthermore the system was able to handle some of the thorny problems such as anaphora and ellipsis which arise in dialogue. We can examine an extract from a protocol of an interaction with SOPHIE (Brown and Burton 1975: 314ff.). The extract includes some of the authors' annotations, in parentheses, which explain the electronic problem involved and also indicate some of the linguistic issues handled by the system:

(7)
WOULD YOU LIKE TO START WITH A FAULTED INSTRUMENT WHICH NEEDS FIXING?
yes
(SOPHIE randomly selects a fault, inserts it into a model of the instrument and tells the student how the controls are set)
THE INSTRUMENT HAS A FAULT AND ITS PRESENT CONTROL SETTINGS ARE:
(SOPHIE lists the control settings)
. . . .
what is the output?
THE OUTPUT VOLTAGE IS 11.7 VOLTS
(notice that *the output* was disambiguated as the output voltage)
what is it in a working instrument?
IN A WORKING CIRCUIT THE OUTPUT VOLTAGE IS 19.9 VOLTS
(note the student's use of the pronoun *it* to refer to the previous measurement)
. . . .
(following further questions the student proposes a solution)
replace Q6
I AM GOING TO ASK YOU SOME QUESTIONS ABOUT HOW Q6 IS FAULTED
(before a component is replaced the system queries the student as to how he thinks it is faulted)
ARE ANY JUNCTIONS SHORTED?
yes
ARE ANY TERMINALS OPEN?
yes
WHICH TERMINALS ARE OPEN?
the base
Q6 IS NOT FAULTED IN THAT MANNER. Q6 NOT REPLACED
(after learning that Q6 does not have an open base, the student asks if this was at least a reasonable hypothesis)
is it possible that Q6 has an open base?

(before the system's evaluation procedures can be applied to his idea or hypothesis, the hypothesis must be completely specified. To help the student out, the system suggests a plausible complete specification of it)
IS THE COMPLETE FAULT MODE EB/EC/BC = OP/OK/OP WHAT YOU INTENDED?
sure

As can be seen, SOPHIE can perform at a fairly sophisticated level as a tutor in electronics, and, as Brown and Burton point out, the reasoning and linguistic mechanisms could be applied to domains outside electronics. Let us look more closely at how the semantic grammar works.

It will be recalled from chapter 2 that the categories in a semantic grammar are not syntactic categories such as noun and verb, but semantic categories which represent concepts within the domain of application (e.g. *measurement, circuit elements, transistors* and *hypotheses*). Such a list would quickly grow to enormous proportions for a general natural language processor but, as far as SOPHIE was concerned, there were about 50 relevant concepts. The grammar specifies ways in which these concepts can be combined in sentences and also provides information about which of the elements can be deleted or pronominalized.

We shall now examine how this works. SOPHIE functioned mainly as a top-down, left-to-right parser. This allowed it to make predictions about what should come next. A syntactic parser might, for example, predict that following a determiner there would be a noun. In SOPHIE's semantic grammar a higher level constituent was the concept *measurement*. This permitted a structure such as *the voltage at x,* where x had to be a phrase specifying a location in the circuit. This type of prediction assisted in the resolution of anaphoric pronouns. If the system encountered the phrase *the voltage at it* it would be able to restrict the class of possible referents to locations. Similar strategies were used to handle ellipsis.

SOPHIE provided a convenient and efficient mode of communication for tutorial interaction. Its linguistic capabilities were limited and depended on the use of a limited domain and a restriction of activities within that domain – in this case, to taking measurements and developing hypotheses. Thus SOPHIE is a good example of a working system which does not necessarily have to reflect linguistic or psychological theory. As Brown et al. (1982: 239) write:

The goal of SOPHIE's natural language interface is to successfully understand whatever sentences users type into the system. It presupposes that users have a fair amount of knowledge of electronics and are seriously engaged in troubleshooting a circuit.

These assumptions are an integral part of the 'world view' that has been designed into SOPHIE, limiting the scope of interactions. The natural language interface was built by using an engineering approach that took advantage of these constraints. . . . We refer to these techniques as natural language engineering techniques because their goal is the production of useful widgets, not necessarily the furthering of our understanding of the language-understanding process. In particular, there are many problems in linguistics and the psychology of language for which semantic grammars are inadequate, and there are classes of dialogue phenomena not addressed by our dialogue mechanism.

Despite the fact that SOPHIE is limited linguistically, the system embodies many of the principles which underlie the more 'cognitive' systems to be discussed in the next few chapters. In particular we will see how world knowledge can be used to drive language processing. But first we will look at SHRDLU, a system which was endowed with far greater linguistic capabilities than any of the systems discussed in this chapter but which shared some of their characteristics in that its domain was limited to a tiny world in which the user could only converse with the system about coloured blocks and pyramids.

Further Reading

Early work on natural language systems, including the work discussed in this chapter, has been collected in edited volumes such as Feigenbaum and Feldman (1963), Minsky (1968) and Rustin (1973). Discussions of ELIZA can be found in almost every AI text. For Weizenbaum's own account, see Weizenbaum (1966, 1967, 1984).

5

SHRDLU: the Blocks World

SHRDLU, developed at MIT in the early 1970s, represented a major advance in natural language understanding since, for the first time, a program had been written which attempted to model language understanding on a computer (Winograd 1972). Previous systems, as we have seen, embodied little more than engineering techniques aimed at eliciting language-like behaviour but nobody claimed that these techniques were psychologically valid.

In what ways was Winograd's system different and how did it attempt to model the psychological processes of language understanding? To answer these questions we need to look first at how the system was organized. Recall the serial model of language understanding presented in chapter 2 (figure 2.3) in which an utterance is processed by a hearer through a series of stages. In this model, when an utterance is perceived by a hearer, it is first analysed syntactically and a full representation of its grammatical structure is constructed. This forms the input to the semantic analysis which constructs the meaning of the utterance. Finally, the pragmatic component analyses the utterance in terms of the context of its use. By following this path the hearer arrives at an interpretation of the utterance.

Winograd's system was more like the interactive model in which information could be passed between the modules as required. For example, while the syntactic component was in the process of constructing a grammatical structure, it could pass on its results to the semantic component to check whether the interpretation made sense. Further checks could be made with the pragmatic component to see whether the constructed interpretation fitted with the actual state of the world (or context). One of Winograd's examples will illustrate this process. Take the sentence:

(1) He gave the boy plants to water.

If this sentence were analysed on a purely syntactic basis, two structures would be possible. In one of these, the words *boy* and *plants* would be analysed as one constituent, as in the phrase *boy scouts*, or as in the phrase *house plants* in, for example, the sentence *he gave the house plants to charity*. Of course our common sense would make us reject this interpretation in favour of the analysis in which *the boy* is one constituent (the indirect object) and *plants* another (direct object). However, a parsing system with no immediate access to common-sense knowledge would produce the two structures as equally plausible, and the decision would be left to the semantic component. In more complex sentences many such alternative structures would occur and the number of syntactic representations would reach enormous proportions. For example: in a sentence with four constituents each open to three different interpretations, the number of syntactic representations would be $3 \times 3 \times 3 \times 3 = 81$. This combinatorial explosion was avoided by allowing a check on the plausibility of a structure such as *the boy plants* before the analysis went any further. Thus the system worked more efficiently and approximated more closely to human processing, since we usually make one interpretation only by allowing our syntactic and semantic knowledge to interact; we seldom entertain multiple choices and then decide between them.

The term *knowledge* has been introduced here; this is one of the key terms in SHRDLU and indeed in any serious work in language understanding. Two types of knowledge – syntactic and semantic – were used to make the interpretation of example 1. A third type of knowledge, embodied in the pragmatic component, is a combination of deep knowledge of the domain of discourse and the ability to reason and make deductions about what was said. To take a couple of Winograd's examples, when we hear the sentence:

(2) Sam and Bill wanted to take the girls to the movies, but they didn't have any money,

we assume that *they* refers to *Sam* and *Bill* and not *the girls*. Our assumption is based on our world knowledge; we know that when someone invites someone else, it is the inviter who pays. Consider also the following:

(3) The city councilmen refused the women a permit because:
(a) they feared violence;
(b) they advocated revolution.

Here we have to draw on our knowledge of the world in order to work out that the *they* in version a refers to *the city councilmen* and the *they* in version b to *the women*. These inferences are guided by our knowledge about the usual goals and motives of people. For example, most city councilmen are respected citizens and they have responsibilities such as keeping the peace, therefore they would not wish to provoke a potentially violent situation and they would be unlikely to be advocating revolution. To be certain that our second inference was correct we would need to know which women were involved, if for example, they were members of the Women's Rights Movement, since we would hardly wish to ascribe the goal of revolution to all women.

Thus non-linguistic world knowledge interacts with linguistic knowledge in the language understanding process. As we shall see, the incorporation of world knowledge into language understanding programs was a major advance in natural language processing. It also brought many problems stemming from the immense difficulties in representing this knowledge formally in a computer program. Some of these problems will be discussed towards the end of this chapter.

But if knowledge representation is such a difficult task for the system-designer how is it that Winograd's system was so successful? The answer is that the world knowledge was highly restricted. The domain of discourse was a tiny world containing various coloured blocks, pyramids and a box which could be manipulated by a one-armed robot. This scene was simulated on a television screen and the robot was able to converse with a human on a teletype. The robot could be given instructions such as *pick up the red block*, could be asked questions like *does anything support the blue pyramid which is in the box?* and could be told simple facts such as *I own everything which is green and large*, which it would then add to its store of knowledge. It could also answer questions about its actions, *why did you pick up the red cube?* or *how did you clear off the large blue block?* The strength of the system was that it used a combination of sophisticated techniques of syntactic, semantic and pragmatic analysis in order to produce these effects, thus addressing the issue of how language is used within a context of physical objects, events and a continuing dialogue. The main disadvantage was that it was limited to this tiny discourse world and was unable to talk about anything outside this domain. In order to appreciate how SHRDLU works, we will need to look a little more closely at each of its components.

Syntax

Unlike systems which we have encountered so far, SHRDLU incorporated a fairly comprehensive grammar of English, based on Halliday's Systemic

Grammar. We will not be concerned here with details of the theoretical differences between the work of Halliday and that of linguists such as Chomsky, except to point out that, whereas, for Chomsky, language is primarily a means of organizing and manipulating abstract symbols, for Halliday it is a means of conveying meanings. In other words, for Halliday and Winograd syntax is not viewed in isolation but in interaction with a semantic system. This intimate interaction between form and meaning guides the parsing process, as we have already seen.

The syntactic parser works by looking for items which fill slots in structure. A fairly simple example is the noun phrase, which has the following structure:

Det   Ord   Num   Adj*   Clasf*   Noun   Q*

Some of these units are optional and some, indicated by the asterisk, can occur more than once. What this says is that a noun phrase can have a determiner (e.g. *the*), followed by an ordinal (e.g. *first*), followed by a number (e.g. *five*), followed by one or more adjectives (e.g. *small, green*), followed by a noun used as a classifier (as in *iron cubes*), followed by a noun (e.g. *cubes*) which can then be followed by one or more qualifiers (e.g. *in the garage, which I bought*). Thus, the parser, on encountering a noun phrase such as *the first five iron cubes* would fill in the slots according to the structures permitted by the grammar. These are then assigned features relevant to the meaning. For example: *the* is a determiner with the feature DEFINITE as opposed to *a* which is also a determiner but has the feature INDEFINITE.

We can follow through a simple example – *pick up a big red block*. The parser begins by trying to parse a sentence and looks at the first word. If this is a preposition, it then calls a program to parse a prepositional phrase. In the present case it finds a verb and calls the structure for imperative clauses. For this structure it has to find a verb of the right type – here it will have to have features such as MAIN VERB, INFINITIVE, TRANSITIVE and PARTICLE. These say that, in a sentence which is imperative, the verb must be a main verb in infinitive form (with no tense markings). The other features, TRANSITIVE and PARTICLE, come from the dictionary definition of *pick* which requires a direct object and a particle (*up*). The next word *up* fills this latter requirement and so the parser moves on to find a noun phrase which will function as direct object. There are two possibilities for a verb such as *pick* – either a simple noun phrase as illustrated above, or a clause beginning with a WH-word (as in *pick up what I told you to*). The second possibility is excluded by the next word *a* which is classified as a determiner. As it has the feature INDEFINITE the slots for numeral and ordinal cannot be filled (we cannot say *a next three blocks*) so the parser moves on to the category adjective and succeed with *big*. It repeats this process with the next word *red* and tries again with *block*. This fails, as *block* is not listed as an adjective. Similarly, it is not listed as a classifier, so the system goes on to parse *block* as a noun and the parsing of the clause is complete. This analysis is then passed on to the semantic module to check whether it makes sense.

Semantics

There are certain commands which SHRDLU rejects as meaningless within the blocks world. Examples of these are *pick up the table* and *can the table pick up blocks?* In order to do this, the system uses semantic knowledge about the objects in its domain, for example, which objects are manipulable and whether a verb such as *pick up* requires an animate subject. Thus the dictionary information for *cube* would contain the following information:

> Cube
> > object
> > manipulable
> > rectangular
> > block
> > equidimensional

Other information should be added, for example, that blocks have colours, sizes, shapes and locations, thus permitting combinations such as *the big red cube in the box*.

The definition for verbs such as *contain* would also provide for different word meanings. One meaning involves physical containers and objects, as in *the box contains three pyramids*. The other applies to constructs such as stacks, piles or rows, as in *the stack contains a cube*. These meanings would be represented roughly as follows:

> Contain
> > transitive
> > > relation 1: container (object 1)
> > >   physical object (object 1)
> > >   object 1 contains object 2
> > > relation 2: construct (object 1)
> > >   physical object (object 2)
> > >   object 2 is part of object 1

Semantic knowledge is also used to identify the objects referred to by words such as *one* (e.g. *the big one*) and *the* (e.g. *the blue cube*). When the pro-form *one* is encountered, as in *a big red block and a little one*, a program is called to look back at what objects have been previously mentioned as candidates for the referent of *one*. In this case the phrase must be understood as meaning *a little red block* and not *a little big red block*. As far as *the* is concerned, the system looks either for a unique object in the data base (such as *the box*) or for an object which is unique from the speaker's viewpoint (usually because it has been mentioned recently). Thus at the beginning of a dialogue the instruction *grasp the pyramid* would be rejected as there is no uniquely identifiable pyramid (there are several in the scene), whereas following a command about a pyramid (such as *pick up a green pyramid*), a command using *the* (e.g. *put the pyramid in the box*) is meaningful.

Pragmatics

The pragmatic component contains non-linguistic information about the blocks world. Some of this is in the form of statements about the objects, such as:

B1 is a block.
B2 is a pyramid.
B1 is at location x,y,z.
B1 supports B2.
B2 is cleartop (i.e. there is nothing on it).
Box contains B4.
B1 has the colour red.
Blue is the colour.

A second type of information is represented in procedures for actions such as CLEARTOP (meaning to clear objects off the top of something). The procedure for CLEARTOP would ask the question:

Does X support an object Y?

If the answer is *no*, then the procedure returns *Assert that X is cleartop*. If the response is *yes*, then the procedure calls a further procedure GET-RID-OF Y. In other words, if we are asked to clear the top of an object, we look first to see if it already clear. If it is, we need proceed no further. If it is not, then we have to get rid of whatever is on top of the object.

Let us look a little more closely at what is involved in the procedure

GRASP. If asked to grasp an object, the first question the procedure asks is whether the object is manipulable. This can be ascertained by consulting the dictionary entry for the object. If the object is not manipulable, then the action cannot proceed and the request fails. If the answer is positive, then the next question is whether the robot is already holding the object. If the answer is positive, then the request succeeds and the system asserts that it is grasping the object. If the answer is negative, then we ask whether the robot is holding another object (remember that this is a one-armed robot). If the answer is *no*, then the robot can move its arm to the top centre of the object in order to lift it. However, if the answer is *yes* then the robot has first to get rid of that object. This involves a further procedure GET-RID-OF which would have a similar structure to the procedure for GRASP. (Getting rid of an object in this domain involves simply putting it on the table.)

As we can see, actions such as GRASP involve other actions such as GET-RID-OF and this in turn involves actions such as PUT-ON – in other words, there are goals and sub-goals, which can be represented in a table of goals, as follows:

Grasp object 1.
    Get rid of object 2.
        Put object 2 on a table.

In other words, to grasp object 1, first get rid of object 2. To get rid of object 2, put it on the table. A table of goals and sub-goals such as this provides a basis for responses to *why*-questions. If asked *why did you put object 2 on the table?* the system can consult the table of goals, match the question with the procedure PUT-ON and then move one step up to find the answer (*to get rid of object 2*). If asked *why did you get rid of object 2?* it matches the question with the procedure GET-RID-OF, which is one step up in the table of goals, and it responds *to grasp it*. In other words, actions are carried out because they accomplish higher level goals, so the answer to a question about why an action was carried out involves consulting the goal which that action was intended to achieve. Convesely answers to *how*-questions work in the opposite direction. When asked *how did you get rid of object 2?* the system would look to the sub-goal for GET-RID-OF and locate the procedure PUT-ON, which would lead to the response *by putting it on the table*. In other words, in order to achieve a goal you have to perform a particular action. Stating this action is a way of saying how the goal was achieved.

It is worth noting at this point that procedures such as GRASP and GET-RID-OF can be considered in terms of the actions they embody along with the preconditions for these actions and their subsequent effects. All of this information has to be made explicit. Take a simple example, the request *put the green block on the red block*. Here the preconditions for this action would be something like:

    Is the green block cleartop?
    Is the red block cleartop?
    Is your hand free?

Assuming that these preconditions are fulfilled, then the action can be carried out by invoking procedures such as GRASP and PUT-ON. But now the world has changed and will incorporate statements such as:

    The green block is on the red block.
    The green block is cleartop.
    The hand is empty.

This is a very simple example. If other procedures had been invoked, for example, in order to clear something off the green block before grasping it, then further changes would have been made to the state of the world and the whole interaction of preconditions and effects would become quite complex. This way of viewing actions has been mentioned here because it will be taken up later in chapter 8 which discusses computational work on speech acts, where actions such as making a request will be analysed similarly to actions such as picking up blocks, that is, in terms of their preconditions and effects. In this way, as we will see, physical and speech actions can be represented in similar terms.

Interaction of the modules

Let us look at how these modules interact in the interpretation of a sentence. We will take a sentence which is potentially ambiguous:

(4) Put the blue pyramid on the block in the box.

This could refer to either of the situations represented in figure 5.1: either the blue pyramid is already on the block and it is to be put into the box, or there is a blue pyramid and it has to be put on to a block which is in the box. The problem lies in how the grammatical constituents are bracketed.

The two different structures can be represented as follows:

    Put (the blue pyramid on the block) in (the box).
    Put (the blue pyramid) on (the block in the box).

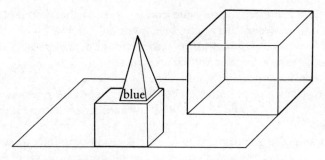

(a) *Put (the blue pyramid on the block) in the box*

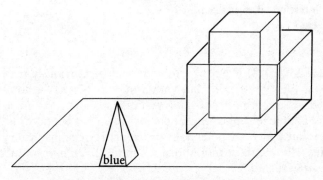

(b) *Put the blue pyramid (on the block in the box)*

Figure 5.1   Pragmatic interpretation of Put the blue pyramid on the block in the box

How would SHRDLU proceed? First the syntactic analyser would look for a suitable noun phrase to fit the slot of object of the verb *put*. It would come up first with *the blue pyramid on the block* which has the structure

Det	Adj	Noun	Q
The	blue	pyramid	on the block

The semantic analyser would check whether such an object is possible. The answer in this case would be positive, as pyramids can have a colour and they can be supported by other objects such as blocks. The next move would be to get the pragmatic component to check the blocks world to see whether this meaning is possible in the present state of the world. If the present world-state corresponds to the representation in figure 5.1(a), where there is a blue pyramid on the block, then the meaning *the blue pyramid on the block* would be accepted. If however the world-state were that represented in figure 5.1(b), where the blue pyramid is not on a block but there is a block in the box, then the structure (*the blue pyramid on the block*) would be rejected and the syntactic analyser would have to look for another structure (in this case, *the block in the box*). In this way the system comes up with the appropriate interpretation by allowing the modules to interact with each other, thus preventing a wasteful accumulation of unusable interpretations. It is assumed that this approximates to human understanding in that on hearing an utterance we check to make sense of that utterance in terms of the objects and persons being referred to and only entertain a second interpretation if the first is unacceptable.

Conversational aspects

What was SHRDLU like as a conversationalist? Obviously the range of topics was highly restricted, but within the tiny blocks world SHRDLU exhibited several aspects of conversational competence. In a general sense it was able to deal with phenomena which did not occur in isolated sentences but which are potentially problematic in conversation, such as pronouns, ellipsis, substitution forms (e.g. *the green one*) and the use of the definite article.

A second feature was the ability to cope with potential ambiguities. It had two ways of doing this. In the first, it would point out the ambiguity so that the user would be informed and could keep track of what was happening. It would then choose and act upon the more plausible interpretation. The following is an example:

(5)
find a block which is taller than the one you are holding and put it into the box
BY 'IT' I ASSUME YOU MEAN THE BLOCK WHICH IS TALLER THAN THE ONE I AM HOLDING
OK

There were two possible referents for *it*, the taller block and the block the system was holding. The program had heuristics for selecting the more plausible interpretation.

When SHRDLU required a response from the user before it could proceed, it would asked the user to choose between interpretations offered. In response to the question *how many things are on top of green cubes?* the system replied:

(6)

I'M NOT SURE WHAT YOU MEAN BY 'ON TOP OF' IN THE PHRASE 'ON TOP OF GREEN CUBES'
  1 DIRECTLY ON THE SURFACE?
  2 ANYWHERE ON TOP OF?

These responses were achieved by means of combining parts of the input question with pieces of the definitions of words stored in the dictionary. Although the end result is still far removed from the devices with which humans cope with conversational breakdown (see chapters 9 and 10), it is interesting that the system is endowed with a knowledge of some of the ways in which breakdown can arise – in the use of pronouns and of ambiguous or imprecise natural language expressions. Thus one aspect of conversational repair, the identification of sources of potential misunderstanding, is addressed by the program.

The most interesting conversational aspect of SHRDLU concerns its question-answering techniques. Answering questions does not just involve simple information retrieval from a store of knowledge – it also involves some assessment of what sort of responses people expect. SHRDLU's abilities in this respect can be seen in the answering of *yes/no*-questions. At first sight it might seem that a question such as *does the block support three pyramids?* requires only *yes* or *no* as an answer. But what if the block supports either two or four pyramids? In this case the answer *no* is not very helpful. Instead the system would reply either *no, only two of them* or *four of them*. Indeed the system was capable of more; it could also specify which blocks were involved (e.g. *two of them: a large red one and the green one*), which would be even more helpful. In other words, a response to a *yes/no* question could have three parts:

  1 yes or no
  2 a number
  3 a description

This was achieved by treating a question such as *does the pyramid support a block?* as logically equivalent to the questions *which block does the pyramid support?* or *how many blocks does the pyramid support?* which supply the descriptions and number respectively. There were also ways of avoiding redundant information as in the exchange *are there three blocks? – yes, three of them: a green one and two large red ones*. Also, questions involving phrases such as *exactly one block* would generate no description as it would be assumed that here the number is more important than the description of the objects.

We have looked at SHRDLU in some detail as it exemplifies an integrated approach to language understanding. The syntactic analysis of the input is not treated as primary or autonomous but is performed in consultation with the semantic and pragmatic levels. However, syntactic analysis is viewed as contributing significantly to language understanding. In this way SHRDLU is an advance on simpler keyword-matching programs. We have also seen how SHRDLU incorporated some basic principles of conversation which enable it to engage in a more co-operative dialogue with the user. We will be returning to this aspect of natural language systems in chapter 8.

There were, however, many aspects of conversation which SHRDLU could not handle; it lacked the ability to contribute further to the current topic, to cope with the sorts of ill-formed input which usually cause no problems for people and to understand the goals and plans which underlie the utterances of a dialogue partner. We will see in later chapters how these issues have been dealt with by other systems. But first we will need to look at some developments in another area pioneered by SHRDLU – the use of knowledge to guide the language understanding process.

The role of knowledge in language understanding

We need many different types of knowledge in order to participate in dialogue – knowledge about objects, their typical functions and attributes and their relationships to other objects; knowledge about events and stereotypical sequences of events; and knowledge about people, their typical wishes, motivations, goals and plans. All this is part of a normal person's knowledge of the world and it is brought to bear when we interpret stories, situations and everyday events. When we engage in dialogue we need an additional kind of knowledge – we need to know something about our dialogue partners, about what they know and what they do not know – in order to make our talk relevant and appropriate to their needs.

Knowledge can be used in several ways in natural language processing.

1 To restrict the domain sufficiently so that all the information which is relevant to the domain can be built in.
2 To enable connections to be made between objects and events where the links are often left implicit.
3 To permit new knowledge to be derived on the basis what is already known.

In the first case knowledge constrains language understanding by specifying which particular structures and meanings are to be expected in a particular context. This insight, which has guided some of the simpler domain-specific systems described so far, also applies to more sophisticated systems which embody stereotyped knowledge of everyday objects and events. Indeed many successful working systems have been based on this principle. When a system is required to handle questions on such fields as baseball games, electronic circuits, supplementary benefit, and these fields themselves are limited in a specified way, there is no need to provide it with a more general language understanding capability. For example, BASEBALL 'knew' that it was going to be asked questions about the times, places and results of baseball games and so it simply had to analyse any input in terms of these topics. Because the amount of analysis that had to be done on the input was constrained fairly complex queries could be handled. One amusing example of the use of this technique is the story (probably apocryphal) of a voice-activated chess-playing system which would interpret any input as instructions to move a chess piece. On receiving the input *take the banana off the board* the system carried out the move *move the pawn to kind 4*, presumably because the input was roughly similar phonetically to this opening chess move.

More generally systems can embody stereotyped information such as our knowledge of everyday objects and events, or they can include knowledge about what has already been said in the discourse by each participant. Both kinds of knowledge can be stored in memory and called upon, when necessary, to interpret new input; thus understanding does not have to begin afresh with each new input. We will be looking later at *frames* and *scripts* which are well-known ways of representing such knowledge.

Knowledge can also be used as a means of making sense of input in which the connections are implicit as in the following example:

(7) John couldn't start the car. The battery was flat.

In order to understand how these two sentences are related, we need the knowledge that a battery is a part of a car and that if the battery is flat the car will probably not start. This knowledge is quite specific. If we substitute a different averse condition the story no longer makes sense for example:

(8) John couldn't start the car. The windscreen was dirty.

The knowledge required to understand 7 involves the representation of the meanings of the words *car*, *battery* and *flat* in such a way as to show

how they are interrelated. Semantic networks, to which we will return later, are one way of representing the interrelation of this knowledge.

The next example needs a different type of knowledge structure to make the connection between two sentences clear:

(9) Jim wanted to buy a new car. He rang his bank manager.

It is unlikely that there would be a direct link in any knowledge structure between cars and bank managers, or indeed between bank managers and anything else for which a person might require money. We have to take a more circuitous route to understand example 9. We assume that Jim called the bank manager because he wanted to buy a car, that to buy a car a person needs money and that bank managers are a potential source of money. Thus we set up a goal and a plan to achieve that goal which in turn involves a series of sub-goals. Some goals can be stated at a fairly general level, but associated with the items in example 9 might be further information about some of the conditions which are involved when obtaining a loan from a bank manager, e.g. repayment and interest rates. A different plan for obtaining money could be to rob the bank. This plan would carry associated risks such as possible detection and imprisonment. Jim's choice of plan (i.e. ringing his bank manager) might therefore also involve an explanation of why he chose one method rather than another.

Often, when we do not have the specific knowledge which might enable us to make sense of what we hear we have to rely on our expectation that conversational participants usually follow a principle of co-operative behaviour which involves their making relevant and appropriate contributions. Consider the following example from Stubbs (1983: 124):

(10) You ought to read Wombats Galore. Bruce McQuarry is a great author.

Our interpretation of example 10 is that Bruce McQuarry is the author of a book called Wombats Galore. Yet, as Stubbs argues, we cannot have reached this interpretation via stored information as neither the book nor the author exist. What happens is that we seem to assume that sentences which are juxtaposed in this way are related, unless we are given reason to assume the contrary, and we make this assumption because of the principle of co-operative behaviour in conversation. This would precede any further reasoning involving general world knowledge by means of which the mention of reading might evoke books, newspapers and other reading material, which in turn could evoke names of authors, publishers and other information. In other words, the knowledge that we use to make the required links between the two sentences might be representable at a more general level than is the case in current computer programs and may involve more general rules of reasoning than those which have been proposed so far.

We come now to the third way in which knowledge can be used in language processing, that is, to enable us to reason from what we already know and thus create new knowledge. Indeed it can be argued that the ability to reason is a primary indication of intelligence. One aspect of reasoning involves making logical deductions. To take a simple example: if we know that a poodle is a dog and that a dog is a pet, then we can conclude, on the basis of a simple law of logic, that a poodle is a pet. This sort of deduction can be made, irrespective of the actual words of the statements or content of our knowledge, on the basis of universal principles of logic as we shall see later in the book. Other deductions are more content-specific and are not governed by laws of logic but by our knowledge of everyday information. In order to appreciate this, consider the situation where you hear the sentence *Chris is pregnant*. On hearing it you would be likely to add the information to your store of knowledge and if asked later whether Chris was pregnant, you would remember what you had been told and answer in the affirmative. But we do much more than store and retrieve information which we hear – we process it and create new knowledge out of it. In some cases this might be in the form of conclusions which follow logically from what we know. In other cases the knowledge takes the form of assumptions which may or may not be true. For example, we might make the following assumptions about Chris; some of them follow logically, not all will necessarily be true:

1 Chris is female.
2 Chris is of a certain age, probably between 14 and 40 years.
3 Chris has had sexual relations with a male.
4 Chris is no longer menstruating.
5 Chris may be experiencing nausea, especially in the morning.
6 Chris is going to have a baby (or an abortion).
7 If Chris remains pregnant, her body shape will change.
8 If Chris gives birth to a baby, she will be a mother and the baby will be her child.

This list is incomplete, but notice how much knowledge is normally assumed in the concept *pregnant*. The list deals mainly with physical actions and states, but clearly other factors can come into play. If we knew more about Chris's circumstances, we might make other assumptions. If she is a woman in her thirties who is anxious to have a child, then we would imagine that she is pleased that she is pregnant, but if she is a 13-year-old schoolgirl then she might be worried or unhappy. We would also entertain different assumptions in these two scenarios in respect of other people associated with her.

It might be argued that what has been said so far is familiar to anyone who has been concerned with the use of language in communication. For example: in speech act theory and discourse and conversation analysis reference is often made to the importance of background knowledge and of people's ability to make inferences. However it should be noted that these issues have usually been treated in a rather cavalier way in this literature. Little or no attempt is made to characterize background knowledge explicitly or to spell out how it is used to make inferences. In AI, on the other hand, such things have to be made explicit, even if, as we noted before, they may seem obvious to us. For this reason it will be helpful to examine from an AI perspective what would have to be represented when we refer to things such as background knowledge and inferences. Indeed knowledge representation is currently one of the most rapidly developing areas in AI. It would go beyond the scope of this book to present a full account of knowledge representation techniques in AI (see, for example, Barr and Feigenbaum 1981; Rich 1983; Rumelhart and Norman 1983). Instead those issues which are most relevant to the systems described in this book will be presented briefly and fairly informally as a preparation for later chapters which deal more specifically with different types of knowledge structures used in natural language processing.

Inference

The term inference is used widely to explain the interpretative work which hearers and readers do when they try to understand a text. It is important to distinguish between different types of inference. We can make a preliminary distinction between logical and pragmatic inferences. Logical inferences (or deductions) are the result of laws of inference as specified in formal logic. Given the following premisses

(11)
All teachers are impoverished.
John is a teacher.

we can deduce, on the basis of one of the laws of logic, that John is impoverished. This works as follows: if we know that the statement all *xs are p* is true, and further that the statement *John is an x* is also true, then by the law of universal instantiation (which states that if something is true for all members of a class then it is true for individual members of that class) we can validly deduce that *John is p* (in this case, that he is impoverished). These laws of deductive logic are content-independent and can be used to deduce any conclusion on the basis of premises known to be true. Laws of logical inference such as these have been used extensively in AI for automated theorem proving. Here facts that are known to be true are operated on by rules of inference in order to deduce further facts which can be guaranteed to be true.

Notice, however, that these laws do not necessarily apply in a natural conversation. Suppose, for example, that the statements about John and teachers were part of a dialogue like the following:

(12)
A   All teachers are impoverished.
B   John is a teacher.

Now suppose that it is known to both A and B that John has a lot of money. Then it would be absurd to conclude that John is impoverished – rather we would more naturally conclude that the first statement, that all teachers are impoverished, is not true, or at least does not hold universally. In other words, B's utterance is to be taken as a qualification of what A has said; B is in fact saying that not all teachers are impoverished.

What we are encountering here is the difference between logical and pragmatic inferences. Logical inferences are obviously important because they enable people to arrive at certain conclusions by applying universal laws of logic to known facts. However, in many cases people arrive at conclusions which are not necessarily true, as in deductive logic, but are only potentially true. Pragmatic inferences are neither content-nor context-independent and so are possibly more difficult to represent formally. They often involve a process of filling in details which are not explicit in the surface text, such as associations between words (or, more accurately, concepts) in the text and ideas which are relevant to an understanding of the text. Thus, if we hear that John is afraid of thunder, we can assume that this is because he feels that thunder might be harmful to him. If we hear that Jim has had a lot to drink, we might infer that he has been drinking for a reason, that he will be intoxicated and will possibly behave uncharacteristically, and that next day he might have a hangover. These are inferences which deal with the possible reasons for and effects of what we are hearing. As Schank (1980: 257) puts it

'Inference, then, is the fitting of new information into a context that explains it and predicts other facts that follow from it.'

Semantic networks

It was mentioned earlier that not all knowledge needs to be stored explicitly but that some knowledge can be inferred on the basis of more general principles. This has important consequences both for theories of human processing and for the representation of knowledge in computers, as it is possible to represent the knowledge more economically. This was in fact one of the strengths of semantic network theory, which was one of the most prominent systems for the representation of knowledge in the late sixties and early seventies. Semantic networks consist of a series of nodes representing objects, concepts or events, and of links between the nodes, representing their interrelations. These representations were often intended as an explicitly psychological model of human associative memory (see, for example, Quillian 1968).

Some simple examples will illustrate how semantic networks were used to represent knowledge about objects and about meanings of words. If we wish to represent the fact that a poodle is a dog, we could do this with the following network (figure 5.2).

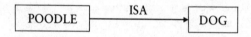

Figure 5.2   Semantic network 1

This simple network has nodes for poodle and dog and these are linked by the ISA relation. Further nodes and links could represent further facts such as:

A poodle is a dog.
A dog is a pet.
A pet is an animal.

Thus ISA links can be used to represent relationships between objects in a hierarchical taxonomy (see figure 5.3).

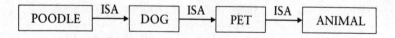

Figure 5.3   Semantic network 2

A further type of link, the ISPART relation, deals with properties of objects, in particular the relationships between an object and its components. The following examples are illustrated in figure 5.4:

A hand is part of a body.
A finger is part of a hand.

Figure 5.4   Semantic network 3

Semantic relations such as these were the basis for the reasoning processes in SIR (see chapter 4). Given facts such as:

John is a boy.
A boy is a person.
A hand is part of a person.
A finger is part of a hand.
A person has two hands.
A hand has five fingers.

SIR could work out the answer to the question *how many fingers has John?* This was done by passing information from higher categories in the network such as *person* down to lower categories or instances such as *John*. For example, if it is known that John is a boy and that a boy is a person, then it can be deduced that John is a person on the basis of a simple rule along the lines of:

If x is a y and y is a z then x is a z.

Thus information which is not explicitly stated in the representation can be deduced. Taking this one stage further, the properties associated with an object represented in a higher node can be passed down to an object in a lower node. This is referred to as *property inheritance*. To take an example: if it is known that a person has two hands and that John is a person, then it can be deduced that John has two hands. Furthermore, if it is known that there are five fingers on a hand a simple calculation can be made to work out how many fingers John has. Thus information about persons can be stored under a general category and can be passed down (or inherited), as required. This allows for greater economy in the representation and at the same time incorporates principles of general reasoning which transform a static database into a more dynamic one. Semantic networks have also been used to represent other types of knowledge such as the content of sentences in terms of case frames (see, for example, Simmons 1973). More recent work on semantic networks has been described in Findler (1979).

Frames and scripts

Suppose your neighbour asked you to come out and see his new car. What would you expect to see? You would probably expect a vehicle of a certain size and shape. You would expect it to have certain properties such as wheels, lights, doors and bumpers. As you approached the car you would probably be able to see only two of the wheels, but what you knew about cars would lead you to expect to be surprised if you found on further inspection that there were no two wheels on the other side. Then as you looked into the car you would expect to see more things, such as a steering wheel, seats, pedals, a gear lever and a variety of instruments and dials. You might even notice that one of the instruments was a clock. You would be surprised if there were no steering wheel or if there were more than one.

This example illustrates what is meant by the notion of a frame. Frames are large-scale knowledge structures which represent stereotyped information. Minsky, who first proposed frames as a way of representing knowledge, wrote:

> when one encounters a new situation (or makes a substantial change in one's view of the present problem) one selects from memory a substantial structure called a frame. . . . A frame is a data-structure for representing a stereotyped situation like being in a certain kind of living-room, or going to a child's birthday party. (1975: 212)

Frames are like complex semantic nets in which each node has its own internal structure. A frame consists of slots to be filled. In some cases these slots will already have default values, that is, values which are to be assumed unless there is any information to the contrary. In the car frame the slot for number of doors may be four, but this can be altered to suit a particular instance, such as a two-door car. Within one frame other frames can be evoked. The car frame might lead to a frame for car engines, which might include frames for parts of the engine. We use frames, when we encounter new situations, by selecting from memory an appropriate frame and comparing it with reality. Often the frame stored in memory will not directly match reality. For example: the car frame might not correspond exactly to our neighbour's car, but it will provide a typical description of a car into which details can be added as appropriate.

In what ways can frames be used to help understanding? Frames were originally proposed to assist in the field of computer vision. We can look at a simple example which provides a basic principle which is extendable to language processing. Take again the example of our neighbour's car. When we first approached it we could only see two wheels, yet our knowledge of cars told us to expect four. Not only would we expect to see two more wheels if we went round to the other side of the car, we would expect them to be in a certain place. We would also know that the two wheels which we saw at first and which were now out of sight were still in place where we first saw them. In other words our general knowledge about objects enables us to assume things which we cannot actually see. More generally, our sensory input is inadequate – it is varied and distorted and it changes as we adopt a different perspective. But this does not cause us any problems because we impose order on this inadequate sensory input through out internal representations of objects which are based on our prior knowledge and experiences.

So far we have talked about frames for objects. However the principle can be applied to other stored knowledge. There can be frames for syntactic structures, for stereotypic situations, for how people typically behave. In each case the frame will have slots with default values which can be altered as more information becomes available.

How do frames relate to language? Basically frames have been used in natural language programs to facilitate the understanding process. By using frames we do not need to work things out from first principles – instead we can use stores of knowledge representing previous experience to guide us in making sense of what we hear. This is what is known as top-down processing. We know something about the situation we are in, about the objects and events that appear in this situation, and this prior knowledge leads us to have expectations and to make predictions that will guide our interpretations of what we hear. In this way our understanding is facilitated and we do not have to analyse the input entirely from scratch. We will look at an example of the use of frames in the natural language understanding system GUS which is to be described in chapter 7.

We can look briefly at the related concept of scripts, which will be discussed in greater detail in the next chapter. Scripts are concerned with stereotypic events. As Schank and Abelson (1977: 41) have written:

> A script is a structure that describes appropriate sequences of events in a particular context. . . . Scripts handle everyday situations. They are not subject to much change, nor do they provide the apparatus for handling totally novel situations. Thus a script is a predetermined stereotyped sequence of actions that defines a well-known situation.

We can see how scripts might help in natural language processing if we consider how we work out the referents of the pronouns in the following example:

(13) Max got on a bus. The conductor came over. He gave him a ticket.

We have no difficulty in understanding that the conductor gave Max a ticket and not vice versa. In other words, *he* refers back to *the conductor* and *him* to Max. It could be argued that we know this because the conductor is the focus of the previous sentence and the next sentence, which contains the pronouns, maintains this focus through parallel syntax. However, we would have no greater comprehension difficulty if the third sentence had read *he gave him a five pound note*. In this case we would understand that *he* referred to Max and *him* to his conductor.

But how do we know? we know through our knowledge about travelling on buses. People who are passengers on buses pay fares and conductors give them tickets as a token that they have paid. This knowledge enables us to sort out the roles in the short story in 13 and to work out who is giving what to whom, and why?

Scripts represent sequences of events. They can be used in many ways in language understanding and the resolution of pronouns is only one example. A more widely cited use of scripts is to supply the information which is implicit in a story. For example, in the above story we can assume that Max waited for the bus at a bus stop, that he got on to the bus when it stopped, that he gave the conductor some money, and so on. Although we have not been told these things happened, we can assume that they did on the basis of our knowledge of this everyday situation. In the next chapter the use of scripts and similar knowledge structures will be examined in greater detail.

Further Reading

SHRDLU

Like ELIZA, SHRDLU is discussed widely in AI textbooks. The original account is Winograd (1972). A shorter version of this appears in

Winograd (1973), while Winograd (1981) presents a critical review of the shortcomings of this work.

Knowledge representation

Bobrow and Collins (1975) in an early collection of papers on this topic, including Minsky's classic paper on frames. For good overviews see the chapter on this topic in Barr and Feigenbaum (1981), chapters 5–7 of Rich (1983), as well as Rumelhart and Norman (1983).

6

Knowledge Structures:
Events, Goals and Plans

Some of the most interesting work on natural language processing has been carried out by Schank and his colleagues at Yale. We have already encountered Schank's conceptual dependency theory (see chapter 2). Basically this is an approach to natural language which emphasizes content rather than form. We saw that one of the main features of the theory is that it addressed the issue of the role of world knowledge in language understanding and production by associating with the conceptual representation of a sentence the inferences which that sentence could give rise to. There were two major problems, however. First, there was no control over the inferences which could be generated from any one sentence. Each sentence could give rise to a large number of inferences, each of which could in turn give rise to more inferences, thus leading quickly to combinatorial explosion. As well as controlling the number of inferences which ought to be made, there needed to be a way of determining which were the most sensible inferences to generate. The second problem was that the theory dealt only with isolated sentences, whereas in the communicative use of language we are concerned with larger units such as stories and conversations. The work to be described in this chapter builds on conceptual dependency theory to take account of these two problems. As we will see, the two problems turn out to be related. Work on larger units of language has not only extended analysis beyond the level of the sentence; what has emerged is that it is only by considering larger units that we can interpret sentences in the first place and exert some control on the inferences which we generate from them. It will be impossible to do full justice to the work of the Yale language understanding programs within this chapter. A popular account is provided in Schank (1984), while a more technical account, on which much of the following is based, is to be found in Schank and Riesbeck (1981).

Scripts

Scripts were introduced briefly at the end of the last chapter. Scripts have been used widely as a means of representing sequences of events in stereotyped situations, such as going to a restaurant or travelling by bus. Here is another short story about travelling on a bus which will show how scripts are used in language understanding.

(1)
Terence got on a bus to go to work. He sat down. When the conductor came, he realized that he had left his money at home, so he had to walk to work.

The reader should have little difficulty in understanding this story. But what do we mean by understanding? One important test is whether we can answer questions about the story, thus demonstrating our understanding. The first two questions should pose no problem:

Q   Did Terence get on to a bus to go to work?
Q   Who came up to Terence?

Now consider the next two:

Q   Did the conductor give Terence a ticket?
Q   Why did Terence walk to work?

Again, we should have little difficulty in answering these questions. However, the information required to answer them is not contained in the text. Instead, in order to answer the second set of questions, we have to supply information based on our knowledge of what is involved in travelling on a bus. Schank claims that humans have thousands of such scripts stored in their brains and that these are brought into play when familiar situations are encountered. In other words, much of human understanding is heavily script-based. Scripts are concerned with what can happen in everyday situations – with the order of events, and with the people and objects involved. There are also mechanisms for coping with interference, that is, with what happens when an expected event does not, or cannot, occur and how this can be. The bus story can serve as an example. A script for an event such as a bus journey would include roles for the people involved, settings for the events, and props (the objects involved in the script). The following list sets out roles, settings and props for a bus script:

Roles
   travellers
   bus driver
   conductor
   bus company

Settings
   bus stop at origin of journey
   inside of bus
   bus stop at destination

Props
   money for bus fare
   ticket exchanged for bus fare
   seat on bus
   door

All of these items are slots which can be filled during the course of a story about a bus journey and we can expect to hear about them in the story. The script accounts for the fact that when we hear about *the conductor* we are not surprised, whereas we would be if we heard about *the waiter*. Note that it also accounts for the use of the definite article *the* in this sentence. A simple guideline for the use of the definite article in a text is that it can normally only be used when referring back to something which has been previously mentioned. An extension to this rule is that the definite article can also be used when the speaker believes that the hearer can locate the person or object being referred to. Scripts, which set out the persons and objects which we can expect to hear about in a story, account for this use of the definite article.

One aspect of scripts which we have not mentioned so far is *scenes* – the events which have to occur in a script. For the bus script, these would include the following:

Wait for bus at bus stop.
Get on bus.
Pay fare.
Get off bus at destination.

This is not a complete list, and there are some events which are optional, such as taking a seat. Furthermore, each scene can be sub-divided into component actions. For example, paying the fare involves the conductor approaching the traveller, the traveller taking out money, handing it to the conductor and receiving a ticket in return and possibly some change. All of these details would be listed as actions which happen during the course of a bus journey. Of course, not all of the actions are likely to be mentioned and even the crucial ones for a bus script, such as paying the fare, may not be explicitly mentioned. Such actions are, however, assumed by default, so that if we hear a story such as:

(2) John took the bus to work. He arrived early.

we assume that John did things like getting on the bus, paying his fare and getting off at his destination, even though we have not been told this as such. It is the knowledge contained in scripts which enables us to understand stories about everyday events in which much is left unsaid.

So far we have used a constructed example to illustrate and explain the basic principles of scripts. It might now be helpful to look in a little more detail at an actual example of the workings of SAM, the Yale program for applying and understanding scripts. SAM (Script Applier Mechanism) consists of three components. The first, ELI (English Language Interpreter), analyses the input sentence by sentence. ELI extracts the conceptual content of each sentence, representing this content in terms of Conceptual Dependency structures. Thus if the first sentence was *John gave Mary a book*, ELI would construct a representation around the conceptual act ATRANS, which deals with transfer of possession and which has slots to be filled for the actor, object and recipient roles as well as for the direction of transfer. This representation is based on the content of the sentence rather than its form; it is language-independent. We understand from it that transfer of possession is involved and the surface verb could be, for example, *give, sell, present, receive, take, buy*, etc. This level of representation is important as it is claimed that we do not understand stories by recognizing the surface forms of sentences but by seeing the stories as chains of causal events and perceiving the links.

SAM's second component is PP-Memory. Briefly, this component deals with the roles and props mentioned in the story. These are called the Picture-Producers (PPs). PP-Memory notes each mention of a Picture Producer and hands this information on to the third component, the Script Applier. In example 1, for example, *Terence* would be marked with a token on first mention in the first sentence. *He* in the second sentence would also be given a token but at this stage would not be connected with *Terence*. If, in the third sentence, we read that *the young man realised that he had left his money at home*, a further token would be created for the role *the young man*. All of these references would be tied together by the Script Applier.

The Script Applier is the component which does most of the higher-level understanding for SAM. A script is applied from a database of scripts to the output from ELI and predictions are set up about likely inputs to follow. References to PPs are resolved at this point. In the case of example 1, the expectation would be that Terence would sit down, so *Terence* in the first sentence and *he* in the second are linked. The same thing happens in example 3 which reads:

(3) When the conductor came, he realized that he had left his money at home and so he had to walk to work.

We do not assume that *he* in any of its three occurrences refers to the conductor, although there is nothing in the syntactic structure of the sentence to prevent this interpretation. Rather, our knowledge of the bus script leads us to expect that it will be the traveller who needs money for the fare and who will have to leave the bus if he has no money to pay the fare.

SAM was able to read newspaper stories about events such as car accidents, plane crashes, train wrecks, oil spills and state visits, to provide summaries, paraphrases and translations of the stories, and to answer questions abou them. We can illustrate this with an actual example based on a VIP visit script (Cullingford 1981).

VIP visit

The following is a three-sentence story about a state visit of the Premier of Albania to China.

(4)
Sunday morning Enver Hoxha, the Premier of Albania, and Mrs Hoxha arrived in Peking at the invitation of Communist China. The Albanian party was welcomed at Peking Airport by Foreign Minister Huang. Chairman Hua and Mr Hoxha discussed economic relations between China and Albania for three hours.

Although this seems to be a simple story, there are several points where script knowledge is required in order to understand what is going on. The following informal account explains how SAM handles such a story. ELI begins by analysing the first sentence and on encountering *arrived* outputs an appropriate conceptualization – that a group of people, consisting of Premier and Mrs Hoxha, PTRANSed themselves to Peking (PTRANS is the act dealing with transfer of location). The arrival is seen in some temporal relation to an invitation by Communist China. No inferences are made at this stage about where the Hoxhas came from or how they got to China, nor that the invitation preceded their arrival, as this information is not contained in the surface string. Next PP-Memory deals with reference to PPs, looking for those in permanent memory such as Enver Hoxha, Peking, Albania and China. At this stage no inference is made connecting the group which has arrived with the group which has been invited. Finally, Script Applier receives a representation of the first sentence. A search is made for *invitation* in the database of scripts. Other scripts might be tried first (e.g. TRAINWRECK); eventually VIPVISIT is tried and *invitation* is recognized as a relevant concept, so VIPVISIT is activated, and the analyser now looks for words and phrases which are appropriate to a state-visit context. *Arrival* is found and predictions are made about what can come next, for example, the mode of travel. In addition, a check is made for a VIP to fit the role required in a VIPVISIT script, as otherwise the story could be about a tourist arriving in another country.

The second sentence is treated in the same way. Script Applier looks for mention of a group reaching an arrival point and can make the inferences that, as the group is at Peking Airport they must have arrived there and that they are likely to have travelled by plane. PP-Memory can now match information about the Hoxhas with the token for the Albanian group, showing that both refer to the same persons.

The third sentence describes a two-way transfer of information (MTRANS), involving Hoxha and Hua, about an economic contract. APPLY searches for this event in VIPVISIT. An economic agreement is one of the main events expected in the script and can be seen as a possible reason for the state visit – other reasons could be the signing of a treaty. Thus this story consists of three episodes:

1 a VIP group travels to Peking.
2 an official greeting episode.
3 an official talks episode.

Various inferences are made during the application of the script. For example, there is no mention in the story of where talks were held, so Script Applier assumes it was in the city where the Hoxha party arrived. This is, of course, only a probable inference, but it can be assumed by default because any contrary information would probably be supplied explicitly.

The next stage is that SAM provides a summary of the text (example 5) in which only the main event (MAINCON) is expressed, supplemented by information about where the discussion took place and additional information about the names and roles of the participants:

(5)

Premier Enver Hoxha, the Albanian government head, and Chairman Hua Kuo-Feng, the China government head, discussed Albania/Communist China economic affairs in Peking, China two days ago.

SAM's question answering abilities are also worth illustrating with some examples:

(6)

who went to China?
PREMIER ENVER HOXHA AND MRS HOXHA

Note here that the story does not actually say that anyone went to China, only that the Hoxhas arrived in Peking. In other words, a causal-chain inference has to be made that arrival in the capital of a country must be preceded by entering that country.

(7)

how did they get to China?
MRS HOXHA AND PREMIER ENVER HOXHA FLEW TO COMMUNIST CHINA

This answer depends on three inferences:

1 *They* must be recognized as referring to the Hoxha party.
2 China must be recognized as Communist China and not Nationalist China.
3 The mode of travel has to be inferred from the phrase *welcomed at Peking Airport*, which is stored as the instrumental part of the travelling part of the VIPVISIT.

These examples show how knowledge structures such as scripts can be used in the understanding of connected discourse. Understanding is seen as more than analysing the syntactic structure of sentences. It involves finding causal links between events and making assumptions on the basis of default reasoning about events which have not been mentioned explicitly. It is claimed that humans have access to thousands of scripts which they use to understand situations similar to those which they have previously encountered. However, there is still the problem of how people manage to make sense of situations which they have not previously encountered. This brings us to the notions of plans, goals and themes, which have been implemented in a program called PAM (Plan Applier Mechanism) to which we now turn.

Plans, goals and themes

Consider the following story:

(8) Harry was hoping for promotion. He asked his boss round for dinner.

Unless we have a Promotion script to apply to this story, in order to understand it we need to rely on non-stereotypical common-sense knowledge of what people might do to enhance their chances of getting promotion – impressing the boss might help, inviting the boss to dinner might impress him and so on. On hearing the first sentence we might expect that what follows has something to do with Harry's plan to get promotion, but there is no way of predicting his exact behaviour, as there could be many different ways of achieving this goal. What is needed is general information about how people achieve goals and what sort of goals they try to achieve. This sort of knowledge can be handled by PAM. The following example is taken from a description of PAM by Wilensky (1981).

(9)

INPUT	John wanted money. He got a gun and walked into a liquor store. He told the owner he wanted some money. The owner gave John the money and John left
INPUT	why did John get a gun?
OUTPUT	BECAUSE JOHN WANTED TO ROB THE LIQUOR STORE
INPUT	why did John threaten the storekeeper?
OUTPUT	BECAUSE JOHN NEEDED TO GET SOME MONEY
INPUT	why did the shopkeeper give John some money?
OUTPUT	BECAUSE THE SHOPKEEPER DIDN'T WANT TO GET HURT
INPUT	why did John leave?
OUTPUT	BECAUSE JOHN DIDN'T WANT TO GET CAUGHT.
OUTPUT	STORY FROM JOHN'S POINT OF VIEW: I NEEDED TO GET SOME DOUGH. SO I GOT MYSELF THIS GUN, AND I WALKED DOWN TO THE LIQUOR STORE. I TOLD THE SHOPKEEPER THAT IF HE DIDN'T LET ME HAVE THE MONEY THEN I WOULD SHOOT HIM. SO HE HANDED IT OVER. THEN I LEFT
OUTPUT	STORY FROM THE OWNER'S POINT OF VIEW: I WAS MINDING THE STORE WHEN A MAN ENTERED. HE THREATENED ME WITH A GUN AND DEMANDED ALL THE CASH RECEIPTS. WELL, I DIDN'T WANT TO GET HURT, SO I GAVE HIM THE MONEY. THEN HE ESCAPED

As can be seen, common-sense knowledge about goals and plans is made explicit in PAM. Notice, for example, that we are not told why John got a gun, what his goal was in telling the owner that he wanted some money, why the owner gave him the money, and why John left. We assume explanations for these actions and our assumptions are based on fairly sophisticated knowledge of people's goals and plans. Take the question about why John gets a gun. One general rule which is built into PAM can be stated as follows:

> If a character has the goal of possessing a functional object, then that character probably wants to use that object for its intended purpose.

PAM includes about 180 such rules. Of course, this is a general rule, but we can see how it applies to John's action of obtaining a gun. Elsewhere would be stored information about guns and what they can be used for – for example, to threaten people. Linked to threatening is the goal of obtaining something (e.g. money or goods). The goal of obtaining something can be achieved in several ways – by asking, by offering an exchange, by threatening or by overpowering. At a higher level there are goals such as satisfaction (getting food and sleep), enjoyment (travel, entertainment, exercise), achievement (possessions, power positions, good job). Some goals take precedence over others – for example, the goal of self-preservation usually takes precedence over achievement and so the storekeeper parts with his money. Goals can also involve sub-goals. For example, in order to get money, John obtains a gun. In order to threaten the storekeeper, he has to tell him what he wants and show him his gun. To do this, he has to enter the store. Later, in order to preserve his freedom, John leaves the store to avoid subsequent capture.

In some cases there is a fairly fixed sequence of instrumental goals which combine with a particular plan and these goals can in turn involve further plans which are subject to general rules and so have become known as *Planboxes*. To take an example: for John to be able to use a gun to threaten the storekeeper, he had to use the general plan USE. This plan consists of the following goals:

> In order to use an object you must:
>   know where the object is.
>   be near the object.
>   get control of the object.
>   have the object ready for use.
>   do the desired action.

Each of these goals might involve a further plan. For example, to know about something can involve asking about it. ASK is a general plan subject to rules which are set out in a Planbox, as shown below.

Planbox for ASK

GOAL	X wants to find out P from Y	
ACT	ask questions of Y	
PRE-	1 be near to Y	(under control of X)
CONDITIONS	2 Y knows P	(under control of Y)
	3 Y wants to tell P to X	(mediating pre-condition)
RESULT	Y tells P to X	

As can be seen, the information about ASK in the planbox is similar to the sets of conditions proposed by Searle and others to account for the use of speech acts (see further chapter 8).

QUALM

QUALM is a question-answering system which was used in conjunction with SAM and PAM (Lehnert 1980). Like these two systems QUALM worked at a conceptual level independently of the words and sentences in the questions and answers it processed. In other words, the aim was to model language-independent processes specific to question answering. In this way QUALM differs from conventional question-answering systems where the emphasis is on the design of the database and on information retrieval techniques. In these systems the main function of the natural language interface is to translate the user's input into a formal query language which is appropriate to the structure of the database. Ellipsis and anaphora are important linguistic problems which have been addressed here. QUALM, however, is more concerned with issues such as how information is stored in the human mind and how concepts are organized in memory.

When answering questions, QUALM goes through four stages. In the first, the question is analysed according to its type. For example, one type of question, the *causal antecedent*, is about the causation of some event (e.g. *why did John leave? what caused the accident?*). Following this an inferential analysis is performed to determine whether a literal analysis of the question is appropriate and, if it is not, to pursue the 'intended' meaning. This part of the system deals with questions such as *do you know what time it is?* which, if taken literally, are requests for a *yes/no* response but in fact are intended to be interpreted in other ways.

Another type of question which QUALM could handle is called *universal set inference*. The following are some examples, followed by inappropriate, though literally correct, responses:

(10)
Q1   who wasn't in class yesterday?
A1   Margaret Thatcher
Q2   what did Mary forget to put in the cake?
A2   an oil filter

These questions are subjected in stage two to the process of *Concept Completion*, which requires the filling of a slot marked by words such as *who* and *what*. Notice that the questions in example 10 have negative modality, though in Q2 this is at the conceptual rather than at the surface level. Questions of this type carry certain constraints on their range of possible answers, and these constraints are derived from script roles such as classrooms and cake-making. In other words, the implicit meanings of the questions are:

(11)
Q1   who wasn't in class yesterday (who should have been)?
Q2   what did Mary forget to put in the cake (that should have gone in)?

In this way inappropriate answers are avoided by applying the commonsense knowledge represented in scripts.

The third stage is called *content specification*. This deals with the amount of information which is required in the response and allows the system to operate in three modes – minimally responsive, co-operative and talkative. For example: suppose we have a story beginning with the sentence *John went to New York by bus*. On being asked the question *Did John go to New York?* the system would answer *Yes* if operating in minimally responsive mode, while in talkative mode it would answer *Yes, John went to New York by bus*. What the system does is to search in the representation of the story for a conceptualization which matches the conceptual question. If a match is found, then the answer is *Yes*. In talkative mode, however, any additional information in the matched conceptualization is printed out, so that we are told not only that John went to New York but also how he went. Thus the system appears to volunteer information. This procedure works when conceptualizations can be matched straightforwardly, as in this example, but problems would arise if there were several possible items of additional information and the system had to decide which to include and which to omit. This would require some notion of what is relevant information in terms of what the listener knows and may need to know. (See further the work on user modelling discussed in chapter 8.)

The fourth and final stage, *retrieval heuristics*, is concerned with extracting a conceptual answer from memory. One aspect of this can be illustrated by looking at the way in which QUALM answered expectational questions. Expectational questions ask about expectations that are aroused during the understanding process and then violated by an unexpected turn of events. For instance, in a story about a bus journey we might expect the passenger to board the bus, pay the fare and get off at his destination. If something unexpected happens, such as the passenger having to leave the bus because he has no money to pay the fare, questions might be asked like *why didn't he pay the fare?* and *why didn't he take the bus to his destination?* The answers to these questions would not necessarily be included in the text of the story but could be answered on the basis of knowledge of what normally happens on a bus journey. In other words, the system's memory representation for the story would have to include:

1 conceptualizations about events that actually occurred.
2 inferences about events that probably occurred but were not actually mentioned.
3 failed expectations that were aroused during understanding.

The third element, which involves stereotypic variations from the normal path of a script, is referred to as *ghost path generation*. We can illustrate this with a story based on the restaurant script (Lehnert 1980: 57–62).

(12)
John went to a restaurant and the waitress gave him a menu. He ordered a hot dog, but the waitress said they didn't have any, so he ordered a hamburger instead. But when the hamburger came, it was so burnt that he left.

In order to answer questions such as:

Why didn't John eat the hot dog?
Why didn't John eat the hamburger?
Why didn't John pay the bill?

we need to refer to expectations of what should normally have happened and to interference points in these expectations. A simplified outline of how the story might be represented is shown in figure 6.1.

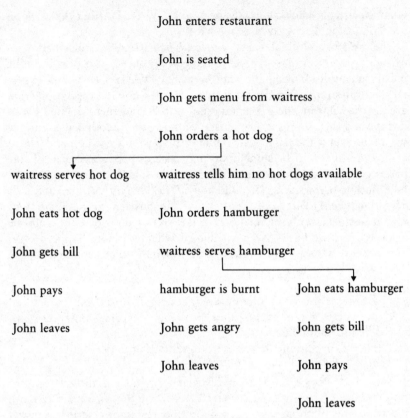

Figure 6.1   Ghost path generations in the restaurant story
(Lehnert 1981: 159)

The actual story is represented in the middle column. At the point where the waitress tells John there are no hot dogs, a ghost path is generated in the left-hand column, representing what would have been expected if the story had not taken this unexpected turn. The same applies later when the burnt hamburger is served and a ghost path is generated in the right-hand column. When QUALM processes a question such as *why didn't John eat the hot dog* it locates the reference to John eating a hot dog in the ghost path, works up this path to where it branched off from the main story (at the point *John orders a hot dog*) and returns the event below this point (*the waitress told him there were no hot dogs*). In this way valid expectational questions can be answered appropriately. Furthermore, invalid questions such as *why didn't John jump into the lake?* would not be answered as there would not have been valid expectations involving such an event in the restaurant script.

One final problem which arises in question-answering is *knowledge state assessment*. In a normal human conversation, when people answer questions they usually try to assess what the questioner does and does not know in order to provide an appropriate answer; for example they usually try to keep track of what has been said previously in the discourse. The following sequence would be unusual in dialogue between humans but could occur in a dialogue with a machine which faithfully retrieves answers to the user's questions but does not keep track of what has been said previously.

(13)
Q   who hit Mary?
A   John
Q   who hit Mary?
A   John
Q   who hit Mary?
A   John

In normal human dialogue the answer to the repeated question would be something like *I just told you*.

A further aspect of knowledge state assessment concerns the selection of one answer from among several possible alternatives. Consider the following conclusion to a restaurant story which has been preceded by a subway ride, in the course of which John had his pocket picked.

(14)
When the bill came, John discovered he couldn't pay. The management told him he would have to wash dishes. When he left, he caught the bus to New Haven.

There might be several possible answers to the question *why did John wash dishes?*

(15)
A1   because he couldn't pay the bill.
A2   because he had no money.
A3   because he lost his money on the train.

Which is the most appropriate? Lehnert argues that the first two answers are relatively uninformative for people who have basic scriptal knowledge and therefore already know that being unable to pay a restaurant bill because one has no money can stereotypically lead to one's having to wash dishes. More is learned – the reason why John did not have any money – from the third answer. However, for a person who did not possess basic scriptal knowledge, for example a young child or a person from another culture, either of the first two answers would be appropriate and informative. Thus for the answer to a question to be appropriate and as informative as possible account must be taken of the questioner. We will examine some other ways in which this aspect of dialogue has been handled in chapter 8.

POLITICS

To conclude this chapter we will examine a program which deals with the representation of political beliefs and in particular with the way different people make different interpretations of the same event. This is referred to as *subjective understanding*. The program POLITICS deals with conservative and liberal interpretations of events. Space will only permit a brief overview of the system and for a more detailed and annotated account the reader is referred to Carbonell (1981).

The following is an example of the behaviour of POLITICS. The system takes an event such as:

(16) The US Congress is expected to approve the Panama Canal Treaty.

and interprets this event from the point of view of a conservative or a liberal ideology. The following question–answer series illustrates the system in conservative mode.

(17)
Q1   should the US approve the treaty?
A1   NO, THE TREATY IS BAD FOR THE UNITED STATES
Q2   why is the treaty bad for the US?
A2   THE UNITED STATES WOULD LOSE THE CANAL TO PANAMA AND THE UNITED STATES WILL BE WEAKER
Q3   what might happen if the United States loses the Canal?
A3   RUSSIA WILL TRY TO CONTROL THE CANAL
Q4   why would Russia try to take over the Canal?
A4   RUSSIA WANTS TO EXPAND ITS MILITARY CONTROL. THE PANAMA CANAL HAS HIGH MILITARY VALUE
Q5   how might this happen?
A5   THE UNITED STATES MIGHT NOT BE ABLE TO STOP ANYONE TAKING OVER THE PANAMA CANAL. TORRIJOS IS A COMMUNIST. TORRIJOS WILL LET RUSSIA CONTROL PANAMA
Q6   why should the US worry about Russia taking over the Canal?
A6   BECAUSE RUSSIA WANTS TO CONTROL THE WORLD

Q7   what should the US do to stop Russia from taking over the Canal?
A7   CONGRESS SHOULD VOTE AGAINST THE PANAMA CANAL
       TREATY

We will present the liberal interpretation of the same event shortly. But first we need to examine the knowledge structures on which POLITICS draws. The main knowledge structures are

Counterplanning strategies

These involve high-level plans about how to thwart an adversary and to achieve goals in spite of an adversary's interference.

Goal trees

Goal trees are the means of encoding ideologies. For example: under US conservative ideology, the goal tree for Soviet politicians includes world domination, leadership of the Communist world, and a strong military. The US goal tree under the same ideology includes Communist containment, preservation of free enterprise, and a strong military. In contrast, the US goal tree in US liberal ideology includes establishing and maintaining world peace, defence of human rights, minimizing unemployment in the US, minimizing disease and hunger in the world, and opposing the creation of totalitarian regimes.

Situation scripts

These are similar to the scripts mentioned earlier in the chapter except that they encode knowledge of stereotypical political situations. These scripts used by POLITICS involve situations such as military invasions, military aid, economic aid, negotiation, espionage and arms-race. In addition the scripts include two types of inference rules, context-dependent rules and context-switching rules. Context-dependent rules are activated in particular contexts and deal with events which might be expected in those contexts. For example, in the context of government funding, if the goal of the funding is of a military nature, then it can be expected that a military agency will be authorized to spend the money. Context-switching rules determine which script is to be applied in a given situation. For example, on receiving the input *Russia massed troops on the Czech border* they would decide whether invasion or military aid is involved. In this case the rule which would activate the invasion script is as follows:

(18)
(X is a small country and Y is a large country)

IF	Y moves armed forces near to or inside of X
AND	having X militarily stronger does not help Y achieve one of its goals
AND	expanding its political control is a high-level goal for Y
THEN	Y has the goal of a military takeover of X.

Let us now look at a liberal interpretation of example 16, the Panama Canal story. The goals of US liberal ideology include reducing political tension, avoiding conflicts and improving relations. Furthermore, liberal ideology sees Russia as having the goals of maintaining world peace and avoiding military and political conflict and it rates these higher than the Russian goal of expanding military and political control, and for this reason the treaty is viewed as favourable.

(19)

Q1	should the US approve the treaty?
A1	YES, THE PANAMA CANAL TREATY IS GOOD FOR THE UNITED STATES
Q2	why is the treaty good?
A2	THE PANAMA CANAL TREATY IMPROVES RELATIONS WITH LATIN AMERICAN COUNTRIES
Q3	what happens if the US keeps the Canal?
A3	THIS WILL CAUSE DISCONTENT AND CONFLICT IN PANAMA AND LATIN AMERICA
Q4	why would this lead to conflict?
A4	THE CANAL ZONE IS A UNITED STATES COLONY. LATIN AMERICA DOES NOT LIKE COLONIALISM. THE UNITED STATES WOULD MAINTAIN COLONIALISM
Q5	what if Russia tries to take over the Canal?
A5	RUSSIA DOES NOT WANT CONFLICT WITH THE US. RUSSIA WILL STAY OUT OF THE CANAL IF THE UNITED STATES DEFENDS IT. THE UNITED STATES DEFENDING THE CANAL IS PART OF THE TREATY

These two extracts provide striking examples of subjective understanding; as we can see, the same event is interpreted in radically different ways by the two ideologies. The knowledge structures which underlie POLITICS are of various sorts, ranging from high-level planning strategies for conflict situations to domain-specific knowledge and context-dependent inference rules. Sometimes, however, POLITICS made mistakes when understanding events such as the input *Russia massed troops on the Czech border*. In liberal mode the following question-answer sequence resulted.

(20)
Q   what should the US do about it?
A   THE UNITED STATES SHOULD CONGRATULATE BREZHNEV

This answer was produced because liberal ideology opposes military conflict in favour of the use of diplomatic means. It was arrived at thus: countries must have good relations before they can enter diplomatic negotiations; this precondition was blocked and congratulating Brezhnev was seen as a way of bringing about good relations in order to achieve the goal of using diplomatic means to stop a Russian invasion of Czechoslovakia. As Carbonell points out, the system's reasoning was not sufficiently integrated and this had to be rectified by making the system check that no preconditons to a high-level goal were violated by the choice of a plan for an instrumental goal, as happened in this example. Carbonell also makes the point that this sort of problem cannot be easily foreseen and that the construction of a working program is an integral part of testing consistency and completeness in a theory of human reasoning. This is a good example of cognitive simulation, in which the program tests the theory and suggests modifications. Such a test can then provide essential input to a working model and thus contribute to the parallel goal of computational achievement.

In this chapter we have examined in some detail the knowledge structures which have been implemented in some natural language understanding systems, focusing particularly on the work of Schank and colleagues. Knowledge structures such as these are essential for any system which is to be used for handling dialogue. However, there are additional problems associated with dialogue and these will be the subject of the next two chapters.

Further Reading

The work of Schank and his colleagues is reported in a wide range of sources. The early work on Conceptual Dependency Theory is discussed fully in Schank (1972), Schank (1973) and Schank and Rieger (1974), while Schank (1975) is a detailed account of the early system MARGIE (Memory, Analysis, Response Generation, and Inference in English). Schank and Abelson (1977) is the classic account of scripts and similar knowledge structures. These are also reviewed in Schank and Riesbeck (1981), a major feature of which is an introduction to how the models were built, including actual code, flow diagrams and exercises which allow the reader to construct miniature versions of the programs.

Schank's more recent work on language has been concerned with memory structures (see Schank 1982). A popular account of the Yale language understanding project and of the relationships between AI research, commerce and education can be found in Schank (1984).

7

Knowledge of Discourse Structure

In the previous chapter it was shown how the understanding of connected discourse is guided by knowledge of stereotypical events, everyday goals and plans for the achievement of these goals. Thus knowledge of what is involved in eating in a restaurant enables us to understand the connections between the different events described in a story about restaurants and knowledge of political goals and motives helps us understand a news account of a political event. This knowledge is external to stories and reports and as such it contrasts with a different type of knowledge, knowledge of discourse structure, which is concerned with internal relations between items in a text, whether this text is a narrative, a description, an interview or a casual conversation. Knowledge of discourse structure enables us to recognize whether a story or a conversation is coherent and how this coherence is marked through the use of surface discourse phenomena. In this chapter, then, we will be looking at some ways in which this knowledge of discourse structure has been incorporated into computer programs which understand and produce natural language. As discourse analysis is a relatively new area of linguistics it might be helpful to elaborate briefly on some aspects of the structure of discourse. Further details can be found in the recommended readings listed at the end of the chapter.

The structure of discourse

We will be concerned with two aspects of discourse analysis in this chapter – the structure of conversation and the structure of units of text such as explanations, narratives and descriptions. The latter may occur within a conversation, as, for example, when one participant takes an extended turn to tell a story or to explain a point.

A considerable amount of research has been carried out in recent years on the analysis of conversation (Coulthard 1985; Levinson 1983; Stubbs 1983). This research has shown that utterances in conversation do not occur randomly or in isolation. In fact some have gone so far as to draw an analogy between the rules which govern conversation and the sequencing rules which have been described in syntax, where there are constraints on which items can occur in particular slots in a structure. So, for example, just as in syntax there are rules stating that a determiner has to be followed by a noun, a noun phrase by a verb phrase, and a transitive verb by an object noun phrase, so there are rules of discourse which stipulate that a question should be followed by an answer, an offer by an acceptance or rejection, a complaint by an apology, an excuse or a counter-complaint, and so on. In other words, it has been argued that analytic concepts such as distribution, co-occurrence constraints and hierarchical structure, can be found in conversation as well as in sentences. We will see later, for example, how the ATN formalism, which has been used mainly to describe sequencing rules at the levels of syntax and semantics, can also be used at the level of discourse.

Several types of structural unit have been proposed for conversation. The Birmingham discourse analysts have proposed the notion of the *exchange*, which is the minimal unit of interaction, consisting of at least one move by one speaker which initiates the exchange, and a second move by another speaker which responds to this initiation (see, for example, Stubbs 1983; Coulthard 1985). This basic notion has been greatly extended and used widely in linguistic analyses of conversation and has also been used as a basis for some of the work to be described later.

A similar term, which has been proposed by conversation analysts such as Sacks and Schegloff, is the *adjacency pair*. This term is used to describe pairs of utterances which belong together, such as greeting-greeting, question-answer, offer-acceptance/refusal (Schegloff and Sacks 1973). The conversation analysts have also extended this basic concept to include units such as pre-sequences and inserted sequences. Pre-sequences involve utterances which prepare the way for a subsequent utterance. For example, an utterance such as *are you doing anything tonight?* might be a preliminary to an invitation. Inserted sequences interrupt the normal flow of the discourse, usually because something is unclear and it is necessary to request clarification (see further chapter 9).

A further refinement is the notion of *preference*, which has been used to refer to the relationships between response types which occur in the same structural position but which are non-equivalent in terms of their formal and sequential properties. A simple example will illustrate. We might expect that an utterance such as an invitation will be followed by either an acceptance or a refusal. The choice between an acceptance and a refusal does indeed exist, but whichever response type is chosen has a bearing on the form of the utterance, as the following examples from Atkinson and Drew (1979: 58) illustrate.

(1)
A   why don't you come up and see me some / /times?
B   I would like to

(2)
A   uh if you'd care to come and visit a little while this morning I'll give you a
     cup of coffee
B   heh   well   that's awfully sweet of you
     (DELAY)   (MARKER)   (APPRECIATION)
     I don't think I can make it this morning
     (REFUSAL)
     .hh uhm I'm running an ad in the paper and – and uh I have to stay near the
     phone
     (ACCOUNT)

The response to the invitation in example 1 is an acceptance. It occurs promptly, with a slight overlap of the prior turn, and it is simple in form. In contrast, the response to the invitation in 2 is marked in several ways – it is delayed, an appreciation is proffered and the refusal is explained. Similar features mark a variety of dispreferred responses as we will see later when we look at the issue of conversational breakdown and repair (chapters 9 and 10).

What has been said so far applies particularly to the analysis of casual conversation; eventually computers will need to be able to deal with the complex structures of casual conversation. At present, however, most systems have involved more formal discourse types within fairly restricted domains such as booking a flight through a travel agency or making a hotel reservation. GUS, a system which simulates a travel agent, will be described in the next section, while the HAM-ANS system, which plays the role of a hotel reservation clerk, will be described in chapter 8. In these and similar systems the dialogue structure is more predictable and can be specified as a series of obligatory and optional elements like the events in a script. Although casual conversation is less predictable and there are fewer constraints on what can be said at any given point, it is clear from what was said earlier that conversation is highly organized and that knowledge of this structure will be an essential component of future natural language understanding systems.

Why is knowledge of conversational structure relevant to language understanding? There are two reasons. First, knowledge of what items can co-occur permits us to recognize well-formed discourse and to distinguish it from ill-formed discourse like that produced, for example, by a thought-disordered schizophrenic or an inarticulate computer. Whether the concept of well-formedness can be applied as clearly in discourse as it can in syntax is a controversial issue (see the discussion in Stubbs 1983, chapter 5), especially when a conversation involves the interaction of two or more participants.

This leads, however, to the second issue, which is that structure determines meaning. What this means is that speakers have a choice in what they can say at any given point in a conversation, but what they do say will be interpreted in the light of predictions set up by the preceding discourse. The following example illustrates this point (Coulthard and Brazil 1979: 16).

(3)
A   so the meeting is on Friday?
B   Tom will be back in town

Here the predictive power of the structural framework is such that, following A's request for information, B's response will be heard as either *yes* or *no*. (Which of these it is depends on the speakers' shared knowledge of Tom and how he is involved in the meeting in question.) Similarly, in the following example, taken from Levinson (1983: 320), a silence in a conversation can be interpreted as meaningful on account of its sequential position in the discourse.

(4)
A   so I was wondering would you be in your office on Monday
      (.) by any chance?
      (2.0)
      probably not
B   hmm yes

In the first turn A asks a question which is followed by a two-second pause. This pause is taken to indicate a negative answer to the question, although, as B's response shows, this inference was incorrect. However this inference derives from the speaker's knowledge of the structural characteristics of conversation, in particular, the preference organization described earlier. More specifically, the preferred form of an acceptance is that it follows immediately, whereas refusals are often marked, as B's response is, by delays. For this reason A interprets the silence as a refusal.

Most work on conversational structure has been concerned with relations between fairly short turns as illustrated in the examples so far. There are, however, many cases where speakers take extended turns which have their own internal structure. In answer to a question a person may give a response which puts forward a particular point of view and he may then go on to support the response with a justification for the viewpoint expressed, perhaps using an analogy as an illustration. All of this could be considered a response to the initial question, but clearly there is structure within this response. Reichman's work, which deals with the issue of coherency in conversation in such extended turns, will be discussed later in this chapter.

Two distinctions need to be made before we look at some systems which incorporate knowledge of discourse structure. These are the distinctions between linear and non-linear discourse and between static and dynamic analysis. We saw earlier how inserted sequences can interrupt the flow of discourse, so that it is possible, for example, for a question to be followed by a question (recall example 1 in chapter 2). This means that discourse is not strictly linear as the normal flow can be interrupted in order to clarify a misunderstanding. The same applies to the development of conversational topics, where the discussion of one topic may be suspended while a sub-topic is discussed. Where discussion is action-centred, as in the situation to be described later when an expert gives an apprentice instructions on how to install a pump, the organization of the discourse may be closely related to the organization of the task. In other words, the task may consist of sub-tasks which may be related to each other in a variety of ways. This in turn affects the discourse which will similarly break down into a series of interrelated sub-topics. As we will see, this non-linear (or hierarchical) structure also affects the use of pronominal and other anaphoric devices. Furthermore, the structure of the discourse will often be marked by words such as *by the way*, which indicate that the next turn is not strictly relevant to the current topic, or *anyway*, which indicates a move away from a sub-topic and back to a main topic.

The distinction between static and dynamic analysis is related to the distinction made in chapter 2 between descriptive and process models of language. Much of the work which has been carried out in discourse analysis involves detailed text descriptions aimed at revealing the complex structure of the texts. This work treats discourse as product whereas a process model accounts for the dynamic way in which discourse is processed and produced by speakers interacting in real time. The distinction can be illustrated with reference to the notion of adjacency pairs. Adjacency pairs could be seen as part of a descriptive framework for the structural analysis of conversation. However, as we saw earlier, adjacency pairs also reflect the dynamic processes of conversational interaction by means of which speakers are involved in an ongoing process or prediction and interpretation. In other words, the first part of an adjacency pair not only predicts the occurrence of the second pair part, it also projects an expected interpretation on it. The speaker of the first utterance will inspect the next utterance to see whether it fulfills its predicted function and will then respond to that second utterance according to how it in turn has been interpreted. Thus speakers in a conversation are engaged in a continuous process of monitoring each other's utterances within the predictions set up by preceding utterances and are continually displaying to each other their understanding of these utterances. As the conversation proceeds, what was said previously moves out of focus to be superseded by the current utterance. Similarly, in an extended conversational turn, if a second support for an argument is put forward then the first support is put into the discourse background. Thus a dynamic rather than a structural-descriptive approach is required to capture the moment-by-moment progression of a discourse through time. We will see how some attempt has been made to take account of these dynamic processes of discourse when we come to look at the work of Grosz and Reichman.

Several systems will be described in this chapter. The first, GUS, involves a fairly structured type of dialogue, an interaction with a travel agent, and uses the notion of frames to capture this structure. Following this we will look at the DIALOGUE GAMES system which shows how different dialogue types share basic features but differ from each other in specific ways. This will lead on to a discussion of discourse structures and of the ways in which objects and persons referred to in the discourse can be identified on the basis of the structure of the discourse. Finally we will look at how coherence is maintained in extended conversational turns and how discourse structure is often marked by a variety of clue-words such as *but first, yes, but* and *anyway*.

Booking a flight with GUS

GUS (Genial Understander System) is a frame-driven system which acts as a travel agent and conducts a dialogue with a client who wants to make a simple return trip from Palo Alto to a single city in California. The following is a transcript of a dialogue with GUS (Bobrow et al. 1977).

(5)
1 HELLO. MY NAME IS GUS. I CAN HELP YOU PLAN A SIMPLE TRIP BY
  AIR. WHERE DO YOU WANT TO GO?

2 I want to go to San Diego on May 28
3 WHAT TIME DO YOU WANT TO LEAVE?
4 I must be in San Diego before 10 am
5 WOULD YOU LIKE PSA FLIGHT 102 THAT ARRIVES AT 9.15?
6 what is the next flight?
7 AIR CALIFORNIA FLIGHT 310 THAT LEAVES AT 8.30 AM AND ARRIVES AT 10.00 AM
8 I'll take the first one
9 IN WHAT NAME SHOULD I MAKE A RESERVATION, PLEASE?
10 Dan Bobrow
11 I HAVE CONFIRMED THE FOLLOWING FLIGHT: PSA FLIGHT 102 ON WEDNESDAY MAY 28 FROM SAN JOSE TO SAN DIEGO THAT LEAVES AT 7.30 AM AND ARRIVES AT 9.15 AM
12 WHAT DATE DO YOU WANT TO RETURN ON?
13 on Friday in the evening
14 WOULD YOU LIKE THE FLIGHT THAT LEAVES AT 7.45 PM?
15 that's fine
16 I HAVE CONFIRMED THE FOLLOWING FLIGHT: PSA FLIGHT 307 ON FRIDAY MAY 30 FROM SAN DIEGO TO SAN JOSE THAT LEAVES AT 7.45 PM AND ARRIVES AT 9.30 PM
17 THANK YOU FOR CALLING. GOODBYE

Before examining how GUS uses frames to participate in such a dialogue, let us consider two of the linguistic features of this extract – the ability to respond appropriately to indirect speech acts and the ability to resolve anaphora. Examples of indirect speech acts can be found in lines 2 and 4. In line 2 the client states that he wants to go to San Diego. This is treated by GUS as a request to make a reservation, not just as a statement of the client's wishes. The interpretation derives from the overall topic of the conversation; in this case planning a journey, so a statement of a wish to travel to a particular destination will be taken to mean that a flight reservation to that destination is required. Line 4 is a little more complex. GUS asks when the client wants to leave and the client answers *I must be in San Diego before 10 am*. This response does not directly answer the question about departure time. However, given that the immediate goal of this exchange is to find a departure time and assuming that the client is behaving co-operatively by making a response that is somehow relevant, a suitable departure time can be inferred from the arrival time. GUS presents such a solution in line 7. Thus the interpretation of indirect speech acts is constrained here by expectations about the general topic of the dialogue and by a knowledge of the client's goals.

There are several samples of anaphora in this extract. For example, the client's phrase *the next flight* in line 6 refers to the flight following the one mentioned in line 5. In this case *next* is interpreted in terms of the order of flights in the airline timetable. However *the first one* in line 8 (the *one* stands for *flight*) refers to the first-mentioned flight in the conversation. As a matter of fact no ambiguity arises here, as the first-mentioned and the earlier flight are the same; problems could have arisen if this had not been so. It is not clear from the published account of GUS how *first one* would have been interpreted if there had been ambiguity or indeed whether the system would recognize the ambiguity and have some means of resolving it. Finally, the phrase *Friday in the evening* in response to the question *what date do you want to return?* has to be interpreted as being the Friday following the date of departure (May 28 i.e. May 30). If, in response to the system's first question the client had answered *I want to go to San Diego on Friday*, then the date for Friday would have been calculated as the Friday following the date of the conversation. We will return shortly to how GUS uses frames to resolve this issue of dates.

GUS uses frames in several different ways. First, general frames are used to determine the sequence of the conversation. These frames are concerned with the overall structure of the dialogue but allow some flexibility to cater for occasions when the client volunteers information or asks questions. The second use of frames is to represent the attributes of particular blocks of knowledge associated with this dialogue type, such as dates, trips and travellers.

Let us look first at how frames are used to guide the dialogue. There is a general dialogue frame which has slots for the client, the current date and the topic, a trip specification. This last slot is in turn a further frame with slots to be filled, including one for a trip leg, which is itself another frame. A simplified version of the frame for trip specification appears below.

Trip specification

Slots	Fillers
Homeport	City
Foreignport	City
Outward leg	Tripleg
Awaystay	Placestay
Inward leg	Tripleg

Each has to be filled during the course of the conversation. The Homeport is assumed by default to be Palo Alto but the slot for Foreignport is left unfilled until the information is supplied from the Tripleg frame (see below). Once a destination has been established, that same city can be used as the *Placestay* filler and as the *Tripleg* filler the city of departure for the return journey. (A more complex journey, with a point of return on the inward leg differing from the place of destination on the outward leg, would cause problems for this system and would require much more elaborate structuring.) In order to see how the dialogue proceeds, we need to examine the frame for Tripleg, which appears below.

Frame for Tripleg

Slots	Fillers
Fromplace	City
Toplace	City
Traveldate	Date
Departure	Time range
Arrival	Time range
Proposed flights	Set of flights
Flight chosen	Flight
Traveller	Person

So far nothing has been said in the dialogue beyond the introductory sentences *Hello. My name is GUS. I can help you plan a simple trip by air*. The system has automatically filled in the slots in the dialogue frame for the current date, the topic of the dialogue and the city of departure. The next piece of information which is required is the destination. Naturally the system cannot fill in this slot without asking the client, so at this point a procedure is triggered which generates the question *where do you want to go to*? Following this, the system works its way through the slots – asking for information about the travel date, departure and arrival times – to a flight confirmation. In some cases a dialogue can be completed without all the slots having to be filled. So, for example, unless the time of arrival is relevant to the booking, as happens in the cited example, this slot can be left unfilled. The control of the dialogue is also susceptible to the nature of the client's responses. In line 2, for example, the client gives the requested information, the destination, and in addition some relevant but unrequested information, the date. This is automatically filled in and the question about the date, which would have come later in the dialogue, is not generated.

Let us now look at the more specific frames for items such as dates. A simplified version of the date frame is set out below.

Frame for date

Month	Name
Day	Number (between 1 and 31)
Year	Number
Weekday	One of (Sunday, Monday, Tuesday, etc.)

The first three items are simple. The slot for Month requires the name of a month, for Day a number between 1 and 31, and Year is filled by default as the current year. Weekday is more complicated as there are procedures attached to this slot to deal with possible problems raised by the client's response. Recall in the extract how the client specifies the date of return as *Friday* rather than a regular date with a number for the day and a month name. When this happens, a procedure is called to find the date from the specified day using the type of contextual information which was described earlier. There is also a procedure to get the name of the weekday from the date, although this is only called if the name of the weekday is required. There are similar frames and procedures to determine the flight time. For example, when the client asks for a return flight for *Friday in the evening*, the phrase *in the evening* is interpreted as being equivalent to *around 7.30 p.m.* and GUS looks for a flight departure nearest to that time.

We have focused mainly on the way in which frames were used in GUS to direct the dialogue and to handle bundles of information relevant to the dialogue topic, although it should be pointed out that the system also incorporated sophisticated morphological and syntactic analysers. It should be clear, however, that the success of the system derives in large part from the fact that it is frame-driven in the ways described here. By limiting the domain of discourse and the goals which the client might have, the system can guide the conversation within the limits of its own language processing capabilities. The authors make clear that, although the system illustrates the essential components of an intelligent system, it is not sufficiently developed for use with real clients. Some of the problems which GUS would not be able to handle were raised in an experiment in which a human simulated the system, thus permitting more flexible and more realistic responses from the clients. An experiment like this is interesting as it reveals what is required to make computers behave in a more human-like way. This issue will be considered further in chapter 10.

Dialogue Games

GUS was concerned with one type of dialogue and a single subject domain. The next system to be described, Dialogue Games (Levin and Moore 1977), embodies the notion that conversation consists of a series of different types of dialogue which share certain basic features but differ in specific ways.

Levin and Moore (1977: 399–400) list the following types of dialogue:

1 *Helping*: Person 1 wants to solve a problem, and interacts with Person 2 in attempting to arrive at a solution.
2 *Action-seeking*: Person 1 wants some action performed and interacts with Person 2 to get him to perform it.
3 *Information-seeking*: Person 1 wants to know some specific information and interacts with Person 2 in order to learn it.
4 *Information-probing*: Person 1 wants to know whether Person 2 knows some particular information and interacts with him to find out.
5 *Instructing*: Person 1 wants Person 2 to know some information and interacts with him to impart the information.
6 *Griping*: Person 1 is unhappy about some state of affairs and interacts with Person 2 to convey that unhappiness.

As can be seen, these represent basic goals which arise in dialogue such as making requests, asking for and imparting information, and complaining about things. Each of these dialogue types is represented in the model according to the following sets of information:

1 parameters – a list of the participants (Roles) and the task (Topic).
2 parameter specifications – the specific goals and knowledge states of the participants within a particular dialogue type.
3 components – the sub-goals of the participants.

To take an example: in the Helping dialogue game listed above, the parameters are Helpee, Helper and Task. The parameter specifications consist of a series of statements to the effect that a helpee is a person who wants to perform a task that he is permitted, but unable, to do. A helper is a person who is both able and willing to enable the helper do his task. Finally the components specify stages in the achieving of these goals – a diagnosis of the problem stage and a treatment stage. The former usually consists of the description by the helpee of a state of affairs which he wishes to achieve (Context) followed by a description of an unexpected and undesired result (Violation). The following is an example of a Helping dialogue in which A (Helpee) is communicating with B (operator and Helper) about a problem arising in the use of a computer system (Levin and Moore 1977: 406–7).

(6)
1   A   are you there? Go ahead
2   B   yep, what's up?
3   A   know anything about the TELNET SUBSYS? Go ahead

4   B   try me
5   A   I just connected to (computer site name) via TELNET and tried the
          DIVERT.OUTPUT.STREAM.TO.FILE command. Strange things
          happened. Esp., my TELNET typescript is 'busy'. Go ahead
6   B   TELNET TYPESCRIPT will always be busy until you do a RESET. But
          when you do that, be careful not to EXP, since that is a temporary file.
          Go ahead
7   A   I see . . . it's not enough for me just to do a DISCONNECT? Go ahead
8   B   correct. Is that the only problem?

This dialogue consists of an opening section (lines 1 and 2), followed
by an INFO-SEEKing dialogue (lines 3–4) which serve as a pre-sequence
to the main dialogue. A's statement of the problem in 5 consists of a
description of the desired state of affairs and its violation. B provides the
solution to the problem in 6 along with some additional information
which might be useful to A. Following A's check for clarification in 7, B
tries to conclude the dialogue as A's initial goal has now been satisfied.

Let us look a little more closely at how the system operates. The system
consists of the following parts:

1 a long-term memory (LTM), which contains a representation in
   semantic network form of the knowledge brought to each dialogue
   type by the participants, including world knowledge, relevant
   objects, processes and concepts, the cognitive state of the dialogue
   partner, rules of inference and knowledge of the overall dialogue
   structure.
2 a workspace (WS), in which partial and temporary information
   gathered in the course of the dialogue is stored.
3 processors which work on and modify the information to WS, and
   which are influenced by the contents of WS as well as by knowledge
   in LTM.

Thus dialogue processing is viewed as being knowledge-driven in as
much as the static knowledge contained in LTM is used to guide the
processing. In addition, however, this process also uses information in
WS in a dynamic way in order to make decisions during the course of the
dialogue – for example, about which dialogue game is in operation,
whether the participants' goals have been achieved and whether the
dialogue can be terminated.

We can see what is involved if we consider the initial stages, in which
the system has to determine which dialogue game is to be played. As
much of this information is conveyed implicitly in natural language

dialogues, the system has to be able to make inferences based on the information which it has available. For example, if faced with the utterance *I tried to send a message to P at S and it didn't go* the system first decomposes the utterance into a set of elementary propositions such as the following (Levin and Moore 1977: 142):

(7)

1 A tried to do X.
2 A wanted to do X.
3 A wants to do X.
4 HELPEE wants to do TASK.
5 It didn't go.
6 What A tried to do didn't work.
7 X didn't work.
8 A can't X.
9 A didn't know how to X.
10 HELPEE doesn't know how to do TASK.

These would be matched with propositions in LTM and if a suitable match could be found then a dialogue game would be nominated. In this case, the appropriate game would be Helping. Problems arise when more than one match can be found and alternative hypotheses have to be evaluated – that is, the system cannot be sure at first which dialogue game is involved. As an example, a question such as *how do I get RUNOFF to work?* could be treated either as a request for information or as a probe question. The parameter specifications for the two differ; in the former the questioner does not know the answer whereas in the latter he does. Accordingly the system would have to search for information about the questioner's state of knowledge in relation to the question in order to reach a decision about which dialogue game to eliminate.

Once a particular dialogue game has been selected, further information is inferred and added to the workspace. For example, if the system already knows that the speaker does not know how to do a task but wants to know how to do it, then it can be inferred from the Parameter Specifications for the Helping dialogue game that the speaker believes the hearer knows how to do the task, is able and willing to tell the hearer, and so on. This information is communicated implicitly but can be predicted by the system.

Dialogue Games is based on a functional view of language and builds on concepts from speech act theory. The system can handle indirect speech acts on the basis of predicting the underlying goals of a speaker within the constraints set by a particular dialogue type. Thus the processing is expectation-driven and this enables the system to control the generation of inferences by terminating its processes of inference once a speaker's goal has been established. It is also able to focus its inferencing in a particular direction by looking for the goals which are possible within a specific dialogue game. The system's knowledge of dialogue structure also assists the comprehension process. For example, an utterance such as *thank you for your help* after a problem has been solved would be interpreted not only as an expression of thanks but also as an attempt to bring the dialogue to a close. Thus sequential information about what items occur in what order in a dialogue is brought to bear on the interpretation process.

This structure also accounts for topic shifts within a conversation as a new game is initiated once a goal has been achieved in a preceding game. Levin and Moore point out that dialogue structure is neither linear nor hierarchical, as new dialogue games can be initiated without the old ones being terminated. An old game is simply overriden by a new one and drops out of the conversation. In the next section we will examine a system which is also concerned with a non-linear approach to dialogue structure and with how speakers keep track of topic shifts and implicit references, although, unlike the Levin and Moore system, it is based on the notion that conversation is organized hierarchically.

Keeping track

In this section we will examine a different approach to the identification of the objects and persons referred to by a speaker. This approach relies on the notion of *focus*, which is determined by the position of an item within the structure of a dialogue. Focusing influences the interpretation and generation of utterances in a dialogue; it is important since people often move from one topic to another during a conversation without explicitly marking the shift. They also use pronouns and other expressions such as definite noun phrases to refer to objects and persons which have been previously mentioned. Both of these characteristics of everyday conversation could cause potential havoc in a system which was trying to keep track of the topic of the conversation and of what objects and persons were being discussed. Yet if we examine transcripts of naturally occurring conversations between humans, we will find that such problems rarely arise and, even when they do, there are routine ways for resolving the difficulty. To illustrate this issue, let us examine a piece of dialogue in which an expert instructs an apprentice in the assembly of an air compressor (Grosz 1978: 246).

(8)

E   good morning. I would like for you to reassemble the compressor
    . . .

E   I suggest you begin by attaching the pump to the platform . . . (other sub-tasks)

E   good. All that remains then is to attach the belt housing cover to the belt housing frame

A   all right. I assume the hole in the housing cover opens to the pump pulley rather than to the motor pulley

E   yes that is correct. The pump pulley also acts as a fan to cool the pump

A   fine. Thank you

A   all right the belt housing cover is on and tightened down
    (30 minutes and 60 utterances after beginning)

E   fine. Now let's see if it works

The problem is: what does the pronoun *it* in the last line refer to? It certainly does not refer to the most recently mentioned noun phrase *the belt housing cover* nor to other recent noun phrases such as *the pump pulley, the fan* or *the pump*. Rather *it* refers right back to the compressor which was last mentioned thirty minutes and sixty utterances previously. But how does A know this and is E justified in using a pronoun in this way? Moreover, how would a computer system keep track of such use of pronouns which appear to be able to refer back to entities mentioned at any arbitrary distance away? The answer is that the item which the pronoun refers back to, in this case the compressor, is still in focus as far as E and A are concerned, despite the intervening talk concerned with installing the belt housing cover. This raises the question of how items come to be in focus, how they remain there and how they go out of focus. In other words, how do we know what is being talked about at any given time in a dialogue? In the remainder of this chapter we will discuss two ways in which this question has been addressed; first we will look at the structure of task-oriented dialogues as illustrated in example 8, and then we shall look more generally at the issue of how conversational coherence is maintained.

Focus in task-oriented dialogue

The dialogue about air compressors (example 8) formed part of a large-scale research project on speech understanding which was carried out at SRI International (Walker 1978). We will be concerned here only with the discourse problems which were tackled in this research. These involved issues such as the identification of the referents of pronouns and definite noun phrases as well as the interpretation of utterance fragments and their expansion into complete utterances. As far as the first issue is concerned, the main difficulty arose from referring-expressions which did not identify objects that could have satisfied the description (see the instance in example 8). The main solution proposed was based on the assumption that dialogues, and in particular task-oriented dialogues of the type exemplified here, have a clearly recognizable structure which permits participants in the dialogue to keep track of what is being talked about as items move into and out of focus. Let us look more closely at how this works.

A task such as the construction of an air compressor can be broken down into a series of sub-tasks which may themselves be further broken down. This hierarchical structure, which is illustrated in figure 7.1, is mirrored in the dialogue structure; the dialogue as a whole is subdivided into sub-dialogues. As each sub-task is tackled, different objects and actions come into focus and then fade from focus when the sub-task has been completed. However, while the sub-tasks are being performed, the higher-level task remains in focus so when referring expressions such as pronouns and definite noun phrases are used to identify objects in the higher-level task they are correctly interpreted even though attention has been most recently directed to the objects involved in a sub-task. It is this mechanism that enables the apprentice to understand that the pronoun refers back to the *air compressor* (example 8), as the construction of the air compressor is the higher-level task which consists of various sub-tasks such as the installation of the belt housing cover. Furthermore, as Grosz (1978) argues, sub-dialogues are in themselves coherent. It is possible to

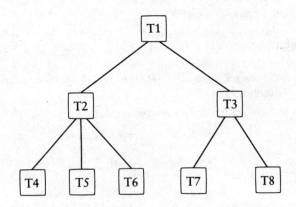

Figure 7.1   A simple model of task structure
(Grosz 1978: 254)

remove an entire sub-dialogue without affecting the coherence of the dialogue as a whole, but the removal of part of a sub-dialogue affects coherency.

A crucial question is how do the participants know when a new sub-dialogue is about to begin or an old one is to be closed. As we can imagine, focus will shift during the course of a dialogue and there will be no predetermined sequences of events. For example, if the apprentice experiences difficulties with the identification of a particular object, this can open a further sub-dialogue aimed at clarification. The participants have to be on the lookout for any clues to the structure of the dialogue which might facilitate their identification of which objects are being referred to. Grosz shows that speakers provide various clues to what items are currently in focus. An expression such as *now* or *next* can indicate that a new sub-task is about to begin. (Similar devices are used by speakers in other types of discourse to indicate boundaries and shifts – see, for example, Sinclair and Coulthard 1975 on the structure of classroom discourse.) Questions by the apprentice e.g. *what should I do now?* or *how do I remove the pump?* can introduce the next task.

There are also clues for indicating that a sub-task is to be closed. A frequently used clue-word was *OK*, although *OK* was found to have several different meanings such as:

1 I heard you.
2 I heard you and I understand.
3 I heard you, I understand, and I am now doing (or will do) what you said.
4 I'm finished (OK what next?)

Problems can arise when signals such as *OK* are misunderstood, although in many cases interpretation is supported by reference to knowledge of the task. For example, if the expert asks the apprentice to carry out a sub-task which both know will take some time to complete, an immediate *OK* cannot mean that the task has been done. The following extract illustrates a misunderstood *OK* (Grosz 1978: 251).

(9)
1 E open the top of the valve and let the water out. Just open the faucet on top. Just like you were going to turn the water on
2 A oh, like I'm going to turn the water on. OK
3 E now, that'll relieve the pressure
4 A OK, some water came out
5 E now the next thing you do, you take an allen wrench
6 A do I leave it on or turn it back off?

7   E   it doesn't make any difference
8   A   OK

In line 4 A indicates that part of the *open-valve* task has been completed and E gives the next task in line 5, thus closing the whole *open-valve* task. However A indicates in line 6 that he believes more is involved in that task. E has to reopen the *open-valve* task in order to interpret the pronoun *it* which refers to the faucet in this task and not, for example, to the allen wrench introduced in line 5 as part of the next sub-task.

Examples 8 and 9 illustrate how the participants in a conversation co-operate with each other. Each participant has his own set of beliefs about what item is in focus and will normally assume that the other has followed any shift in focus. But, as well as maintaining their own beliefs, the participants have to keep track of what they believe about the other's beliefs. Failure to do this blocks the resolution of misunderstandings. In this particular task setting the two participants did not share a visual field. When this is the case the identification of objects often requires co-operative work between the participants, as in the following example where the object in question cannot be identified by the expert by means of a simple shape-based description (Grosz 1981: 88).

(10)
E   OK. Now we need to attach the conduit to the motor. The conduit is the covering around the wires that you . . . were working with earlier. There is a small part . . . oh brother
A   now wait a s . . . the conduit is the cover to the wires?
E   yes and . . .
A   oh I see, there's a part that . . . a part that's supposed to go over it
E   yes
A   I see . . . it looks just the right shape too. Ah hah. Yes
E   wonderful, since I did not know how to describe the part

Although the expert was unable to provide a description, he and the apprentice pooled resources in order to achieve success. Thus participation in dialogue involves working together to achieve commonly agreed meanings. Misunderstandings can arise when the participants think they have achieved agreement but have in fact failed to do so, as we will see in chapter 9.

One final point concerns the adequacy of descriptions. Experimental work in referential communication has shown that speakers, particularly young children, produce information which is unnecessary and therefore redundant when describing objects which have to be differentiated by a listener (Robinson 1981). An adequate description must obviously contain sufficient information to distinguish the required object from other similar objects, but the question is whether a good description should include items which are not necessary for the comparison of criterial attributes. For example, if there is only one red-handled tool available, is it preferable in response to the question *what tool should I use?* to say *the red-handled screwdriver* or *the red handled-one?* In terms of the minimal information required, the second phrase would suffice. However, in terms of the efficient completion of a task a message carrying some redundant information might make identification of objects more rapid by limiting the search – in this case, to screwdrivers. On the other hand, too much information demands more processing by the listener; to identify the only screwdriver *the red-handled screwdriver with the small chip on the bottom and a loose handle* would probably hold up the search as the hearer would have to process too much unnecessary information. As we have seen, a speaker designs his utterance to take account of the listener's needs and may redesign it in the course of a sequence as a result of indications from the listener that the utterance is being misunderstood. Thus a dialogue system must be able to cope with the dynamic nature of dialogue. Throughout a dialogue the participants are actively engaged in the ongoing process of changing the focus and perceiving changes in focus.

Coherency in dialogue

It might be objected that a clear-cut dialogue structure which runs parallel to the task structure is applicable only to discourse types such as task-oriented dialogues. However other dialogues discussed by Grosz (1978) include database dialogues in which questions were answered about a database of ships. The database dialogues contained less segmentation than the task-oriented dialogues, although devices such as ellipsis were widely used to indicate the relatedness of adjacent utterances. Nevertheless the question arises: are there general devices used in dialogue to keep track of what is being talked about and to maintain a sense of overall coherence? One approach to this issue has been addressed by Reichman (1985).

The dialogue systems we have looked at so far have all involved conversations in which the turns at talk have been short – usually in the form of a single sentence. Furthermore, the situations have been highly structured so the sequential organization of the dialogues has been heavily constrained. Much casual conversation consists of longer stretches of discourse in which a speaker might develop several points. Furthermore, participants in a casual conversation have much more choice open to them than would be permitted by the systems considered so far. Reichman (1985) has developed a discourse grammar which aims to account for the structure of casual conversation. As we will see, this model includes many of the features of dialogue discussed so far, such as its nonlinear, hierarchical structure as well as the notion of predictability. A further feature of the model is that it sets out to characterize the knowledge which conversational participants have of discourse structure, based on Reichman's claim that this knowledge is necessary in order to understand how utterances fit together in a conversation. Reichman's discourse grammar is an abstract process module for the generation and interpretation of coherent conversation. To be a fully implemented computer system it would require further modules to handle other levels of language such as syntax and semantics. The discourse module is, however, specified in formal terms and can be used to simulate at the discourse level the processes involved in the generation and interpretation of conversation.

One of the key concepts in Reichman's system is the *conversational move*. Examples of conversational moves are presenting a claim, explaining a claim, giving support to a claim, challenging a claim, shifting a topic and resuming a previous topic. Moves are discourse-internal units which are defined in terms of their functional relations to one another rather than in terms of external relations such as the speakers' communicative goals. A similar notion was proposed by the Birmingham discourse analysts whose system included moves such as initiating and responding (Coulthard 1985). In the Birmingham system, however, the set of moves was rather restricted and could only be applied to fairly structured encounters such as teacher-pupil interaction or doctor-patient interviews. Reichman's moves, on the other hand, are able to account for the structure of more casual conversation in which participants put forward a particular point of view which can then be supported or challenged, and where challenges can be further followed by counter-challenges, or further supports or rejections. As Reichman argues, a conversation can be seen as a sequence of such functionally related moves.

Such a sequence of moves does not, however, constitute the structure of discourse. Reichman's basic constituent element of discourse structure is the *context space*. Roughly speaking, a context space consists of a series of utterances which refer to a single episode or issue. One common type is the *issue context space* in which a particular state of affairs is asserted to be true or false, good or bad, possible or impossible. Each context space is defined by the conversational move which it contains and it can be followed by subsequent context spaces containing moves such as support, challenge or rejection. Additionally a context space will usually refer to some preceding context space to which it is functionally related. For example, a context space containing a support will refer back to the context space containing the claim which is being supported. The following extract, in which the participants are discussing the respective roles of genetics and environment in human development, illustrates this structure (Reichman 1985: 21–2).

(11)

1	R	except, however, John and I just saw this two-hour TV show
2	M	uh hum
3	R	where they showed – it was an excellent French TV documentary –
4		and they showed that in fact the aggressive nature of the child is not
5		really that much influenced by his environment
6	M	how did they show that?
7	R	they showed that by filming kids in kindergarten
8	M	uh hum
9	R	showing his behaviour among other children
10	M	and then?
11	R	and showed him ten years later acting the same way, toward, um,
12	D	well, of course, that's where he learns his behaviour, in kindergarten

Here R makes a claim in lines 4–5 for the genetic argument and this is followed by M's demand for support in line 6 which elicits R's support in lines 7, 9 and 11. This is then followed in line 12 by D's challenge to that support. So, as can be seen, each conversational move is functionally related to preceding moves. Furthermore, the production of a particular move, such as a claim, will constrain what moves are likely to follow – for example, a demand for support, a challenge or a rejection. As Reichman (1985: 30) writes: 'As a conversation progresses, each discourse move thus constrains continuing options of conversational development and sets up expectations of the context relevant for the interpretation of succeeding utterances.' Thus utterances are generated and interpreted in the light of the functional relations they have to preceding discourse units. It is knowledge of such functional relations which, as Reichman claims, enables participants to perceive the coherency of conversation especially when, as so often happens, topic shifts within a conversation are not explicitly marked. The perception of coherency is also made more complex by the fact that these relations are often non-linear. Rather, as Grosz says in the work discussed earlier, discourse structure is hierarchical. Thus a constituent such as a claim, which is an independent unit of discourse, can have associated dependent units such as supports or explanations, just as in syntax a verb can be

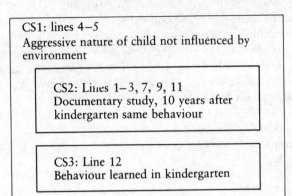

Figure 7.2   The hierarchical structure of example 11
(Reichman 1985: 26)

supported by an adverb, or a noun phrase by a relative clause. The hierarchical structure of example 11 can be illustrated diagrammatically as in figure 7.2.

Here CS2 and CS3 are sub-constituents of CS1, acting respectively as support and challenge. As we will see later, this hierarchical structure has a bearing on the use of anaphoric reference in conversation as well as on the production of discourse markers such as *on the other hand, by the way, anyway* and *but first.* Knowledge of this structure also enables conversational participants to follow the flow of conversation; they can work out whether an utterance is related to its direct predecessor or whether it is related to some utterance which is further removed temporally but which is nevertheless functionally associated in terms of this hierarchical structure.

From what has been said so far it might be argued that Reichman's model is not unlike other frameworks for the analysis of conversation. As mentioned earlier, it uses the concept of a conversational move which was also a basic unit in the descriptive framework of the Birmingham discourse analysts. This unit is also similar to the types of unit proposed by the conversation analysts. The same argument applies to the notion of predictability, which states that the discourse structure sets constraints on what can be said next and also on how subsequent utterances will be interpreted. In other words, Reichman's model would seem to be simply a more elaborate framework capable of handling conversations involving more extended turns.

There are, however, two features of Reichman's model which

distinguish it from the linguistic and ethnomethodological models discussed earlier and which locate her model within AI. First, its components, in particular the structure of units such as context spaces, which are specified so explicitly and exhaustively that they are amenable to a computational implementation. And second, the fact that the model adopts a process view of conversation which can account more adequately for its turn-by-turn construction. While this aspect is addressed in conversation analysis, Reichman's model shows how it might actually be implemented in process terms. Let us look at each of these aspects in a little more detail.

The structure of context spaces

Context spaces are structured like frames, in that they consist of slots to be filled. All context spaces have the following slots (Reichman 1985: 52):

TYPE	the name of the context space
DERIVATION	whether the claims in the context space were explicitly stated by the speaker or inferred by the system
GOAL	the function of the conversational move, e.g. support, challenge
CONTEXTUAL FUNCTION	1 Method: the method used to perform the conversational move, e.g. analogy
	2 Co-relator: specific reference to the context space to which the current move is related
SPEAKERS	a list of speakers who have produced utterances within the context space
STATUS	the role of the context space in the discourse, e.g. whether foreground or background
FOCUS	the status of individual elements within the context space

An issue context space has three additional slots for claim, topic and support context spaces. The last mentioned contains a list of all the context spaces developed in support of the claim made in the issue space. Issue context spaces are sub-divided into debatative and nondebatative issue spaces. Debatative issues spaces have further slots for the protagonists and antagonists in the argument and for counterclaims and countersupports. The following example illustrates the structure of the context space CS2 which includes B's conversational turn (Reichman 1985: 55–6).

(12)

A   I think if you're going to marry someone in the Hindu tradition, you have to – Well, you – they say you give money to the family, to the girl, but in essence, you actually buy her

B   it's the same in the Western tradition. You know, you see these greasy fat millionaires going around with film stars, right? They've essentially bought them by their status

Context Space CS2: B's turn

TYPE	Issue
DERIVATION	Explicit
GOAL	Generalization
CONTEXTUAL-FUNCTION	Method: Analogy
	Co-relator: C1
SPEAKERS	B
STATUS	Active
FOCUS	It (buying and selling of women)–high focus Western tradition–medium focus

We can now look in greater detail at how certain types of conversational move are accomplished within context spaces. The following example illustrates a support move, which is often marked with words such as *because*, *like* and *like when* (Reichman 1985: 37).

(13)

1   D   you and I are very close in this room right now
2   but we don't have the same environment
3   because I'm looking at you, I'm seeing the window
4   behind you. You're not seeing that window behind you

In this extract from the genetics-environment debate, part of which was cited earlier, D makes a claim in lines 1–2 that he and R (the addressee) do not share the same environment. This is followed by a supporting statement in lines 3–4. But the question arises: how is this a supporting statement? In order to understand this, we have to realize that underlying D's argument is the implicit principle that if two people share the same environment then they will see the same things. Assuming now that we have three elements – a claim, a support and a principle – it is still necessary to specify how these are related. To do this two things are required. First, there is a process of *instantiation*, by means of which the general principle which is being assumed (that if two people share the same environment then they will see the same things) is applied to the particular people in this conversation – D and R. This involves a mapping between the general class referred to in the principle (two people) and instances of the class (i.e. D and R) who can now be substituted for that general class. Second, a demonstration of how the argument is carried out is needed. Analogies can often be used to support claims, as we saw earlier. In this case, however, a rule of logic, *Modus-Tollens*, is used. This rule can be stated informally as:

(14)
Given two facts, A and B, and the assertion that A implies B, then if you know that B is not true, you can conclude that A is not true.

Applied to this example we have the following line of argumentation:

(15)
If two people share the same environment, then they will see the same things (If A then B).
(We (D and R) are two people and 'things' is 'the window behind you'. (Instantiation)
I can see the window but you cannot (B is not true).
Therefore: We do not share the same environment (A is not true).

A support context space would thus have slots for claim, fact of support, principle of support, mappings between the claim and the principle, and a method, such as the logic rule Modus-Tollens. Each of these slots would have to be filled, including the implicit information in the underlying principle of support, and there would have to be a way of connecting these elements by means of a process of inference as illustrated here. Once it is clear that a support move is to be performed, then the conversational participants will expect utterances that can be interpreted as support components and that can be related to each other and to the issue context space in conventional ways. The move will not be completed until all the obligatory elements have been supplied. In this way the model can account for the well-formedness of the discourse as well as providing a structural frame for the interpretation of subsequent utterances.

Conversation as process

This brings us to the second major characteristic of Reichman's discourse grammar. It is argued that the model is not just a static description of discourse structure but an attempt to model discourse generation and interpretation as an active, ongoing process. One aspect of this process is that each conversational move selected will have a bearing on subsequent moves, either by making certain moves more likely or by precluding certain others. Furthermore, Reichman claims that the conversational participants update their discourse models accordingly. In other words, the participants' knowledge of discourse structure is not a static model, external to the ongoing conversation, but a model which changes as the discourse proceeds. The mechanism for maintaining this discourse model is the slot within the structure of context spaces for STATUS.

The status slot reflects the role of an utterance in the discourse. This role changes as the conversation proceeds. There are seven values for status in the model (Reichman 1985:54).

1 Active: the context space in which current utterances are being placed.
2 Controlling: the context space in direct relation to the active space being developed.
3 Precontrol: a previously controlling context space whose controlling status has been temporarily usurped, for example, by a digression in the topic.
4 Open: a previously active context space that was interrupted before completion of its corresponding move.
5 Generating: a context space which is indirectly related to an active context space, as, for example, in a subargument.
6 Closed: a context space whose discussion is believed to have been completed.
7 Superseded: a context space whose discussion is concluded by its being replaced by a new context space containing a 'finer restatement' or a 'further generalization'.

The two most important values are active and controlling. These constitute the discourse context, in that at any given time in a conversation there will be one active context space – the context space which is being currently developed – and one controlling context space – the space to which the currently active space is related. Thus at any given time the discourse context consists of these two context spaces but any subsequent conversational moves will change the status of existing context spaces and result in further updating. This is done by associating with each conversational move a description of the updatings it gives rise to. A few examples will illustrate.

Support moves can occur in two different discourse positions. In example 11 R provides support for her claim that children are not influenced by their environment. Thus a support can follow a claim and in this case the support context space becomes active and puts the preceding issue context space into a controlling status. In other words, what is said in the supporting space is influenced by the contents of the preceding issue space. However a support can also be offered as an alternative to a preceding support which has been withdrawn. This happened in the continuation of the genetics-environment debate following D's challenge to R's original support of her claim for the genetic side of the argument (Reichman 1985: 22).

(16)
15	D	well, of course, that's where he learns his behaviour, in kinder-
16		garten
17	M	oh sure
18	R	now, another thing, it wasn't that he didn't have–
19	J	what? what's that? what did you say?
20	R	the aggressive child in kindergarten who acted the same way later
21		on
22	J	yeah, he did
23	R	oh it was twins. The important thing was that there were two
24		children from the same environment, whereas only one of the
25		brothers acted that way, so you couldn't blame it on the child's
26		home

Here R implicitly accepts D's challenge and goes on to offer an alternative support marked by the words *now another thing, oh it was twins*, and *the important thing was*. The effect of this move is to assign closed status to the previous support move and active status to this new support move. The issue context space, which contains the original claim being supported, remains in a controlling status as it still has an influence on the current discourse.

Similar effects are achieved with other moves. For example, an interruption move, which suspends discussion of a context space before it has been completed, causes that context space to be assigned an open status, which means that it can be expected the speaker will return later to that space after the digression. A return, often signalled by words such as *but, anyway* and *any case*, causes the open context space to be assigned an active status again. Thus there are standard effects associated with the selection of particular conversational moves and, as Reichman (1985:66) writes: 'it is in part their knowledge of these standardized effects that allows conversants to share compatible models of the current relevant discourse context as conversation proceeds.'

The context space grammar is implemented in terms of an ATN. It will be recalled from chapter 3 that ATNs are a means of representing grammatical rules in networks which consist of states and arcs. Arcs represent sentence constituents (e.g. NP, VP and PP), category labels (e.g. noun or verb), or words, and a complete traversal of a network corresponds to a sentence. Furthermore there are often conditions which have to be fulfilled before arcs can be crossed and the transition of arcs can cause certain specified actions to be taken. Reichman has applied the same ideas to her discourse grammar. Here the basic unit of analysis is the context space, and arcs indicate what options are available at given points in the discourse. Traversal of the ATN entails the production or parsing of a single conversational move, while a complete conversation would involve many cycles through different paths in the network. Tests on arcs are concerned with whether the appropriate conditions exist for a move to be taken, while the effects of taking a particular arc involve actions such as updating the status slot of a context space. Information relevant to the conversation is kept in registers. For example, information about the expectations set up as a result of taking a particular move is kept in an expectation register. So, for example, there is an expectation that a challenge will be followed by a counter-challenge, and a demand for support of a claim by a support. Where more than one subsequent move is possible, an expectation-list register is kept in which a running history can be maintained of discourse expectations which may be taken up at later points in the conversation. Other information kept in registers includes lists of the protagonists and antagonists on each side of an argument.

It is not possible within the scope of this chapter to do justice to this model of discourse and for full details readers are referred to the comprehensive discussion in Reichman (1985). The main intention has been to show that discourse structure can be modelled explicitly and to support the view that knowledge of this structure is an important aspect of participation in conversation. To conclude, we can look at one further aspect of this work – the way in which the underlying structure of conversation can explain the use of linguistic items such as pronouns and pronominal adverbs (e.g. *here*, *there*). The ability to interpret these items correctly is also essential for conversationalists. To illustrate, we can take the following extract from a conversation between friends, part of which was cited in example 12 (Reichman 1984: 163).

(17)
A I think if you're going to marry someone in the Hindu tradition, you have to – well, you – they say you give money to the family, to the girl, but in essence you actually buy her
B it's the same in the Western tradition. You know, you see these greasy fat millionaires going around with film stars, right? They've essentially bought them by their status
C no, but there the woman is selling herself. In these societies the woman isn't selling herself, her parents are selling her

How do we explain the use of *there* and *these* in C's turn? We would normally expect that *there* would refer to something further away in the discourse and that *these* would refer to something nearer. This would be in keeping with a linear analysis of the conventional flow, such as the following.

Turn 1 (A)	marriage in the Hindu tradition
Turn 2 (B)	the Western tradition
Turn 3 (C)	1 the Western tradition
	2 the Hindu tradition

However the opposite occurs: *there* refers to the Western tradition which has just been mentioned and *these* to the Hindu tradition which had been mentioned two turns earlier. Furthermore, this usage appears quite natural for the conversational participants and does not give rise to any misunderstandings. Why is this?

As Reichman explains, the use of pronominal forms is determined by the structural organization of the discourse in terms of context spaces, as follows.

Turn 1 (A)	Context space C1 – the initiating space
Turn 2 (B)	Context space C2 – the analogy space
	(Marked by the clue-words *it's the same*)
Turn 3 (C)	Context space C3 – the challenge space
	(Marked by the words *no, but*)

The context space C1 is in the foreground (in controlling status) despite the analogy space C2 which precedes C3 on a linear analysis. Unless the analogy is accepted, the main topic remains with C1, so that anaphoric items in C3, which rejects the analogy, are resolved in terms of C1 which is still the controlling context space with an influence on the subsequent discourse.

Reichman's model is premissed on the notion that participants in conversation build a model of the discourse as it proceeds. It assumes that each participant builds the same discourse model. However, if the participants were to have conflicting discourse models the system would have to be amended to allow for separate discourse models for each participant. Dialogue depends to a large extent on the ability of the participants to assume a shared perspective. However another important feature of conversational competence is the ability to recognize when perspectives are not shared and to shape the dialogue accordingly. This involves making judgements about the knowledge, beliefs, goals and plans of the other participants in the conversation. How these character-istics of dialogue partners have been modelled will be the concern of the next chapter.

Further Reading

Discourse analysis

The Birmingham work on discourse analysis was first presented in Sinclair and Coulthard (1975). This is the most comprehensive account of this approach. More recent discussions can be found in Stubbs (1983) and Coulthard (1985).

Conversation analysis

Collections of papers which illustrate the ethnomethodological approach to the analysis of conversation include Sudnow (1972), Schenkein (1978), Psathas (1979), and Atkinson and Heritage (1984). Levinson (1983: chapter 6) provides an extremely coherent account of this work.

Computational pragmatics

The work of Grosz, which was part of a large-scale speech understanding project at SRI, is described along with the other aspects of this project in Walker (1978). Reichman's context space model is presented in

Reichman (1985). Brady and Berwick (1983) is a collection of papers dealing with several aspects of discourse analysis within a computational framework and it includes Kaplan's work on CO-OP as well as Allen's work on speech acts which are to be discussed in chapter 8. See also Joshi et al. (1981) and Lehnert and Ringle (1982).

8

Modelling Dialogue

Dialogue has been defined as a co-operative activity in which two participants exchange ideas and information. Informal conversation also involves activities such as passing on news, relating events and gossip. The notion that dialogue depends on co-operation adds a further dimension to the knowledge structures required for the processing of natural language. In dialogue it is not only a matter of being able to follow a sequence of events, as in a story, and to interpret them as a coherent unit using knowledge of scripts and of the plans and goals of the actors in the story. In dialogue each speaker has to try to assess the other person's intentions, plans and beliefs and to adjust the dialogue accordingly. Each speaker has also to take account of what type of person the dialogue partner is and adjust not only what he says but how he says it. For example, the response to a question about the processes of conception and birth will vary according to whether the dialogue partner is a five-year-old child, a twelve-year-old child, an expectant father or a student of gynaecology. One approach to this issue was discussed in chapter 6 in relation to the question-answering system QUALM.

Another type of adjustment is determined by the speaker's assessment of what the dialogue partner does and does not know. If it is assumed that the partner already has some knowledge of the conversational topic, then various shortcuts can be taken, things can be left unexplained, and objects and persons can be mentioned, with little or no introduction. The listener in a dialogue has to make some assessment of what the speaker is trying to express in order to interpret utterances and respond appropriately. If you think your partner is giving a friendly warning, then you will respond in one way, but if you think he is threatening, you will respond rather differently. But how do you know in the first place whether an utterance is a warning or a threat? As has been shown in the literature on indirect speech acts (see, for example, Cole and Morgan 1975), there is no direct relationship between the form of an utterance and its function.

This being so, listeners have to try and work out what speakers are getting at with their utterances, in other words, what their intentions and goals might be. Intelligent dialogue systems have to cope with issues such as these which underlie conversational interaction. The systems which will be described in this chapter have dealt with these issues in many different ways. Some have been concerned with working out what a user might have intended with a question and deal with the problem that arises when the user asks a question based on false assumptions. A helpful answer would address and correct these false assumptions rather than ignoring them. Such systems, engage in *co-operative dialogue* with the user. Other systems have looked at the question of different user types and how the system's responses have to be tailored to these different user types. This approach has become known as *user modelling*. Yet other systems are concerned with how to work out the user's intentions on the basis of what the most likely interpretation would be, given the specific context of the interaction.

Co-operative dialogue

One approach to co-operative dialogue can be illustrated in the following question-answer sequence from a system called CO-OP, a natural language query system which provides co-operative responses to simple queries requesting information from a database (Kaplan 1983).

(1)
U   how many students got As in Linguistics in 1981?
S   none
U   how many students got Bs?
S   none
U   how many students got Cs?
S   none
U   how many students took Linguistics in 1981?
S   none

After a long sequence it turns out that the user's initial question was based on a false assumption, namely that some students took Linguistics Major in 1981. This assumption is only corrected as a result of the persistent questioning. In the absence of this questioning, the user might have maintained the false assumption. This would be the case following this exchange:

(2)
U   how many students got As in Linguistics in 1981?
S   none

Here the system is clearly being unhelpful; it allows the user to persist with a false assumption because it does not give the reason for the negative answer. A more helpful response would be something like:

(3)
S   no students took Linguistics in 1981

This type of response has been called a *corrective indirect response*. The response is indirect, as it does not give the most direct answer (e.g. *none*), and it is corrective as it corrects the user's false assumptions.

How does CO-OP work? Essentially what happens is that the user's question is translated into an intermediate representation called *Meta Query Language* (MQL). The most important aspect of this representation, as far as dealing with potentially false assumptions in the user's questions is concerned, is that the objects and persons referred to in the question are treated as separate subsets in the data base. In the case of the question about Linguistics Major students there would be four sets: students, the grade A, courses, and the subject Linguistics. If any one of these sets is empty, a null response will be returned. What CO-OP does is to search for the empty set and to produce an appropriate indirect response which will thus address the user's false assumptions. Thus if the set for students is empty, the response will be *I don't know of any students*. If the set for grade A is empty, the answer is *I don't know of any As*. If there are two empty sets CO-OP produces a response incorporating two sets of information, for example, empty sets for students and grade A would produce *I don't know of any students that got As*. In this fairly simple way attention can be drawn to the issue of the user's false assumptions.

A second type of response is the *suggestive indirect response*. This also occurs in the case of a negative answer, but instead of addressing the user's misconceptions the respondent elaborates on the answer by supplying additional potentially relevant information. An example will illustrate this:

(4)
U   is there a newsagent in this street?
S   no, but there is one round the corner

In this exchange, a direct response, a *yes* or *no*, would not endorse any user misconceptions, but it would not be particularly helpful either, as presumably the user is interested in finding a newsagent and any relevant information would be helpful. The facility for indirect suggestive responses is based on the conversational convention that speakers do not normally wish to receive negative or trivial responses and so they phrase their questions in a way that will not elicit these. How this works for CO-OP is that the system looks for the item which is the focus of the question, that is, the item which carries new information. In the case of this example, this would be the phrase *in this street*. This is eliminated from the query which is then executed in modified form to incorporate the information which would probably be requested in a follow-up question. In this example a likely follow-up question would be *is there a newsagent in the neighbourhood?* The system preempts the follow-up question by supplying the information requested in the modified query from which the original focus was eliminated, i.e. *is there a newsagent?* The information *round the corner* is an appropriate response in this case.

Determining the focus of a question is a difficult problem which is not unrelated to the recognition of the user's plans. In the above example, the system has to be sensitive to the probability that the user is looking for a newsagent and not for some other type of shop. So, for example, the response *no, but there is a greengrocer* would not be particularly helpful. As well as this, the focus may be incorrectly selected. This does not produce disastrous results, as the negative response was potentially sufficient in any case, but it could result in the user being inundated with unwanted or irrelevant information.

A final principle which can be mentioned concerns the handling of vague questions by providing supportive indirect responses. Consider the following exchange:

(5)
U   what grades did students get in Linguistics?
S   A,B,B,B,C,A,D,D,C . . . . .

Here the user obviously requires the student names along with the grades, although he does not request the information explicitly in the question. The principle which is used to generate an appropriate response is to assume that if a user explicitly mentions some aspect of the domain in the question, then that aspect should appear in the response. Thus the above query would produce a table of student-grade pairs, as both students and grades are mentioned in the question.

Kaplan attempted to build into CO-OP some of the principles of human conversation, in particular the principle that speakers normally behave co-operatively. The techniques used are language-driven rather than domain-driven. That is to say the nature of the response depends on an analysis of the phrasing of the question, whether this involves the set of entities mentioned, as for corrective indirect responses, the focus of the question, as for suggestive indirect responses, or the entities mentioned, as for supportive indirect responses. These language-driven inferences are motivated by a pragmatic theory of effective language use, in contrast to the large-scale domain-specific knowledge structures described in chapter 6. These conventions and principles are domain-independent; this gives them the advantage of being easily transportable to other domains and does away with the need for a detailed and comprehensive system of background knowledge which would have to be reconstructed for each new domain. However, this economy is achieved by means of restricting the world in which the system operates to that of a database and the goal of the 'system's users to simply finding out information about the attributes of objects in the database. As far as the linguistic analysis of the user's questions is concerned, this is facilitated by there being a close correspondence between database paths and the surface syntactic structure of questions. At the pragmatic level it can be assumed that the user simply wants lists as answers to the database queries, so it is not necessary to deal with the more complex issue of making reasonable inferences about the user's intentions, goals and plans. In order to be able to make such inferences, the system needs to be able to construct an appropriate model of the user and his goals. These issues will be addressed in the next sections of this chapter.

User modelling

When we engage in conversation with another person, we make a series of judgements about that person which guide what we say and how we say it. We try to assess such things as the person's level of education, social background and possible political beliefs in order to tune our talk – select appropriate topics and an appropriate manner of discussing them. If, for example, we are travelling to a conference on artificial intelligence and find ourselves in conversation with a friendly and talkative fellow traveller who describes himself as a grocer, what we choose to say about the conference will be quite different from what we might say if the fellow traveller were a colleague going to the same conference. Assessment of our co-conversationalists facilitates the smooth management of social interaction, and is essential in service encounters. For example, a person selling life insurance will probably only be successful if he is able to assess his customer's needs accurately and recommend an appropriate scheme.

User modelling is an important aspect of computer systems design, especially now that systems are being developed which are sensitive to the needs of individual users. It could be argued that any computer system is planned with specific users in mind since it is normal for a system to be tested and adjusted over a period of time until it appears to meet the needs of its projected user group. This type of modelling caters only for general classes of users and does not produce systems sensitive to individual users. In other words, it is static. A slight ramification of this principle is exemplified by the INTELLECT system (Harris 1984) which can be tuned to a user population studied in advance to determine their level of expertise and familiarity with the system. Once these adjustments have been made, however, they cannot be easily changed.

Generally, what is meant by user modelling is a more dynamic process in which the behaviour of the system is influenced in the course of the dialogue by information about the individual user. This information can be elicited explicitly from the user or inferred from the user's responses. In order to illustrate how such user modelling can be done, two systems will be described – the first plays the role of a librarian and recommends novels to different types of reader while the second plays the role of an hotel employee and books rooms for guests.

GRUNDY: *the automated librarian*

The following is an example of an interaction with GRUNDY, a system which operates as an automated librarian (Rich 1979).

(6)
PLEASE TYPE IN YOUR NAME
John Greene
YOU HAVEN'T USED THIS SYSTEM BEFORE, HAVE YOU?
no
OK
I'D LIKE TO KNOW WHAT SORT OF PERSON YOU THINK YOU ARE.
PLEASE TYPE IN A FEW SINGLE WORDS THAT YOU THINK CHARAC-
TERIZE THE MOST IMPORTANT ASPECTS OF YOURSELF
unconventional open direct honest humorous persistent adventurous
I DON'T KNOW THE WORD UNCONVENTIONAL
I DON'T KNOW THE WORD OPEN
I DON'T KNOW THE WORD DIRECT
WOULD YOU LIKE TO TRY SOME MORE WORDS?
yes
OK GO AHEAD
relaxed jewish friendly playful thoughtful eccentric
HAVE YOU EVER READ EARTH ANGELS BY SUSAN CAHILL?
no
YOU MIGHT LIKE IT
IT IS ABOUT A GIRL WHO GOES TO CATHOLIC ELEMENTARY

SCHOOL, HIGH SCHOOL, AND COLLEGE, THEN GOES ON TO BECOME
A NUN, BUT FINALLY BACKS OUT A FEW DAYS BEFORE FINAL VOWS.
A MAJOR CONFLICT IN IT IS THE RELATIONSHIP OF MAN TO GOD.
ONE OF THE MAJOR STRENGTHS OF ONE OF THE MAIN CHARAC-
TERS IS INTELLIGENCE.
ONE OF THE MAIN STRENGTHS OF ONE OF THE MAIN CHARACTERS
IS INDEPENDENCE.
IT IS POLITICALLY LIBERAL.
IT HAS A MEDIUM-FAST MOVING PLOT.
DOES THAT SOUND GOOD?
no

As can be seen from this extract, GRUNDY's natural language ability
is limited to a fairly simple level of sentence generation and the system
restricts the user's input to single words. What is more important,
however, is how the system copes with the needs of individual users.
GRUNDY elicits the user's name and asks whether he has used the
system before. This input immediately activates two stereotypes – one of
ANY-PERSON, which is activated for any new user, and one for MAN,
activated by the name *John*. Stereotypes are clusters of characteristics
about a person. For example, among the characteristics of a doctor
would be *well-educated, caring, knowledgeable about medicine, fairly
affluent* and *well-respected in the community*. These are assigned values
which are rated according to the certainty with which the assigned values
can be assumed. In addition, the reasons why the system believes what it
believes are recorded, so that a user profile will consist of four
dimensions – attributes, values, ratings and justifications. In the case of
the ANY-PERSON stereotype, activated at the beginning of the extract,
the values will be middle-of-the-road with low ratings, which means that
they can be superseded by any more specific information which emerges
later.

The system then asks the user to input some words which characterize
his most important aspects. In this case some of the words are rejected as
they are unknown to the system and others are elicited. By now the
system has a picture of John. It assumes, because he is male, that in his
taste in literature he will have a fairly high tolerance for violence and
suffering, a preference for thrill, suspense and fast plots, and little interest
in romance. Stereotypes are also elicited by the words *humorous, friendly*
and *playful*. On the basis of these, the system picks out one of John's
attributes which has both a non-middle-of-the-road value and a fairly
high rating and selects a book based on what it knows about the book
and what it thinks John will like. As it happens, John rejects the first
suggestion. In the remainder of the dialogue, which has not been quoted

here, the system tries to find out where it went wrong; it goes through the reasons why it thought John might have liked the book until it isolates its mistake, it then changes its beliefs about John in this respect and goes on to make other suggestions.

There are two main types of information handled by GRUNDY – *stereotypes* and the *model of the individual user*. Examples of stereotypes are SPORTS-PERSON and FEMINIST. SPORTS-PERSON has high values for attributes such as *interest in sport and thrill, toleration of violence* and *admiration of physical strength*, and low values for *romance* and *education*. The value scores range from +5 to −5 and each has an associated rating assessing its degree of certainty. The FEMINIST stereotype has high values for *political causes, conflicts involving sex-roles, toleration of sex, perseverance* and *independence*, but a low value for *piety*. Many attributes are not shared across stereotypes, but may become relevant for a particular user as often more than one stereotype will be activated for any individual. In addition, general information can be overridden by more specific information. For example, the stereotype for RELIGIOUS PERSON includes those for Christian and Jew, and within the category Christian for Catholic and Protestant. However, as Jewish people are often less religious than members of other religious groups the Jewish stereotype will override some of the more general information in the RELIGIOUS PERSON stereotype. Stereotypes activate triggers which are associated with particular situations so that, for example, the scientist stereotype activates an *educated person* or an *atheist* trigger.

The user model, or USS (User Synopsis), is constructed on the basis of information provided directly by the user, of inferences based on what the user says and of predictions derived from stereotypes appropriate to the user. The predictions associated with the MAN stereotype were discussed earlier. An extract from a sample user synopsis is shown in table 8.1. This was constructed on the basis of the user having told GRUNDY she was a feminist and an intellectual. GRUNDY selects the user's most salient characteristics and matches one facet with values for books. Once a set of possible books has been constructed, each facet is compared with them so that the best book can be chosen. GRUNDY then recommends the book and describes its most interesting features, basing its description on the assessment of the user's interests.

One of the most important ways in which GRUNDY differs from more traditional systems is that it permits a dynamic model of the user. The model is dynamic in several ways. First, it is constructed on the basis of predetermined stereotypes which are activated in the course of the dialogue, so that a user profile is built as the system learns more about

Table 8.1   A user synopsis

Facet	Value	Rating	Justifications
Gender	female	1000	inference-female name
Education	5	900	INTELLECTUAL
Seriousness	5	800	INTELLECTUAL
Piety	−3	423	WOMAN
			FEMINIST
			INTELLECTUAL
Politics	Liberal	910	FEMINIST
			INTELLECTUAL
Thrill	−4	839	WOMAN
			INTELLECTUAL
Romance	3	696	WOMAN
Political-causes	5	1000	FEMINIST
Motivations			
Learn	4	700	INTELLECTUAL

Source: Rich 1979: 346

the user. Conflicts between values predicted in different stereotypes for a particular user have to be resolved and give rise to different ratings of certainty for the values. Obviously these ratings will differ from one user to another. Furthermore, if its predictions are not confirmed the system is able to modify its recommendations and make further suggestions. Finally, the stereotypes themselves can be changed as a result of interactions with a series of users. This happened, in fact, with the MAN stereotype after it had been run with about twenty users; the values deriving from the prediction that men would like books that were fast-moving and full of suspense were lowered as a result of this experience.

The HAM-ANS system

HAM-ANS (Hamburg Application-Oriented Natural Language System) is a large-scale natural language system which provides access to a range of software systems, including a hotel reservation system, an image sequence analysis system and a database system (Hoeppner, Morik and Marburger 1984). HAM-ANS is a complex system capable of processing a wide range of natural language input; it incorporates components for lexical, morphological, syntactic and semantic analysis, including ellipsis resolution and quantifier handling. In addition there are various facilities concerned with language generation, involving, for example, the re-arrangement of quantified expressions, definite and indefinite descriptions and the identification of possible ellipsis. In this section we will be concerned mainly with the dialogue capacities of HAM-ANS and, in particular, with the issue of user modelling.

In the following extract the system plays the role of a hotel employee interacting with a client who wishes to book a room. The extract is fairly long but it will be instructive to examine the whole dialogue in order to understand how the system works. (The version presented here is a fairly close translation from the original German and appears in places more stilted and less idiomatic than the original.)

(7)
1 (040 4123 3315)
2 HOTEL ZUM FETTEN OCHSEN, GOOD EVENING
3 hello, this is Karlchen Mueller from Fuchhausen speaking
4 WHAT CAN I DO FOR YOU?
5 I'd like a double room for two days
6 YES OF COURSE, JUST LET ME SEE
7 YOU WOULD LIKE A DOUBLE ROOM UNTIL APRIL 25TH, IS THAT RIGHT?
8 no, that's not the way I meant it
9 SORRY, I MUST HAVE MISUNDERSTOOD YOU
10 I'd like a double room for three nights with a bath
11 YOU WOULD LIKE A DOUBLE ROOM WITH A BATH UNTIL APRIL 26TH, IS THAT RIGHT?
12 yes, exactly
13 YES, WE STILL HAVE SOME VACANCIES, DO YOU HAVE ANY PARTICULAR REQUIREMENTS
14 is there an easy chair or a large chair in the room?
15 A LARGE CHAIR IS NOT AVAILABLE, BUT AN EASY CHAIR
16 how many of the chairs are comfortable?
17 ONE OF THE FOUR IS RELATIVELY COMFORTABLE
18 the easy chair?
19 YES, RELATIVELY COMFORTABLE
20 decidedly comfortable
21 NO, RELATIVELY COMFORTABLE
22 is this easy chair white, perhaps?
23 NO, THE EASY CHAIR IS YELLOW
24 MAY I BOOK A DOUBLE ROOM THEN UNDER THE NAME KARLCHEN MUELLER, FUCHHAUSEN?
25 just a moment, I still have a question
26 YES
27 where?

28 EXCUSE ME, WHAT DO YOU MEAN?
29 where is this easy chair?
30 THE EASY CHAIR IS IN FRONT OF THE WINDOW
31 and what is it next to?
32 THE EASY CHAIR IS NEXT TO A LOW COFFEE TABLE
33 MAY I BOOK A DOUBLE ROOM THEN UNDER THE NAME KARLCHEN MUELLER, FUCHHAUSEN?
34 just a moment, not so fast
35 YES?
36 what is on this coffee table which is next to the easy chair?
37 THERE IS NOTHING ON THIS COFFEE TABLE WHICH IS NEXT TO THE EASY CHAIR
38 the room isn't dark, is it?
39 NO
40 it's bright then?
41 YES, PROBABLY BRIGHT
42 really?
43 ONE OF THE WINDOWS IS LARGE
44 MAY I BOOK A DOUBLE ROOM THEN UNDER THE NAME KARLCHEN MUELLER, FUCHHAUSEN?
45 yes, I have no further questions
46 FINE, I HAVE BOOKED A DOUBLE ROOM FOR APRIL 23 TO 25 UNDER THE NAME KARLCHEN MUELLER, FUCHHAUSEN
47 THANK YOU. GOODBYE
48 goodbye

In the hotel room reservation situation both participants have relatively firm intentions which can be assumed from the outset. These are easily managed in the initial and final parts of the dialogue, which consist of a sequence of speech acts in an obligatory order. For example, the beginning of the dialogue has the following sequence:

1 simulated phonecall
2 hotel greeting
3 caller greeting
4 caller requested to state requirement
5 caller's requirements (to include number of rooms, type, length of stay, room features)
6 paraphrase of requirement as question
7 confirmation or disconfirmation

At this point, there is a choice. If the caller confirms the paraphrase of his requirements, the system confirms room availability and then passes the initiative to the user with the question *do you have any particular requirements?* If the paraphrase is disconfirmed, the system assumes that there has been a misunderstanding and allows the caller to restate the requirements. Once this problem has been resolved, the stage of *consultative dialogue* is entered in which the caller can ask questions about features of the room. Up until this point the workings of the system are not unlike those of GUS, the travel agent, described in chapter 7, as the units of the dialogue consist of a series of predetermined slots to be filled within a frame-like structure.

After answering a fixed number of questions the system tries to take over the initiative and asks whether a room can be booked. As is shown in this example, this has to be repeated several times until the caller complies. This leads to the closing sequence consisting of the following parts:

1 attempt to book room.
2 if room refused (go to 4) otherwise booking approved.
3 paraphrase of booking procedure.
4 hotel goodbye.
5 caller goodbye.

The dialogue structure of this extract appears in figure 8.1 in which numbers refer to lines in the cited extract.

In the consultative part of the dialogue (lines 14–43) the caller appears rather fussy, asking for all sorts of details about the furniture in the room. As we shall see, this part of the dialogue illustrates some important aspects of the language processing abilities of the system and how these interact with its user modelling.

The HAM-ANS system is based on the notion of the typical user (*a priori user modelling*) which is supplemented by information extracted during the course of the dialogue. Of particular importance are the modelling of the user's knowledge and beliefs, including his value judgements. Knowledge of these influences the system's performance linguistically as well as conceptually. At the linguistic level the user profile affects the use of anaphora, ellipsis and definite descriptions, while at the conceptual level it influences the choice of a suitable degree of detail, the order of presentation of items of information, and the recognition of misconceptions.

The linguistic effects of the user profile can be illustrated by examining how referring expressions are selected. It is assumed that the user will be familiar with the typical items in a hotel room, so they can be referred to on first mention using definite descriptions (*the door, the bed*). Familiarity with other items of detail (e.g. chairs and TV sets) cannot be assumed and the system, which has its own referential network of the

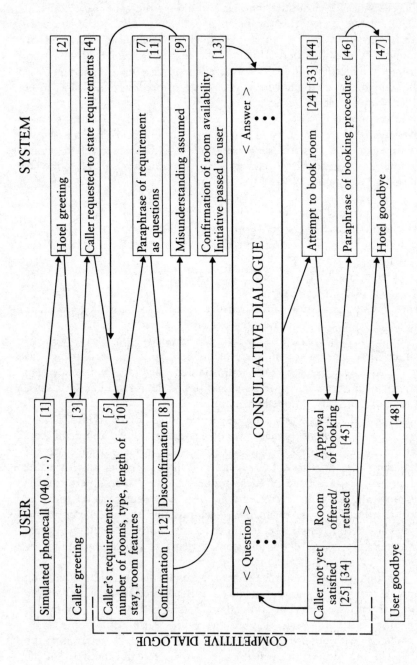

Figure 8.1 *Dialogue structure in the hotel room reservation situation (Hoeppner et al. 1984: 13)*

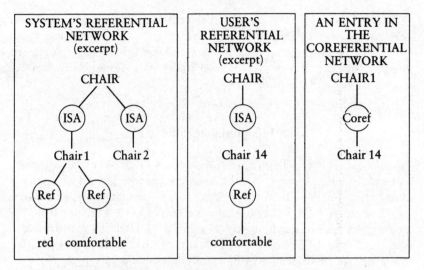

Figure 8.2 Referential knowledge networks of system and user
(Hoeppner et al. 1984: 31)

objects in the room, must keep track of what the user knows. Any time an object is mentioned, such as *the easy chair*, it is added to the user's referential network, indicating that the system knows that the user knows the object exists. In addition there is a coreferential network, indicating what the system and user know in common. An example of these referential networks is given in figure 8.2. For example, the system knows that there are several chairs in the room, but also knows that the user only knows about one chair. This one chair will be represented in the coreferential network and if the user refers to it simply as *the chair* the system can determine which chair is meant because it knows which chair had already been referred to in the dialogue. If an item has no entry in the user's network, indefinite descriptions (e.g. *a lamp*) have to be used. Similarly, if it is to describe a chair, the system must relate the description to the user's knowledge. And if it wishes to refer to a chair which is comfortable and red, and the system knows that the user only knows of a comfortable chair, then the most appropriate expression is not *the red chair* but *the comfortable chair*.

The system also has to keep track of the user's desires and needs in order to recommend the room which best matches them. This requires modelling the user's value judgements, for example, about what constitutes a good room, a large room or a bright room. Various criteria, such as the price class requested or the reason for the stay, can be derived from the dialogue. The system collects these criteria and makes a recommendation; if they are all met the recommendation is unqualified, if most are met a qualified recommendation is made, but if too many criteria are not met the user is consulted and the unfulfillable criteria are listed. Thus the system's recommendation is determined by how it evaluates the user's requirements.

Interpreting intentions

We saw earlier in the chapter how the system CO-OP was able to correct potentially false assumptions in a user's questions; instead of giving a direct response, the system addressed these false assumptions. This is one example of helpful behaviour. However, CO-OP was restricted to dealing with persons and objects mentioned in the user's utterance and with searching for relevant information in the database. A co-operative response was generated when no information could be found.

We will now look at a more general approach to helpful behaviour which involves making assessments about the user's plans and using these assessments to interpret what is said in a dialogue. This approach is based on the assumption that people are rational agents who form and execute plans in order to achieve goals. Many of these plans are stated explicitly in utterances, but sometimes it is the task of a dialogue partner to infer what these plans are and to produce helpful responses by detecting any obstacles to the execution of the plans. Thus participation in dialogue involves the more general notions of plan construction and plan inference. But before considering these notions in more detail, it might be helpful to look at some examples.

Consider the following dialogues, taken from a system which plays the role of a railway employee answering the queries of a user who has one of two possible goals – to board or to meet a train (Allen 1983; Allen and Perrault 1980).

(8)
when does the train to Windsor leave?
3.15 AT GATE 7

(9)
the train to Windsor?
3.15 AT GATE 10

(10)
do you know when the train to Windsor leaves?
3.15 AT GATE 7

In example 8, the user asks for the departure time of the train. However the system reasons that if someone wishes to board a train, then that person will not only need to know the departure time but also the departure location. Lack of knowledge of the departure location would be an obstacle to a user whose goal was boarding a train so the system provides the information. Thus the system gives a helpful response by supplying more than simply the requested information. Example 9 shows that the system is able to deal with utterances which are sentence fragments; what it does is to infer from the fragment what information the user is most likely to require. Finally, example 10 illustrates a helpful response to an indirect speech act; a response to the literal meaning of the request (i.e. a *yes* or *no*) would be inappropriate.

What is involved in providing helpful responses in this way? Recall that the system assumes that the user has one of two possible goals – to board or to meet a train. And it can only deal with questions that relate to these goals. Thus a question such as *did you hear who won the football match?* would be beyond the scope of the system. The elements of these goals are as follows:

Board train	Meet train
get ticket	
find out about destination	
find out departure location	find out arrival location
find out departure time	find out arrival time

What the system has to do is: work out the user's goal from his question, respond to what is explicitly requested in the utterance, look for any obstacles to the execution of the user's goal and provide information which anticipates these obstacles. In order to work out the user's goal, the system constructs his surface intention from the question and then expands this by using a series of rules of inference, yielding a set of alternative interpretations. It begins with the two possible goals and makes inferences from these which yield a set of expectations about the possible goal. These alternatives and expectations are assigned ratings and when the score of one alternative-expectation pair exceeds that of another by a certain amount, then the pair with the higher score is accepted as the more likely plan. The rules of inference used here model what is involved in plan construction and plan inference.

Recall the blocks world which was discussed in chapter 5. If a person had the aim of attaining a certain goal, such as stacking block A on top of block B, then that person might work out that a certain action, such as putting block A on block B, was necessary in order to attain the goal. But before carrying out the action it might be necessary to ensure that certain preconditions associated with the action were fulfilled, for example, that the tops of both blocks were clear and the person had a free hand. Thus goals are attained through actions, but actions have certain preconditions which have to be satisfied before they can be effected. The same applies to the train domain. If the goal is to board a train, it will be necessary to be at the departure location at the right time and in order to do this, it will be necessary to know the departure location and time. This in turn will involve finding the information. In this way the actions to be carried out in order to achieve a goal may themselves become sub-goals, all of which have to be satisfied before the top-level goal can be achieved.

Various rules can be formulated to account for these processes of plan construction, such as the following, which is based on Allen and Perrault (1980: 147).

(11)
If an agent wants to achieve a goal, an some action has that goal as its effect, then the agent will probably want to carry out that action.

There are similar rules for the inference of plans. For example, the rule corresponding to the above planning rule is roughly as follows (Allen and Perrault 1980: 148):

(12)
If A believes that B has a goal of executing some action, and that action has a particular effect, then A may believe that B has the goal of achieving that effect.

A question such as *when does the train to Windsor leave?* would be analysed initially as the action: *user requests system to inform user of departure time of train to Windsor*. Ignoring how the choice between the BOARD and MEET plans is made, this action would be subjected to a cycle of inference and expansions:

infer	system wants to inform user of departure time (effect of action)
expand	system informs user
effect	user knows departure time
infer	knowing the departure time is a precondition for boarding a train assume goal is to board train

action   look for obstacles:
1 time (explicitly requested)
2 location (implicit obstacle)
inform about time
inform about location

Various other types of helpful behaviour can be implemented on the basis of plan inference. Take the question *does the train to Windsor leave at 4*? Assuming the system has worked out that the user wants to know when the train leaves and that the departure location is already known, then there are two obstacles to be dealt with:

1 The user wants to know if the departure time is 4.
2 The user wants to know the departure time.

Both of these are necessary. If the answer to the question is *yes*, then both goals are satisfied simultaneously. However, if the answer is *no*, only the first goal is satisfied and the system has to find a way of satisfying the second goal. In other words, this reflects the general principle that when someone asks about the truth of a proposition that turns out to be false, he is often interested in a related, true proposition. In this case, if the departure time is not 4, the user will probably want to know the true departure time.

Further illustration of the theory that communication involves working out a speaker's plans can be found in a study of how speakers give instructions in a task-oriented dialogue (Cohen 1984). In this dialogue (example 13) an expert was instructing an apprentice in how to assemble a water pump. The instruction were given in two modes – telephone mode, in which communication was via spoken language, and keyboard mode, in which communication was typed. We will look at the difference between these modes in chapter 10. The following is an example of instructions in telephone mode.

(13)
E OK. Take that. Now there's a thing called a plunger. It has a red handle on it, a green bottom, and it's got a blue lid
A OK
E OK now, the small blue cap we talked about before?
A yeah
E put that over the hole on the side of that tube –
A yeah
E – that is the nearest to the top, or nearest to the red handle
A OK

E   OK. Now, now, the smallest of the red pieces?
A   OK

One of the main problems involved here is the identification of the objects which the expert refers to. This identification has to precede any operations on the objects. In many cases, however, the instructions to identify the objects are not given explicitly. Sometimes a sentence fragment is used, as in the expert's final utterance in the above extract, while at other times there is an existential statement (beginning with *there is a . . . .*) followed by a description, as in the expert's first utterance. In order to interpret these utterances, the apprentice has to make inferences about the expert's plans. At the same time, the expert's instructions activate plans for the apprentice. For example: a description such as *the long green tube* would activate a search for green tubes followed by a comparison of their length in order to find a suitable referent for the long one.

In deciding what a speaker intends by an utterance, a hearer attempts to infer the speaker's goals and to work out how the utterance might further these goals. In order to do this the hearer must be able to recognize plans of action and be aware of the relationships between actions and their effects. Two of these rules of inference were quoted in examples 11 and 12. One further rule, which is relevant to the interpretation of requests, is the *Action-effect inference*, which reads roughly as:

(14)
If the observer thinks the agent wants to do an action, the observer can posit that the agent wants that action done in order to achieve its typical effect.

For example, if a speaker utters the words *can you open the door?* the hearer will apply rules of inference to work out the speaker's intentions. These might go roughly as follows:

1 The hearer believes the speaker wants to ask a question about his (the hearer's) ability to open the door.
2 The hearer believes that the speaker wants to know if the hearer can perform the action of opening the door.
3 The hearer infers that the speaker wants this act done.
4 The hearer infers that the speaker wants the act done for its effect, namely that the door be open, which in turn might make possible another act (for example, it might permit the speaker to enter the room).

Thus working out what a speaker means by an utterance involves linking the surface speech act with some expected goal through a chain of means-end reasoning.

The analysis of communication in terms of plans also provides a basis for the repair of miscommunication and for the differential use of instructions. If we consider the instruction to assemble an item, we can see that the speaker's goal can be broken down into three sub-goals:

1 In order to assemble an item, the hearer must be holding it.
2 In order to hold it, the hearer must pick it up.
3 In order to pick it up, the hearer must have identified it.

If an instruction is given at the topmost level, then the hearer has to infer the rest of the plan. If, however, the hearer is unable to implement some of the lower-level parts of the plan, the speaker has to shift to these lower levels in order to repair the failure in communication. The following example shows how the expert begins with an assembly instruction and then shifts down to an identification request because the apprentice has been unable to accomplish the identification (Cohen 1984: 104).

(15)
E   put the ¼ inch long 'post' into the loosely fitting hole
A   I don't understand what you mean
E   the red piece, with the four tiny projections

In this way a communication failure involving a higher-level plan can be repaired by addressing the plan's preconditions, which can be conceived as subordinate plans. Similarly, when dealing with a hearer who has comprehension difficulties, the speaker can formulate all the instructions at a low level in order to monitor whether or not the hearer has been able to achieve the speaker's goals. Other aspects of communication failure and repair will be considered in the next chapter.

9

Communication Failure
in Dialogue

There are many kinds of breakdown in natural language communication. Some of these are fairly trivial and can be easily repaired, as, for example, when two participants start to speak at the same time, or when part of an utterance has been imperfectly heard or understood. Sometimes the breakdown may be more serious – indeed, it may even be recognized by the participants with the result that the misunderstanding will pass unnoticed and remain uncorrected. Computers which use natural language must be able to cope with breakdowns in communication because the input they receive is often ill-formed. For example, in one study, of 1615 inputs only 1093 were parsable (Thompson 1980), while in another 12.3% of the input contained errors (Eastman and McLean 1981). Computers are notorious for their inability to deal with ill-formed input. As the authors of the natural language travelbooking system, GUS, wrote (Bobrow et al. 1977: 172):

> Computer programs in general, and programs intended to model human performance in particular, suffer from an almost intolerable delicacy. If their users depart from the behaviour expected of them in the minutest detail, or if apparently insignificant adjustments are made in their structure, their performance does not usually change commensurately. Instead, they turn to simulating gross aphasia or death.

Many systems deal with ill-formed input such as ungrammatical sentences, misspelt words or ambiguous references by simply rejecting the input, possibly highlighting the source of the mishap, and then leaving the user to try again. What is needed in a natural language system is the human-like ability to make sense of an utterance even if it is ill-formed and to carry out the action the user has requested. In order to appreciate what is involved we must examine the ways in which communication failure is handled in conversations between humans. Following this we will be able to examine some of the ways in which recent natural language interfaces cope with these problems.

Types of communication failure

It might help to begin with an outline of what is involved for a speaker and a listener in communication. In the ideal exchange the speaker encodes the message appropriately, the listener comprehends, and the communication is successful. Temporary failure occurs either when the speaker encodes the message inappropriately and the listener has to request clarification, or when the listener, for some reason, has a problem in interpreting a correctly encoded message and requests clarification. Communication will be successful if the speaker can adjust the message so that the listener can comprehend it. The dynamics of this process are illustrated in figure 9.1.

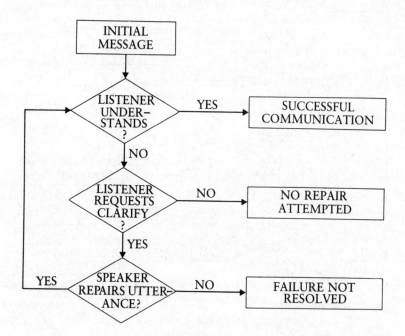

Figure 9.1   The dynamics of communication failure and repair 1

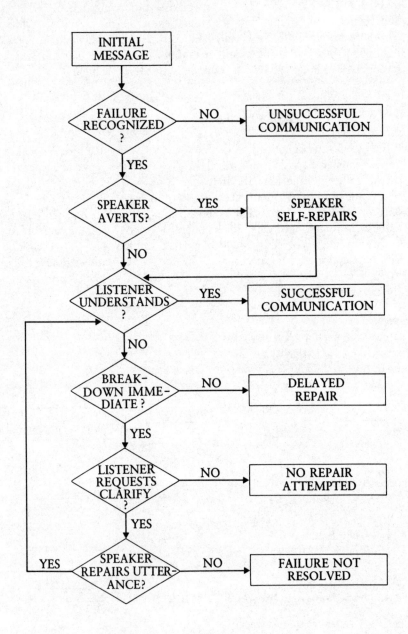

Figure 9.2   The dynamics of communication failure and repair 2

Further problems can arise at several points in this process. The listener may not recognize his failure to understand and if it is not picked up by the speaker then breakdown may result. Unrecognized failure is potentially serious as it permits misconceptions to persist; the best way of avoiding this situation is to develop sophisticated techniques for recognizing failure whenever it occurs. We will encounter some examples later. Some failures can be anticipated and averted. For example, if the speaker thinks that the listener might not know a particular fact, the speaker ought to take particular care when forming an utterance making reference to that fact. This is often referred to as *self-initiated self-repair* – the speaker foresees a potential communication problem and carries out a precautionary repair before any failure actually takes place. There are breakdowns which are not averted in this way. The recognition of the breakdown may be immediate, but sometimes the awareness of a misunderstanding might only dawn after some time – i.e. its recognition is delayed. Separate from the distinction of self-initiated self-repair is the question of whether or not any repair is carried out. The different possibilities which have been outlined are displayed in figure 9.2.

A further set of distinctions arises from this. We have already mentioned self-initiated self-repair which occurs when the current speaker recognizes a potential or an actual communication failure and carries out a repair. But there are other possibilities – the repair may be initiated by the listener (other), i.e. the person who is the recipient of the repairable item, and the repair itself can be carried out either by the speaker (self) or by the listener. This gives rise to a four-way distinction, as set out in figure 9.3. It should also be noted that the terms *request for*

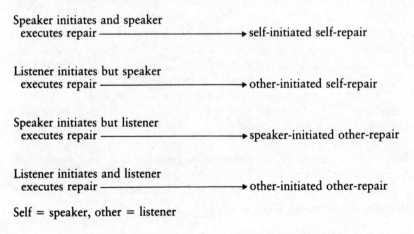

Speaker initiates and speaker
  executes repair ─────────────────→ self-initiated self-repair

Listener initiates but speaker
  executes repair ─────────────────→ other-initiated self-repair

Speaker initiates but listener
  executes repair ─────────────────→ speaker-initiated other-repair

Listener initiates and listener
  executes repair ─────────────────→ other-initiated other-repair

Self = speaker, other = listener

Figure 9.3   Types of communication repair

clarification and *correction* are often used instead of other-initiated self-repair and other-initiated other-repair respectively. Furthermore, research into the occurrence of repairs in naturally occurring conversations between humans has shown that there is a preference for self-repair over other-repair and for self-initiation of repair over other-initiation (Schegloff, Jefferson and Sacks 1977). What is meant by preference here is not the volition or intention of the speaker but the unmarked or default case. In other words, the usual expectation is that repairs will be initiated and executed by self and not by other, and this is borne out empirically by the much higher incidence of self-initiated self-repairs over all other repair types in human conversation. One reason for this is structural; the rules of conversational turn-taking permit the current speaker to continue the turn until a point of possible completion has been reached so the opportunity for self-initiation of repair will occur before that for other-initiation, the current speaker being permitted to effect the repair before the next speaker's turn can legitimately begin. But it also seems to be the case that other-initiated repairs are dispreferred and that they are marked as such – for example, they are often delayed beyond the usual turn transition period as if to give the speaker (self) a further opportunity to effect a self-repair. Furthermore other-initiated other-repairs are often mitigated to make them appear less direct and face-threatening. We will elaborate on the significance of these observations in chapter 10.

So far it has been assumed that breakdown can be attributed to some problem in the speaker's message – it might be ill-formed or poorly designed for the needs of the listener. Such cases involve the issue of message construction and one common way of handling message construction problems in human-computer interaction is to constrain the user's message so that it accords with the interpretive abilities of the computer. But it is also possible to view the listener as the source of some communication breakdowns and when this is the case we are dealing with message interpretation – that is, the ability of the listener to make sense of the input. It is important to consider both sides of the communication process in order to take into account both the speaker's obligation to construct messages appropriate to the listener's needs and abilities as well as the development of more powerful interpretative abilities in the listener. The recognition and resolution of communication failure is the result of a process of negotiation between speaker and listener. For this reason it is essential to consider both sides of the dialogue, message construction as well as message interpretation, in order to model this process accurately.

We are now in a position to examine types of communication failure more closely. They can be divided into two types: *input failures* and *model failures* (Ringle and Bruce 1982). Input failures result when the input is ill-formed in some way and the listener is unable to interpret it. Ill-formedness can occur at any level of language – lexical, syntactic, semantic and pragmatic. Model failures result when the listener is unable to assimilate the input to the coherent belief model intended by the speaker. The listener may have been able to analyse the utterance syntactically and semantically but lacks the background knowledge to make sense of it or to draw the required inferences. Furthermore, failure in natural language interfaces may be relative or absolute. Relative failure results when the input exceeds the potential of the system. For example, the input may contain words or structures with which the system is not familiar. Absolute failure, on the other hand, results when the input is ill-formed and the ill-formedness is such that would be recognized by a native speaker of the language. We will focus mainly on absolute ill-formedness here.

At the lexical level, ill-formedness results in the system being unable to recognize a particular word, because of a misspelling, mistyping, or, in the case of a speech recognition system, a mispronunciation. At the syntactic level, the ill-formedness may lie in a lack of agreement between the subject noun-phrase and the verb (e.g. *The students who live on campus is in trouble*), the ungrammaticality of the word order of sentence constituents, or the omission of some words, such as determiners or prepositions. In a system using an ATN to make a syntactic parse of a sentence, the parse would block on encountering a verb which did not agree with its subject noun-phrase. In such a case the parser would not be able to proceed as there would be no arc which it could follow to complete the network. Normally this would result in a failed parse. The same thing would happen if words in the input were in an order which the ATN did not expect, or if some words were omitted, as in telegram style. An example of semantic ill-formedness would be the violation of selectional restrictions, for example, pairing a verb which requires an animate subject with an inanimate subject-noun, as in *My car drinks petrol*. Finally, pragmatic ill-formedness could involve failed speaker presuppositions, as in the examples cited from CO-OP in chapter 8. In example 1 the speaker makes a false assumption in the input question, asking for the names of students who obtained first class grades in Linguistics in 1984 when no students took Linguistics in that year. Below are listed some examples of types of ill-formed input.

lexical	misspelling, mistyping, mispronunciation
syntactic	word order, subject-verb agreement, omitted words

semantic	violation of selectional restrictions
	inappropriate case frames
pragmatic	failed speaker presuppositions
	failed anaphoric reference

Before we go on to examine the ways in which some of these problems have been tackled in natural language interfaces, it is important to stress that communication failure is a normal feature of human conversation and that it is usually resolved routinely and almost unnoticeably. As Schegloff et al. (1977: 381) have written:

> If language is composed of systems of rules which are integrated, then it will have sources of trouble related to the modes of their integration (at the least). And if it has intrinsic sources of trouble, then it will have a mechanism for dealing with it intrinsically. An adequate theory of the organization of natural language will need to depict how a natural language handles its intrinsic troubles. Such a theory will, then, need an account of the organization of repair.

Thus it is not sufficient to devise means of handling ill-formed natural language input which operate by restricting what the user can say. This is simply avoiding the issue. A system which aims to handle unrestricted natural language input needs to be based on a theory of language which recognizes and handles ill-formedness, for, as Ringle and Bruce (1982: 204) have written:

> Conversation failure, in fact, appears to be the rule rather than the exception. The reason that dialogue is such an effective means of communication is not because the thoughts of the participants are in such perfect harmony, but rather that the lack of harmony can be discovered and addressed when it is necessary.

With these words in mind we can now look at some of the ways in which designers of natural language interfaces have dealt with ill-formed input.

Dealing with communication failure in natural language interfaces: some examples

Communication failure can be handled in two different ways by natural language interfaces. The first involves the processing of ill-formed input by the system while the second deals with the prevention of misunderstandings in the system's output. Taking input first, the system can do the following:

1 It can make an accurate report of the problem and leave it to the user to make corrections and try again.
2 It can engage the user in focused interaction concerning the problem in order to obtain clarification.
3 It can make an intelligent guess at what the user might have meant.

The first is the traditional approach; the system's report can include various degrees of helpful information to assist the user. However, this approach relies basically on the tactic of rejecting the input and asking the user to try again; it is least like the approach used by humans. The second approach would appear to be more efficient than the third, as an intelligent guess could turn out to be wrong. However, the disadvantage of clarification dialogues is that they interrupt the normal flow of the conversation and they are usually avoided in human conversation unless interpretation of the problematic utterance is impossible. If the error is minimal, for example, a slight mispronunciation or the omission of a definite article, a listener will normally attempt to make a reasonable interpretation rather than disrupt the transfer of substantive information. We will look in more detail at these human-like aspects of communication in the next chapter. For the present we will examine the third approach in greater detail.

Coping with extragrammaticality

Extragrammaticality includes misspellings, ungrammatical utterances which may nevertheless be semantically comprehensible, and grammatical utterances which are beyond the scope of the system (Carbonell and Hayes 1984). These problems can be handled as follows:

1 Knowledge of typical errors can be built into the system.
2 Semantics may be allowed to interact more flexibly with syntax so that phrases which fail on a syntactic analysis can be allowed to succeed if they make sense.
3 Additional rules can be built into the grammar which relax the normal constraints imposed by the grammar.

The first solution has often been used in intelligent tutoring systems, where typical student errors are collected in a *bug catalogue* to be matched with the student's input and to evoke subsequent tutorial assistance from the system. The main problem with this solution is that unpredicted errors cannot be handled. The solution of using semantics to assist the analysis is often successful as it brings additional information to bear on the interpretation. The most radical example of semantics used in this way is to be found in expectation-based parsing, as in the work of Schank and colleagues, where semantic rules are used to obtain an interpretation and syntax is overriden. Problems can arise when the syntactic rule is essential for the interpretation, as in the sentences cited by Weischedel and Sondheimer (1983):

(1) List the assets of the company that was purchased by XYZ corporation.
(2) List the assets of the company that were purchased by XYZ corporation.

A system which did not take account of the grammatical rule of subject-verb agreement would fail to distinguish between the interpretation in which assets were purchased and the one in which the company was purchased. The third solution in which the normal rules of language are relaxed, has been used widely to deal with input which is ill-formed syntactically, semantically and pragmatically. We will look at some examples in the next sections.

Lexical problems

Misspellings and mistypings, which result in a character string the system is unable to recognize, are a common source of communication failure for computers. A typical solution is to use partial matching; legitimate words, which are close to the misspelt or mistyped word, are substituted for the unrecognized string. Partial matching is not quite as easy as it might seem, as often many legitimate words can be generated and the system has to decide which one is the most appropriate. The following example illustrates this point (Carbonell and Hayes 1984).

(3) add two fixed haed dual prot disks to the order.

Here there are two problem items – *haed* and *prot*. The system might match *haed* with the following legitimate words: *had, haed, heed, hated, hand*. The only way to make a choice would be to use rules of syntax and semantics. *Had* and *hated* would be ruled out by syntax as a verb would not be expected at this point in the sentence, while *heed* and *hand* would be ruled out by semantics as they would not make sense in this context. This would leave the word *head* which meets both syntactic and semantic constraints and is therefore more likely to be the intended word. This approach is not necessarily efficient, as the correction of *prot* illustrates. It would be possible to generate a set of legitimate words from the system's dictionary and then rule them out as was done for *haed*. However, as Carbonell and Hayes point out, one small on-line dictionary would have produced sixteen possible corrections for *prot*. The use of domain semantics, on the other hand, which would decide which word was most likely in this context, would produce only one word in this position, i.e. *port*. In this case this would be the more efficient method.

A more difficult problem arises when the misspelt or mistyped word results in a character string which is recognized by the system; that is to say the misspelling or mistyping produces a legitimate word which is nevertheless not the word which would be expected in the context in which it occurred. Take the following example:

(4) Copy the files from the accounts directory to my directory.

The word *flies* may be a word the system recognizes, so a less intelligent system might let it pass. *Flies* would also be possible on syntactic grounds; it is a noun which follows a preceding definite article and could function as the object of the verb *copy*. However *flies* would fail on semantic grounds as it does not make sense in this context, the most likely word being *files*.

Syntactic problems

One of the syntactic problems mentioned earlier was subject-verb agreement. A sentence such as *A student living in poor conditions have . . .* would fail on a traditional top-down left-to-right parse as implemented, for example, in an ATN, because one of the conditions on the arc for the verb *have* would be that it should agree with the preceding subject noun-phrase *a student*. Weischedel and Sondheimer (1983) propose ways of relaxing such rules. These involve the use of meta-rules consisting of a set of conditions and a set of actions. The conditions contain a diagnosis of what the problem might be at a particular point in an ATN, (for example, failed subject-verb agreement or failed determiner-noun agreement), while the actions specify how the violated constraint should be relaxed, often through substitution of a new syntactic combination such as a non-agreeing subject-verb pair. The details of how this is implemented and of the controls on this relaxation of constraints are discussed in detail in the original paper but are beyond the scope of the present discussion. The main point is that this approach attempts to relate ill-formed input explicitly to well-formedness rules by relaxing only those constraints which seem to be violated, thus permitting normal controls for well-formedness on the remaining input. The syntax of casual conversation would also cause problems for a parser constructed on the basis of well-formed sentences of formal written language. Typical problems are resumptive pronouns; politeness markers, false starts, and the NP-S construction. Examples of these are presented below:

resumptive pronouns	John's friend Mary married the man that she planned to marry *him*
politeness markers	*would you please* copy this file to my directory
false starts	*add delete* this file from my directory
	add I mean delete the file
NP-S construction	*a man in our street* you should see *him* skiing

Weischedel and Sondheimer (1983) handle resumptive pronouns by relaxing the usual constraint on relative clauses (e.g. *that she planned to marry*) which states that, if the object of the verb *marry* has already been stored (here it is the relative pronoun *that*) it cannot occur again in another form within the same relative clause. An ATN would normally fail on encountering a second object (*him*) for the verb *marry*. A meta-rule would cater for this particular problem. Politeness markers are often simply ignored if they can be explicitly recognized in the input and deleted, leaving an interpretable string. Various rules can also be used to process false starts as in the above example. One such rule proposed by Carbonell and Hayes (1984) states that when a sequence of two constituents of the same syntactic and semantic type is found where only one is permitted, then the first should be ignored. In this example *add* and *delete* occur in sequence in a position where only one verb is permitted. They are similar semantically, in this case being antonyms, so it can be assumed on the basis of this rule that the second should replace the first. A similar rule could presumably be applied to the NP-S construction, except that the rule would specify an isolated noun-phrase and a sentence-internal pronoun which agrees with it. Furthermore, certain explicit corrective phrases (e.g. *I mean*) might be recognized by the system and ignored or used to invoke the rule for false starts.

Generally speaking it can be seen that the application of rules such as these permits several types of ill-formed syntactic input to be handled.

These rules are necessary as natural language input is likely to be ill-formed in such ways. Some of the ill-formedness may arise from non-standard uses of English – for example, the rules of subject-verb agreement differ across many non-standard dialects of English. Other examples involve the syntactic rules of conversational English, which, although not non-standard, differ from those of formal written style. Natural language interfaces, especially speech recognition systems, will need to be able to handle this wide range of syntactic constructions. Some time in the future the important choice will have to be made: to build into a system's rules as legitimate forms or to continue to treat them as cases of extragrammaticality. In any case the general principle remains that a system should not fail on encountering a string which is ill-formed syntactically when it is possible to make sense of the string on other grounds.

Semantic problems

Relaxation techniques can also be employed in cases where semantic constraints are violated. Among the types of semantic problem which have been addressed are selection restrictions and case frames. We can illustrate by looking at selection restrictions.

Selection restrictions ensure that the correct classes of items are used in combination, for example, that a verb requiring an animate subject has a noun marked as animate in subject position. This rule would exclude anomalous sentences such as *The door smiled as I entered the room*. Weischedel and Sondheimer (1983) handled this problem by assuming that semantic class tests are organized in a hierarchy, as in figure 9.4.

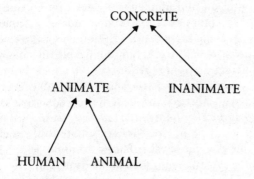

Figure 9.4 A fragment of a semantic hierarchy
(Weischedel and Sondheimer 1983: 170)

The meta-rule which would operate in the case of a violation of semantic class allows the parent of a class, that is, the item which is above the semantic class in question in the hierarchy, to be substituted. Thus, if an animate item were expected, this constraint could be relaxed and a concrete item would be permitted, as in *my car drinks a lot of petrol*. A similar meta-rule was proposed to handle cases of personification; the normal constraint that verbs of believing and thinking can only apply to humans is often relaxed when pets and machines are personified.

Pragmatic problems

Communication failure can also arise from pragmatic problems and as this book is particularly concerned with issues related to pragmatics and dialogue we will examine these in greater detail. Pragmatic problems include failures arising from inaccurate reference identifications, the user's misconceptions and erroneous beliefs, and cases when a user's perceived plan to achieve a particular goal is blocked. Each of these problems calls for an interactional approach, in which the primary goal is that the machine should be able to model the user's beliefs and to use this model to detect the source of actual as well as potential communication failure.

Repairing failure resulting from reference identification

Reference identification problems can be illustrated by examining the task-oriented dialogues involving the construction of a water pump described in chapter 8. Goodman (1986) has examined both instances of imprecision, confusion and ambiguity in descriptions and instructions which gave rise to communication failure and the attempts to correct these problems. In some cases the description was imprecise, in others it contained features which were not applicable in the domain. For example, the instruction *put the red nozzle on the outlet of the rounded clear chamber* was imprecise as there were four objects in the domain which could have satisfied the description *rounded*. Similarly the description *there's another funny little red thing* would not provide much help to the listener as *funny* does not contribute to the identification of the object. In this case the speaker had to continue with a more precise description which eventually resulted in the listener identifying the object *– a little teeny red thing that's some – should be somewhere on the desk, that has um – there's like teeth on one end*. Problems often arose when speaker and listener were confused about focus, either when the speaker shifted focus without letting the listener know and started describing an item which was part of a different sub-task within the overall task, or when the listener wrongly assumed that focus had shifted.

Before a communication failure can be repaired the miscommunication must be detected. In the case of reference identification problems trouble could arise if instructions required actions which were incompatible, or if a requested action were redundant – that is, if an action were requested when its required goal had already been satisfied. Listeners normally assume that speakers do not request redundant goals, if one were requested it would indicate that something had gone wrong in the interpretation of earlier instructions.

Incompatibility can affect descriptions and instructions. In the case of a description there might be no object that corresponded exactly to the description. For example, the description might specify an orange cap when none of the objects are orange, or it might say *the red plug that fits loosely* when all the red plugs fit tightly. As far as imprecise instructions are concerned, a listener might not be able to perform a specified action because of some obstacle, he might perform the action but not arrive at the intended effect, or the action might affect a previous action in some adverse way.

The traditional approach to reference identification in a natural language interface is that identification succeeds if a referent is found, otherwise it fails. But as Goodman points out, humans can often find a correct item even when the speaker's description is inadequate. For this reason he proposes a model, which he calls FWIM (*Find what I mean*), which relaxes the description by ignoring or modifying it in part, thus allowing a further try at identification. This procedure is not followed blindly but is based on the methods and knowledge that people use in such situations. It can involve either negotiation between the speaker and the hearer – a clarification dialogue – or self-negotiation by the listener in which the most suitable candidate is selected, or, if one is not found, the most likely sources of error or confusion are sought.

The process of relaxation through self-negotiation by the listener is based on the insight that people use a combination of knowledge about language and knowledge about the physical world in order to identify objects which have been described imprecisely or inaccurately. On the basis of the principle that the information at the end of a description is usually more important than that at the beginning, linguistic items are relaxed in the following order – adjectives, prepositional phrases, then relative clauses and predicate complements. Thus if the system were unable to match an object with a description such as *a rounded piece with a turquoise base over it*, it would first relax the description *rounded*.

If this did not produce a suitable object, the system would proceed to the prepositional phrase *with a turquoise base over it* and would first examine the adjective *turquoise*. If it were found that there was no turquoise object in the domain world but that there were several candidates which otherwise matched the description, then the colour would be relaxed and substituted by a similar colour. If several potential objects were left after this process, knowledge of the physical world would be applied – in other words, each object would be tested to see whether it could be acted upon according to the speaker's instructions. In this way the process of relaxation is controlled: the system finds potential referent candidates and determines which features to relax and in what order. Goodman (1986) provides a detailed example which illustrates this process. As he points out in his conclusions, the goal of this work is to develop a more robust natural language system which can detect and avoid miscommunication. He does not aim to create a perfect listener, but a more tolerant one. The system also aims to model human performances in this type of communicative task as empirical studies have shown that humans deal with imprecise instructions by relaxing the descriptions and attempting a partial match, then, if necessary, giving up and asking for help. Thus self-negotiation would precede the initiation of a clarification dialogue and Goodman's system models this preference.

Misconceptions and erroneous beliefs

A different type of communication problem arises when a listener detects misconceptions or erroneous beliefs in a speaker's utterance. As we saw from the discussion of CO-OP in chapter 8, the listener's response to such an utterance can support the misconceptions or erroneous beliefs. To take an example from McCoy (1986), if the user makes the query:

(5) Give me the hull-no of all destroyers whose mast-height is above 190.

and no destroyers with such a mast-height exist then a response such as *there are none* is misleading, as the user might continue to believe that such ships could exist. Instead the system ought to reply something like the following.

(6)
There are no destroyers in the database having mast-height above 190. All destroyers in the database have a mast-height between 85 and 90. Were you thinking of an aircraft carrier?

Such communication problems have been referred to as *pragmatic overshoot* (Weischedel and Sondheimer 1983). They arise when utterances which may be syntactically and semantically correct violate pragmatic rules such as the listener's world model – that is, the utterance presumes relationships between objects and their attributes which conflict with what the listener knows about these objects and attributes. As for reference identification failure, detecting the problem precedes taking the decisions as to what type of response the system should produce.

For a system to be able to detect misconceptions it must maintain a model of the user's beliefs which can be matched for discrepancies against its model of its own beliefs. Misconceptions can result either from discrepancies between what the system and the user know about the contents of the database, or from more permanent problems, for example, if the user specifies a relationship that does not exist in the world model. Carberry (1986) gives an example from the real-estate domain in which the utterance *which apartments are for sale?* is pragmatically ill-formed, as in this domain (for American apartments at least), apartments are rented, not sold, though apartment complexes are sold, for example, to property developers. In order to produce a helpful response the system has to infer the user's goal – in this case, either to rent an apartment or to purchase an apartment-complex. The system can then generate an appropriate response on the basis of this inference. Similarly, in an example from an interaction with a co-operative interface to the Unix computer operating system the system infers the user's plan, works through the preconditions which have to be true for the plan to succeed and identifies whichever sub-goal is causing the block. The inference is then used as the basis for the system's response. To take an example from Ramshaw and Weischedel (1984)

(7)
U   please send the file to the laser printer
S   the laser printer is down
    is the line printer satisfactory?

One of the steps in executing the plan to send a file to the laser printer is to ascertain that the laser printer is up-and-running. If this condition is not fulfilled the plan cannot be executed. However the system searches for an alternative means of achieving the sub-goal, i.e. of getting the file printed, and suggests the use of another printer. In this way a co-operative response is provided.

As with some of the systems described earlier, responses to pragmatic overshoot have been based on empirical studies of how humans reply in such situations. McCoy (1986) found that humans often use an utterance consisting of two parts – a denial, followed by a correction containing additional information refuting the faulty reasoning which may have occasioned the user's misconception in the first place. There are two main strategies, depending on whether the misconception involves a wrong object or a wrong attribute. In the first case, which is exemplified in example 6, the strategy is as follows:

1 Deny that the object involved in the misconception has the property stated in the misconception.
2 State the corresponding correct property that the object involved in the misconception does have.
3 Offer an alternative correct query containing the property involved in the misconception and an object that is similar to the object involved in the misconception.

Thus, in this example, the system first denies that destroyers in the database have a mast-height greater than 190. Next it gives the correct mast-height for destroyers. Finally it searches for a similar object – in this case, an aircraft carrier – which does have the mast-height specified in the original query. A similar strategy exists in the case of incorrect attributes, as the example below illustrates:

(8)
U give me the hull-no of all destroyers whose mast-height is above 3500
S all destroyers in the database have a mast-height between 85 and 90. Were you thinking of the displacement?

In this case the specific strategy is:

1 Deny that the object involved in the misconception has the property stated in the misconception.
2 State the corresponding correct property that the object involved in the misconception does have.
3 Offer an alternative correct query containing the object involved in the misconception and a property that is similar to the property involved in the misconception.

Further details of how the choice of alternative objects and attributes is controlled and how responses can differ according to differences in context can be found in McCoy's paper.

We can conclude this section with a brief discussion of how a plan-based model can generate an appropriate response to a query in which an erroneous world model is detected, illustrating with the query *which apartments are for sale?* (Carberry 1986). Carberry's system is based on the Gricean maxim of relevance which suggests that, if an utterance violates the listener's world model (for example, in terms of its relevance), the listener should try to infer the speaker's intent in the belief that the speaker is likely to be attempting to be relevant in a co-operative task, though obviously not succeeding. Carberry's system constructs a model of the speaker's plan based on information derived from the preceding discourse and uses this to infer lower-level sub-goals against which the subsequent dialogue can be matched. For example, if the preceding dialogue contains the following:

(9) I am the manager of a real estate investment trust. We'd like to invest between 30 and 50 million dollars.

then it would be assumed that the query *which apartments are for sale?* would be in keeping with a plan generated from this context for achieving the goal of expanding holdings in real estate. This would include, among other things, plans for buying apartment complexes, shopping centres or office blocks. The system would then consider the possibility of substituting one of these alternative words for the word *apartment* in the original query and would apply an evaluation metric to find the most suitable substitution. In this case *apartment-complex* would be found to be the most similar in semantic terms and it would be selected. A similar process would operate if the preceding context had been a plan to obtain a private dwelling-place. Here the system would expand this plan and produce alternatives such as renting an apartment or buying a house. From these the system would infer that the intended query was *which apartments are for rent?*

Carberry also discusses the type of response a system might make to utterances in which erroneous beliefs are detected. If the errors are not significant enough to warrant correction, they could be overlooked, so that normal information-transfer would not be affected. This would necessitate the use of a failure tolerance threshold along with some means of measuring when it should be applied. If, however, the misconceptions are more serious then the system has to correct them. We have looked at how a system might detect and correct such misconceptions. But there are also cases where the system is unable to produce corrections, possibly because it is uncertain about the nature of the user's misconceptions. In this case the system might enter a clarification dialogue in order to resolve the problem.

Clarification dialogues

Clarification requests arise when the listener (or system) detects a communication problem but is unable to remedy it. The speaker can then be asked to clarify the problematic input and this type of request has often been referred to as *other-initiated self-repair*. Clarification requests may take various forms, depending on the nature of the communication problem. The following are some of the main possibilities (see Garvey 1979 and McTear 1985 for discussions of these request types in children's conversations):

1 request for repetition
2 request for specification
3 request for confirmation
4 request for elaboration

A request for repetition normally occurs in conversation when the listener has misheard or misunderstood an utterance. In human-computer interaction it might also occur as a result of misspelt and mistyped input when the system is unable to work out the correct form. One early system, RENDEZVOUS, was equipped with the assumption that user input might be incomplete, improperly understood by the system or based on false assumptions (Codd 1974). The system was able to initiate a clarification dialogue to ask the user to resolve spelling mistakes and other similar input problems. A request for repetition may ask for the whole of the input to be corrected and repeated, or it may focus on that part which is problematical. Unless the problem is local, such as a mispronunciation, misspelling or mistyping, it will usually be necessary for the speaker/user to rephrase the utterance to take account of the listener's perceived problems. In human conversation a speaker will often respond to a request for repetition by paraphrasing the original utterance, or substituting different words or phrases, or articulating more clearly or making various prosodic adjustments. The nature of the speaker's changes to the original utterance are motivated by an assessment of the nature of the listener's problem. There sometimes follows a lengthy sequence in which meaning is negotiated between the dialogue participants. In human-computer interaction the human user has to work out the nature of the system's problems. A user receiving an error report such as INPUT NOT UNDERSTOOD – PLEASE RE-PHRASE, has to work out how to modify the input in order to make it acceptable to the system. A message which pinpoints the source of the problem is more helpful. This brings us to the second type of clarification request – the request for specification.

Requests for specification often occur in cases of referent identification failure. Some of the examples from Goodman's work discussed earlier are cases in point. A phrase such as *the red plug that fits loosely* would pose problems if no such plug can be located. If the system is unable to find a viable alternative, it might respond with something like WHICH PLUG DO YOU MEAN? or I CANNOT FIND A RED PLUG THAT FITS LOOSELY. This response is in fact a request for specification, as the user has to specify the object more precisely in order for the system to be able to identify it. A request for specification is more helpful than a simple request for repetition or rephrasing as it indicates to the user the nature of the communication problem. The following example from SHRDLU illustrates such a sequence (Winograd 1973: 153):

(10)
U grasp the pyramid
S I don't understand which pyramid you mean

Requests for confirmation are made when the listener or system is reasonably confident about the interpretation of an utterance but seeks confirmation in order to be absolutely sure. Another example from Winograd (1973: 15–4) will provide an illustration:

(11)
U find a block which is taller than the one you are holding and put it into the box
S by 'it' I assume you mean the block which is taller than the one I am holding

In this case there were two possible referents for *it* and the program had heuristics for choosing between them. Requests for confirmation require less from the original speaker than they do from the listener. The listener has to work out what the speaker probably intended and then check whether this is correct; the speaker simply has to confirm or disconfirm. Because of this requests for confirmation are more difficult to implement and so far have only been used in restricted domains such as the blocks world. The following example from the train station domain illustrates this (Allen and Perrault 1980: 173):

(12)
U when is the Windsor train?
S to Windsor?

U   yes
S   3.15

U's first utterance is ambiguous, as it could either be requesting the time of arrival of the train from Windsor or the departure time of the train to Windsor. In the train domain the system tries to work out the user's plans. There are two possibilities only – boarding trains and meeting trains. Usually the user's plan can be worked out without any difficulty, as we saw in chapter 8, but in this example there is no reason to favour one interpretation over the other so the system generates a request for confirmation by assuming the BOARD interpretation first and asking whether the user wishes to go to Windsor. Obviously such a confirmation request is easier to make when the choices are limited, as they are in this example.

The final type of clarification request involves information which was not present in the surface form of the problematic utterance. For example, in response to the statement *I saw John yesterday* a listener might ask *where*? Verbs have associated case frames which specify the agent and patient of the action, its location, time, etc. These may not be mentioned in an utterance and so can be queried. An extreme form of such case frames is to be found in Conceptual Dependency Theory (see chapter 2), where potentially any of the missing but implicit information in an utterance could be queried. Allen's plan recognition model shows how this process can be controlled. The following is another example from the train domain (Litman and Allen 1984: 302).

(13)
Passenger	the eight-fifty to Montreal?
Clerk	eight-fifty to Montreal. Gate seven
Passenger	where is it?
Clerk	down this way to the left. Second one on the left
Passenger	OK. Thank you

The normal information exchange is accomplished in the first two turns of this sequence. The passenger's query *where is it?* poses potential problems for a language understanding system, as it necessitates working out what *it* refers to (it is not Montreal nor the train to Montreal, but gate seven), and this involves realizing that this query is related sequentially to the exchange that has just taken place. The clerk works out the passenger's request within the plan recognition framework as follows:

1 The clerk recognizes that the passenger wishes to board the train for Montreal.
2 To do this the passenger must buy a ticket and get on the train.
3 In order to get on the train the passenger must know its departure location.
4 In order to get to the departure location the passenger must know where it is.

The first three steps are accomplished in the initial exchange once the clerk has worked out that the passenger wishes to board the eight-fifty to Montreal. The fourth step is a prerequisite for step three, and as the passenger does not have the required information it has to be requested. This process could be continued to a further depth if, for example, the passenger were to ask *The second what?* and this in turn could give rise to further queries. The sequence is terminated with the passenger's *OK*, which is a conventional means of indicating termination of the dialogue sequence. However, as can be seen, the queries which arise address sub-plans of the main plan. The system handles higher level sub-plans as a matter of course, giving the times as well as locations of departing trains. Other sub-plans, which arise when a particular passenger is unable to achieve a sub-goal, are generated as necessary and are constrained by the overall plan structure of the domain. As can be imagined, in less restricted domains it would be necessary to constrain queries in order to avoid combinatorial explosion in the generation of queries about implicit information in the input.

Preventing misunderstanding arising from the system's input

The discussion so far has been concerned largely with how the system copes with failure arising from the input it receives. Input problems can range from misspellings, mistypings and mispronunciations through syntactic and semantic errors to cases of pragmatic overshoot, where the user's query exhibits some misconceptions or false assumptions. Various strategies for dealing with such problematic input were described.

We turn now to communication failure which arises as a result of the system's output. A natural language interface should be able to respond truthfully and informatively to the user's queries. But, as we saw in our discussion of the CO-OP system in chapter 8, the system's response could lead the user to draw false conclusions. Furthermore, as Allen's work on plan recognition indicates, a co-operative system should also be able to detect what the user's goal is and give a helpful response, even when the information which is to be given is not requested explicitly by the user. In each case the system is involved in making predictions about what the user might believe and might need to know. Ensuring that the user does not acquire erroneous beliefs is another way of repairing communication failure, although in this case it is potential rather than actual failure. In other words, the system has to predict the problems that might arise as a result of its responses and modify its responses so as to avert these problems. It will help to look at some examples. Consider the following exchange (Joshi et al. 1984).

(14)
U   is Sam an associate professor?
S   yes, but he doesn't have tenure

The direct answer to the question is *yes*. Why then should the system add the additional information that Sam does not have tenure?

In order to understand what is involved here, we need to return to the issue of default reasoning which was introduced in chapter 5 and discussed more fully in relation to scripts in chapter 6. To take a simple example: if we know a variety of facts about dogs, such as that they have tails, bark, eat meat, and can swim and then hear of a particular dog called Fido, we can assume, unless told explicitly to the contrary, that Fido has a tail, barks, eats meat and can swim. It is the same with example 14; the standard default rule is that associate professors are tenured and have PhDs, the system will assume this is shared knowledge between user and system, therefore if it happens that the standard default rule does not apply, the system, if it knows this is the case, will take steps to prevent the user from making a false assumption, i.e. that Sam has tenure. Looked at in another way, the system's beliefs on receiving the user's question, including its beliefs about the user's beliefs, can be characterized as:

1 Sam is an associate professor.
2 The user does not know that Sam is an associate professor.
3 The system and the user mutually believe that associate professors are tenured.
4 Sam is not tenured.
5 The user does not know that Sam is not tenured.

A direct answer to the question would involve beliefs 1 and 2 and as a result 2 would be replaced by:

2a The user knows that Sam is an associate professor.

However, as a result of belief 3 the user will be likely to infer that Sam is tenured. This is in direct conflict to what the system knows (belief 4), so the system should take steps to prevent this false inference with the result that, following the system's answer, belief 5 is replaced by:

5a The user knows that Sam does not have tenure.

The *but* clause in the system's response addresses this problem.

The schema set out here can also be used to constrain the set of inferences the system has to prevent; if these are not constrained the user could draw a potentially unlimited number of conclusions from the system's reponse. Joshi et al. (1984) suggest that only those inferences relating to that part of the system's knowledge base which is currently in focus should be addressed. What this means is that, when responding to a query, the system will need to consult a section of its knowledge base. The system should first retrieve the direct response and should then work out whether the user could infer additional information from this response. If this additional information conflicts with what the system knows to be true, then the system should take appropriate action to prevent the user inferring that additional information. Using the same example, the direct response to the question *is Sam an associate professor?* is *yes*. To give this answer the system would consult information about Sam or about associate professors. It would then attempt to work out what additional information could be inferred from this response. In this case it would be that Sam has tenure, on the basis of the shared beliefs about associate professors. As this information conflicts with what the system knows about Sam, steps have to be taken to prevent the user from making this inference. Thus the inferences which the system has to prevent can be limited to those which could be made on the basis of that part of the system's knowledge base which is currently in focus.

Another situation in which false conclusions have to be prevented arises in consultations with expert systems. In this situation it is assumed that the system is both knowledgeable and co-operative. However it is usually also assumed that the user's query is a valid one – that is, that it is an accurate reflection of his goals. Problems arise when the user's question addresses a plan which is invalid or inappropriate with respect to the goal. A simple example will illustrate.

Let us assume that the user has the goal of travelling to Dublin. A typical query might be *can I take a bus to Dublin?* A direct response would be either *yes* or *no*. However, either of these responses could result in the user reaching false conclusions. Let us consider several possibilities.

1 There is a bus to Dublin and this is the only method of transport – in this case *yes* would be appropriate.
2 There is a bus to Dublin and there is also a train which is faster though more expensive – in this case *yes* would be unhelpful and it would be more appropriate to give an answer like *yes, but there is also a train*, which is much faster though it is also more expensive.
3 There is no bus but there is a train – in this case *no* would be unhelpful and a more appropriate response would be *no but there is a train*.

So far we have seen how the system might provide more helpful responses based on what it knows about modes of transport to Dublin. However it is not just a question of helpful responses. In the second situation a simple *yes* response could cause the user to believe that the bus is the only one mode of transport to Dublin because the user assumes that the system is knowledgeable and helpful and will therefore provide additional information if any is available. The same applies in the third situation where a simple *no* could lead the user to conclude that there is no mode of public transport on which to travel to Dublin. Thus the system has not only to respond truthfully and informatively to the user's questions, it also has to recognize when the user's questions are invalid and to provide responses which are appropriate to the user's goals. To do all this the system has to be able to reason about the user's plans, including those which may be invalid, and also to reason about the sources of their invalidity. Therefore, incorporated in the system's knowledge base, would have to be those misconceptions which can typically occur within the domain of expertise in question. However it would be impossible to anticipate all potential misconceptions. Furthermore it would also be important for the system to be able to distinguish between invalid plans and plans which are potentially valid but which appear to be valid, because they contain information not known to the system. Current research is investigating how problems such as these are handled in conversations between humans (see, for example, Pollack 1986).

To conclude: we have seen that communication failure is inherent in any form of communication, whether between humans or between humans and machines. There is a wide range of communication failure types and a variety of methods have been devised for repairing such failure. Moreover the ability to diagnose an instance of communication failure, or to predict a potential breakdown, depends on the possession and application of the different types of knowledge which have been discussed throughout this book – syntactic, semantic, and pragmatic, including knowledge of typical sequences of actions and of the goals, plans and beliefs of other conversationalists. Thus the study of communication failure has not only the goal of preventing or repairing such failure; it can also make an important contribution to our understanding of the nature of communication itself.

Further Reading

For an excellent collection of articles on the topic of communication failure in dialogue, including several of the papers discussed in this chapter, see Reilly (1986).

10
Humans and Computers:
the Way Ahead

Natural language processing has come a long way in the last twenty or so years and it will be useful to review some of the more important advances and to point to the way ahead. It will be recalled that in chapter 1 we referred to Turing's vision of intelligent machines that could understand and speak language like humans. How near are we to this vision and what has still to be achieved? Many questions have been raised by natural language research during the past two decades and some of these questions will be considered in the first part of this chapter, in particular the following:

1 What is involved in language understanding?
2 What is involved in language generation?
3 In what ways ought machines to be made more human-like in their performance?
4 How is the use of language related to other aspects of human cognition such as learning and memory?

The second part of the chapter will look to the future and examine some of the methods of enquiry which could usefully inform research in natural language processing. These include:

1 studies of human conversation.
2 comparisons of conversation across different modalities, such as face-to-face interactions, telephone conversations and keyboard input.
3 protocols of human-computer interactions and of interactions in which the role of the computer has been simulated by a human.
4 studies of language acquisition in children.
5 studies of language disorders.

What is involved in language understanding?

Early work in natural language processing tended to ignore meaning and concentrated mainly on the manipulation of formal symbols. This was true of the first attempts at machine translation in the 1950s and is also true of purely syntactic approaches to language understanding in which the primary aim would seem to be the computational testing of syntactic theories rather than the development of natural language systems. It will be clear from the work described in this book that our conception of what is involved in language understanding has gradually broadened.

One of the first developments was the inclusion of meaning. Meaning is an obvious factor in any natural language system concerned with the transmission of information as opposed to the analysis of sentences. Early systems which incorporated meaning were fairly limited in that they could only converse about objects or events within predefined domains, such as baseball games or algebra problems. Programs such as Raphael's SIR showed how meanings could be manipulated through the use of a small set of logical operations. This was the beginning of the thinking computer – a system which was able to apply principles of reasoning to what it knew in order to produce new knowledge. Winograd's SHRDLU represented a high point of this early work. Not only did this system embody a comprehensive approach to language understanding in which, for the first time, there were complex and integrated modules for each of the levels of language – syntax, semantics and pragmatics; the system also incorporated procedures for coping with features of natural conversation such as anaphora and ellipsis. However, with the introduction of meaning a vast range of new problems has emerged. What is meant by meaning? Are we concerned with the literal meanings of words and sentences or with those meanings which are inferred in the course of conversation? Indeed, in a more recent paper Winograd (1981) points to deficiencies in the concept of meaning embodied in SHRDLU and suggests that for a hearer in a conversation meaning is the result of a complex process of trying to understand what the speaker is saying and why. This leads Winograd to suggest finally that understanding involves an interaction between utterances and the full range of cognitive processes going on in the language user. We have seen how the work of Allen, Cohen and Perrault on speech acts, where understanding an utterance involves a process of recognizing the speaker's plan, makes some contribution to this concept of meaning. We are left, however, with a sense of awe at all the complexities of the problem which have yet to be addressed.

There was a breakthrough in natural language research when it was recognized how important a role knowledge of the world played in the process of understanding. This led to the belief, developed most extensively in the work of Schank, that language understanding is a knowledge-based process. We have seen that knowledge of objects, events, plans and goals plays a crucial role in our understanding of stories and conversations by enabling us to fill in information which is omitted from the text but which can be assumed from our knowledge of the context of the text — whether it is a story about a visit to a restaurant, a journey on a bus, or a political conflict. Furthermore, knowledge structures such as these play an important role in interpretation by constraining the inferences that can be drawn to those which are the most sensible within the given context. Thus knowledge-based processing has made an important contribution to the solution of some of the problems which have arisen in the study of meaning. For computational systems one of the major problems associated with knowledge structures such as frames and scripts is how to store and apply such large amounts of information, while for those systems which have the aim of cognitive modelling there is, in addition, the question of how such knowledge structures are acquired. We will return to these questions presently.

We have considered two further types of knowledge which are crucial to the understanding of texts such as extended discourse and dialogue. The first of these is knowledge of discourse structure. Whereas knowledge of the world is external to texts, discourse structure knowledge is text-internal, that is, it is concerned with relations between the items in a text. This knowledge enables us to recognize coherence in a story or conversation and it also plays an important role in the tracking of items mentioned in the text, particularly when pronouns and other anaphoric devices are used. Work in this area has mainly used fairly restricted types of text — those generated by such activities as booking a flight or assembling an air compressor. Reichman's model of conversation attempts to overcome these limitations by examining the structure of casual conversation. It incorporates many structural features of conversation, which occur in extended turns, and it also attempts to model the knowledge which conversational participants have of this structure. It remains to be seen whether a model such as this can account for some of the interactional properties of conversation described by conversation analysts and outlined at the beginning of chapter 7.

The second type of knowledge which is relevant to conversation is knowledge of the conversational partner and it involves the modelling of the conversational partner. It is very important to know something about the other person when one is working out what that person is trying to say and when one is deciding how to shape utterances to meet that person's needs. User modelling will be an important area for development, especially for tutoring and advisory systems which must gear their responses and explanations to the perceived level of understanding of the user. The work described in chapter 8 makes a useful contribution to this issue but it is obviously only a first step and is still far removed from the complex 'mind-reading' which people seem to engage in in the course of everyday conversation.

Language understanding by computers is usually an all-or-nothing affair. The system receives input, analyses it and interprets it. If the input is ill-formed in any way, it is usually rejected and interpretation fails. However, as we saw in our discussion of communication failure in chapter 9, language understanding should be a process of trying to make sense of input utterances even if they are ill-formed. We looked at some of the ways in which natural language systems handle extragrammaticality. However, language understanding involves more than the relaxation of a few constraints. Indeed, it has been argued that in conversation meaning is shared between the participants and has to be negotiated and agreed on a turn-by-turn basis. Thus ill-formedness is relative in conversation. If a listener can make sense of what is said, the conversation can proceed. Moreover, as a listener responds, the previous speaker can inspect this response for its relevance. In this way the participants in a conversation monitor each other's turns for their relevance and display in their own turns their interpretations of each other's utterances. This leads to continual adjustments being made as the conversation proceeds. For example, if an utterance is interpreted as a question and this interpretation is ratified by the speaker of that utterance, then it stands as a question. But if the initial interpretation is not ratified, reinterpretation has to take place and continue until the speakers agree. It is important that natural language systems – and particularly expert and database systems – must be able to engage in this process of interpretation. Such systems know what questions are possible and have to interpret any questions which are asked in terms of these possibilities. In contexts which are more symmetrical, where knowledge is more evenly distributed between system and user as it is in an advisory context, the system has to try to build a model of the user. Here it is important to understand that meaning is arrived at by a dynamic process of negotiation between the participants.

This leads us to the final issue in our discussion of what is involved in language understanding. Generally speaking communication with computers can be seen as a transfer of information. The main focus of the communication is transactional; meaning is equated with the propositional content of an utterance and the purpose of the communication is to accomplish some task, such as booking a flight or assembling an air compressor. The problems which are associated with this transactional focus have to do with propositional ambiguity and with the nature and validity of the speakers' presuppositions and belief systems. However much of human conversation is not transactional but interactional and the focus is not on the transmission of information but on the establishment and maintenance of social relationships. This is not to suggest that computers of the future could act as companions to the lonely, though any attempt to model the human language facility computationally will have to take social-interactional as well as transactional aspects of communication into account. One step in this direction is Dyer's system BORIS which can read and understand complex narratives involving emotions, interpersonal relationships and social roles (Dyer 1983). In any case, even those systems which are designed mainly for information-transfer might usefully be equipped with some knowledge of social-interactional aspects of communication to make them better able to appreciate what effects their output might have on human users. To take a couple of examples. Many people imagine that questions are straightforward requests for information. Yet questions rarely function in this way. In many contexts, especially where the person asking the question enjoys a higher social status than the respondent, a question can function as a mode of control. To take a fairly extreme example, questions asked of suspects in a police interrogation do not function solely as a means of acquiring information – indeed their primary function, from the point of view of the interrogator, is to establish a suspect's guilt. Even in information-transfer contexts, such as database queries, a question from the system such as *do you have legal access to these files?* will hardly be considered as a neutral information request by the user. Repeated questions also have an effect on the respondent. Imagine a system asking a question and receiving the answer *I don't know.* If it repeats the question the user will be unlikely to view the repeated question as neutrally as he did the initial question, since, as Labov and Fanshel (1977: 95) have pointed out, repeated requests are usually heard as challenges and are thus treated as aggravating.

Examples such as these highlight the importance of the social-interactional aspects of communication, even for systems which are primarily geared for information transfer. However now the notion of meaning has been extended even further. Earlier conceptions of meaning could be handled within a formal compositional semantics which was concerned solely with the literal meanings of words and sentences. Work in natural language understanding has gradually moved from literal meanings to indirectly conveyed meanings, which are arrived at through a process of assessing the speaker's goals. Eventually it will also be necessary to consider those meanings which are social and interpersonal in nature rather than propositional. We will need this wider view of what it means to understand language if we are to grasp important functions of human communication such as the establishment and maintenance of social relationships, and to appreciate interpersonal aspects of language use such as emotional reactions.

What is involved in language generation?

Language generation has been until recently a largely neglected side of natural language processing as it has been assumed that getting a computer to understand input in natural language is more difficult than getting it to produce output, particularly since fairly simple methods such as canned text or sentence templates can often be used to achieve the desired results. Many of the issues we have discussed that relate to language understanding, such as the role of world knowledge, are also relevant to language generation. However it should not be assumed, as it frequently is, that language generation is simply language understanding in reverse. Understanding is a matter of working out what a piece of input means, while generation involves choosing from a set of options what to say and then organizing it as a coherent and effective message.

Nevertheless the progress of research in language generation mirrors in part that of language understanding. Early work was concerned with testing grammars – with seeing whether the rules of a grammar when applied would produce strings that were grammatical in the language. Simmons and Slocum (1972) showed how ATNs could be used to generate sentences, the content of which was represented in the semantic networks. Different surface strings, such as the active and passive versions of the same sentence, could be produced from the same network.

It was obvious to those concerned with natural language as a means of communication and to those interested in modelling the language production facility that this sentence-based approach had little to offer. What was the point of producing isolated grammatically correct sentences which did not communicate anything? Moreover, this concentration on isolated sentences avoided one of the central problems in language generation – how to produce sentences which were relevant to what had been said previously and which communicated their speaker's intent. Early communication systems used ad hoc strategies to produce fairly satisfactory language output in predictable situations. One of these strategies involved the use of canned text which was printed out at appropriate times. For example, when the system detected some sort of error, it could print out a piece of English text which described the error and perhaps suggest what the user should do next. Obviously such a strategy is highly inflexible and is restricted to those situations which can be easily predicted by the designer of the system. A slightly more flexible approach, which was used by systems such as SIR, ELIZA and SHRDLU, as well as by Rich's GRUNDY and most expert systems, involved the use of templates with variables that could be instantiated according to the situation. If, for example, the system did not understand a word in the input, it would select a template of the form I DO NOT UNDERSTAND THE WORD X in which the unrecognized word in the input would be substituted for the variable X. Quite complex output could be generated in this way, as we saw in some of the extracts cited in earlier chapters. Nevertheless this method also depends on the ability to predict what the system might have to say and it avoids the key issues in language generation which were raised earlier, namely that generation involves making decisions about what to say and then realizing these decisions as a grammatically accurate, semantically coherent and relevant piece of text. In the remainder of this section we will look at some approaches to these issues. This review will be extremely selective, however, as it would not be possible to cover the many recent developments in generation research and for some of the work not covered here the reader is referred to the sources recommended at the end of the chapter.

Generating text

The generation of text involves issues such as the internal coherency of the text, its relevance to the preceding discourse and its tailoring to the needs of the individual user. McKeown's system TEXT, which generates responses to queries about the structure of a database, is an attempt to meet these requirements (McKeown 1985). TEXT is based on the notion that people have schemata for producing particular types of text such as definitions, descriptions, comparisons or instructions. As an example, an *identification* schema, which is used mainly in texts having the function of providing definitions, would have slots such as *identification, particular illustration, evidence* and *analogy*. McKeown found when she had analysed a large number of texts that there were regularly occurring patterns, although each schema would contain a number of alternatives which reflected the variety of options open to speakers. The following is part of a response generated by the system to the query *what is a ship?* (McKeown 1985: 52):

(1)
A ship is a water-going vehicle that travels on the surface. Its surface-going
capacities are provided by the DB (database) attributes DRAFT and DISPLACE-
MENT.

Many of the techniques discussed in earlier chapters were used to
generate such responses. The system drew on a pool of knowledge which
was represented in terms of a semantic net. In this case the superordinate
node was WATER-VEHICLE to which SHIP was related in terms of an
ISA link (see chapter 5). This would be used to produce the first item in
the identification schema – class of object. The item SHIP would inherit
properties from its superordinate node – in this case that the travel
medium for a WATER VEHICLE is water – and other attributes peculiar
to SHIP would be cited, for example, that its travel mode is SURFACE.
The identification schema also has a slot for *evidence* and in this case this
slot was filled by reference to database items related to SHIP–DRAFT
and DISPLACEMENT. Once the items to be described were assembled,
the system would then call up the dictionary and grammar modules to
produce an English text. The details of this process need not concern us
here, but a full account can be found in the original source (McKeown
1985).

As we have seen, TEXT incorporates a body of knowledge on which it
draws to answer the user's questions and a set of schemas which search
this knowledge base for information which is relevant to the question.
There is also a focusing mechanism which makes decisions about what to
say when there are several available options. At the discourse level focus
is used to provide constraints on what can be said next by relating
possible options to the item which is currently in the speaker's centre of
attention, while at the level of message production focus information
affects the use of different syntactic structures, such as a passive as
opposed to an active construction. Thus the production of text will vary
from one occasion to the next according to the constraints set up by the
focusing mechanism. This provides for greater flexibility in the generation
process compared with that of other systems where the production of
text would simply trace the knowledge representation. In other words,
information does not need to be described in exactly the same way as it is
stored.

McKeown points out that there are several ways in which the present
system is inadequate and these reflect some of the issues which have been
raised in earlier chapters. One problem is the repetition of information
during the same session. Decisions about when to omit and when to
repeat information are difficult and depend on factors such as the length
of time which has passed since the information was first presented. In

order to deal with this issue it would be necessary to track the discourse history of a session. This would involve recording what had been said in a session with a user and using that information when generating further responses. Keeping a record of the discourse history would be in keeping with the insight that the previous discourse affects the structure and content of what is being currently said. As can be seen, work along these lines highlights the inadequacy of systems which can only cope with isolated question-answer pairs.

A second area for development is user modelling. An explicit model of the user is needed before decisions can be made as to how much information to provide in a response. If the user is unfamiliar with the material, detailed explanations are required, whereas these would be unnecessary for a knowledgeable user. To illustrate with one of McKeown's examples: when defining a Hobie Cat to someone who knows nothing about sailing, it would not be helpful to say that a Hobie Cat is a kind of catamaran and leave it at that. What would have to come next would be a definition of a catamaran. However if the user were familiar with sailing terminology, then the Hobie Cat could simply be defined as a kind of catamaran. In this way a user model could be used to tailor responses to the needs of different individuals. However, as we saw in chapter 8, work on user modelling is still in its infancy and one of the major problems will be to determine how information about users can be extracted dynamically from the ongoing discourse.

The TEXT system has thus demonstrated how it is possible to generate coherent stretches of English text using knowledge about discourse structure to guide the generation process and to focus constraints in order to ensure discourse coherency. At the same time several issues have been raised which will need to be addressed by future research.

Planning English sentences

Appelt (1985) describes a different approach based on the notion that language generation involves the production of a coherent plan which is passed through a series of stages until it is realized as an English utterance. This system – which is called KAMP (Knowledge and Modalities Planner) – is similar to McKeown's TEXT system in that it includes two levels of generation – one in which decisions are made about which illocutionary act is to be performed and the second which involves the construction of an utterance to express this act. However the control structure of KAMP differs from that of TEXT; in KAMP interaction is permitted between these levels whereas in TEXT, which is structured modularly, there is a strict separation between the levels.

Furthermore, TEXT is based on the notion that speakers have knowledge of discourse structure in the form of schemata for units such as descriptions and definitions, but KAMP builds on the literature on planning and relates this to what is involved in the planning of speech acts such as requesting and informing, and, in particular, to the use of noun phrases as referring expressions.

Let us look at what is involved in the planning of speech acts and referring expressions. There are two main issues – how to plan actions and how to reason about mutual knowledge. It will be recalled from earlier discussions of planning that problem solving can be described in terms of an initial state, reflecting a desired state of affairs. In the blocks world, for example, the initial state might be that block A is on top of block B and the goal state might be that block B should be on top of block A. In addition to these states there are actions which can be performed to effect transition from one state to another. Each action has a set of preconditions which have to be fulfilled before the action can be performed, and a set of effects which become true once the action has been performed. So, for example, the preconditions for grasping block A are that the agent has a free hand and there is no other object on top of block A. The effect of grasping block A is that the agent now holds that block and, in addition, the top of block B is clear. Speech acts can be viewed in the same way. For example, the preconditions on A informing B of something are that A and B are at the same location (assuming face-to-face communication), that A knows the information, that A intends B to know the information and that B wants to know the information. However the situation in the world of dialogue is more complicated than that in the physical world of objects and actions, because dialogue planning has to take into account the mental states of the participants, in particular, what they know or believe. Moreover, working out exactly what someone else knows is not a trivial issue – indeed, in real–world situations it is clearly not possible. For this reason current systems such as KAMP constrain the problem, by assuming, for example, that the participants are engaged in a co-operative task such as assembling a water pump in which the goals of each participant are shared and can be mutually inferred.

What are the effects of performing a speech act such as informing? Recall how the effects of performing actions in the blocks world (or similar physical contexts) can be stated in purely physical terms, such as the changed locations of objects. With speech acts the effects of actions are stated in terms of knowledge about knowledge. If A tells B something, A can reason that B now believes that A had intended to transmit that information. In other words, the effect of performing the illocutionary act of informing is that the hearer acquires knowledge of the speaker's intention to inform. The intended perlocutionary effect of informing – that B should believe what A says – cannot be guaranteed, though this will happen in the ideal case. In other words, the process that is involved is that the hearer recognizes the speaker's surface speech act, infers what illocutionary act it is intended to perform (in this case, informing), and this leads to a change of the hearer's intentions and beliefs which will correspond to the speaker's intended perlocutionary effect. The result is that the speaker and hearer know the same piece of information and, in addition, that each knows that the other knows that information. In other words, they will have shared knowledge.

Problems can arise in a dialogue situation when knowledge is not shared. For example, if A performs some action which B does not know about, A will be aware of the effects of this action but will also need to be able to reason that as B does not know that the action has been performed, then for B the world is still as it was before the action was performed. Thus planning utterances in dialogue involves keeping track of what is mutually known as well as what is not mutually known.

We can illustrate the planning of referring expressions with an example. The situation in which KAMP operates involves a robot, Rob, and a human, John. Rob is an expert who instructs John how to repair an air compressor. Rob wants John to remove the pump from the platform to which it is attached. How does he get him to do this?

Rob's goal is that the pump should be removed from the platform. In order to get John to do this action, he must bring it about that John should intend to do the action. This is accomplished by making a request, so Rob's first decision is that he should request John to remove the pump.

The next stage is to expand the action of removing. Removing involves unfastening a bolt using the appropriate tool. The preconditions for the action are that John should know what the right tool is and that he should know where to find the tool, so Rob has to inform John that the appropriate tool is a wrench. By now the system has devised a plan in which John takes on Rob's goal of removing the pump from its platform. As a result of further planning the system discovers that John requires some additional information to carry out this action so it must plan to provide him with this information.

At this stage the system can begin to plan the surface utterance. The grammar proposes an imperative sentence with the structure V NP (PP), the first part of which can be realized as *remove the pump*. Note that the definite noun phrase *the pump* can be used as Rob is referring to a mutually known object. However, there remains the actions of informing John that he should use the wrench and of telling him where the wrench is. This could be accomplished in two additional utterances, but the structure which has been proposed allows for a prepositional phrase representing the instrumental case of *remove*, so a process of action-subsumption is tried to see if an act of informing can be accomplished within the overall plan to perform a request. This succeeds and the utterance now reads *remove the pump with the wrench*. Next the system has to inform John of the location of the wrench. Again this can be done by action-subsumption, thus avoiding an additional informing utterance, by attaching a further prepositional phrase to the noun phrase *the wrench*. With the plan complete, Rob can now say to John *remove the pump with the wrench in the toolbox.*

Many details have been omitted from this simplified account of the planning involved in the production of this utterance but enough has been said to illustrate the complexity of this process in which the system begins with a description of the speaker's goals and a set of axioms about the objects in the world, knowledge of what Rob and John know about the objects and what actions can be performed on them. In order to produce an utterance the system has to be able to reason about agents' beliefs and intentions and to integrate the planning of actions and goal satisfaction with the linguistic choices available in the grammar. The subsumption of speech acts such as informing within other speech acts such as requesting, as in the example discussed here, shows how speakers can satisfy multiple goals at different levels of communication with their utterances. Thus language generation is an extremely complex research area if by generation we mean the production of utterances that are natural and similar to those that humans would produce within a given communicative context. Many of the knowledge sources relevant to language understanding are involved, though, as we have seen, generation and interpretation are not simply two sides of the same coin.

Towards more human-like natural language interfaces

Earlier we considered some ways in which future research in natural language processing would have to confront the social-interactional aspects of conversation in addition to its transactional aspects, if computers were to be enabled to conduct dialogues in a more human-like way. Current systems are rigid and fragile – they usually demand input which conforms strictly to the grammatical rules embodied in them and they have difficulty in coping with any communication failures. In chapter 9 we reviewed some approaches to these problems and in this section we will examine some of the ways in which humans cope with communication failure and suggest that future research might fruitfully examine these human strategies.

The term *graceful interaction* has been used to describe the ability of a system to deal appropriately with anything a human user happens to say, irrespective of whether it is ill-formed or not (Hayes and Reddy 1983). Graceful interaction includes the ability to clarify misunderstandings, to deal with input that is not fully understood, to explain what the system can and cannot do, to keep track of what has been discussed and to produce appropriate output. We have already seen that many systems have one or other of these abilities. Often these solutions are computationally motivated, whereas the ideas to be considered here are based on the ways in which humans deal with communication failure.

Hayes and Reddy (1983) use the term *robust communication* to refer to the strategies a speaker employs to ensure that a listener receives his message and interprets it correctly. They point out that, although it is not uncommon for people to misunderstand each other, failures in communication are usually resolved without much difficulty and people generally manage to get their message across. As was pointed out earlier, meanings are negotiated in human conversation on a turn-by-turn basis and speakers have ways of indicating when communication has broken down. The techniques used by humans are usually implicit, whereas the checking procedures used by computers are more explicit. For the sake of comparison, we can look at the following example of how Kaplan's CO-OP system dealt with problematic input (Kaplan 1981: 138):

(2)
(Q=question; P=paraphrase; R=response)
Q   who advises projects in area 36?
P   assuming that there are projects that are in area 36, who advises those projects?
R   I don't know of any area 36

CO-OP responds to queries by first paraphrasing them and making their assumptions explicit, and then, if necessary, providing a corrective indirect response. The paraphrase is presented to the user for verification before the query is executed and thus potential misunderstandings are avoided. However, this explicit checking, while effective, is at the expense of rapid information transfer and of gracefulness in interaction. A more human-like strategy, as Hayes and Reddy point out, would be to use more implicit confirmation. What forms does implicit confirmation take?

In chapter 7 we introduced the notion of *preference organization* in conversation. This refers to the way in which choices at particular points in a conversation are non-equivalent. So, for example, when communication failure arises, there are four possibilities for repair (Schegloff et al. 1977):

1 Self-initiated self-repair
2 Other-initiated self-repair
3 Self-initiated other-repair
4 Other-initiated other-repair

However, there are constraints on which types are likely to be used in particular circumstances. Generally, self-initiation of repair is preferred to other-initiation and self repair is preferred to other-repair. What this means is that preferred categories are those which are expected to occur in the normal case – in other words, this is the default category. Applying this notion to acknowledgments and checking moves, we can say that explicit acknowledgements and checking moves are dispreferred and that human conversationalists normally proceed with the default assumption that a message has been received and interpreted correctly unless the listener indicates otherwise. Furthermore, as mentioned earlier, the sequential organization of conversation provides listeners with the opportunity to display in their next turn how they have received and interpreted a preceding utterance and in so doing they also provide the speaker of that utterance with the opportunity to check whether the message has been received and interpreted as intended. Thus each successive utterance in a conversation provides an opportunity for checking, but normally this checking is done implicitly without interrupting the flow of substantive information transfers. Moreover human conversationalists will often tolerate minor conversational failure in the expectation that it is only of local importance or that it will be resolved subsequently. As Hayes and Reddy (1983: 235) write: 'If the speaker believes his message has been received at all by the listener, he believes that it has been received correctly, unless the listener indicates otherwise.'

The notion of preference can also be extended to the ways in which listeners display incomprehension. Explicit requests for clarification interrupt the discourse whereas more implicit indications of incomprehension need only be addressed if the original interpretation turns out to be correct. An *echo* is an example of such an implicit form, as in

(3)
U   what is the extension for John Smith?
S   John Smith
    the extension is 2244
U   2244
    thank you

Here both user and system use direct echoes which display their understanding of the preceding turn for subsequent confirmation, modification or rejection. If the understanding is correct, the original speaker, by not commenting on it, can confirm it implicitly, as happens in the above example.

An even more indirect form, which does not intrude on the normal flow of the conversation, is the *indirect echo*, in which the part of the utterance being displayed for confirmation is incorporated into the listener's next turn (Hayes and Reddy 1983: 242):

(4)
U   what is the (garble) for John Smith?
S   the number for John Smith is 2957

Here the system attempts to cope with problematic input by presenting the user with a reasonable interpretation for implicit confirmation. Indeed, in the case of indirect echoes, the original speaker does not even have the opportunity to confirm explicitly, although explicit correction is still, of course, possible if the indirect echo turns out to have been inaccurate.

We might consider what would be involved in equipping natural language systems with the types of discourse abilities which have been outlined in this section. Some of the types of knowledge which we considered in earlier chapters – such as knowledge of discourse structure and knowledge of the conversational partner – are relevant here. Indeed these two types of knowledge would have to be integrated so that the system could estimate at a given point in the conversation, on the basis of its knowledge of conversational structure, what its conventional partner is likely to be thinking. This meta-knowledge would then be updated on a turn-by-turn basis as the conversation progressed and as elements came into and disappeared from focus. Several of the systems which were described earlier incorporate individual components of graceful inter-action but the integration of these into a truly gracefully interacting system is still beyond the current state of the art. Research on how humans accomplish such tasks will yield important information which will point the way to the development of gracefully interacting systems. We will return to this point shortly.

Language, learning and memory

By now it should be clear that the ability to use language in everyday situations depends on many different sorts of knowledge. Designers of natural language systems have adopted the technique of constructing systems which draw on selected areas such as knowledge of typical events and goals, knowledge of typical discourse structures and knowledge of typical conversational partners. There are two major problems. First, each of these approaches has been necessarily selective and has led to the development of systems which incorporate deep knowledge within restricted domains. What is eventually going to be needed is a model in which different knowledge structures are integrated in a more general language processing system which, like a human being, has the ability to converse on different levels with all sorts of people on a wide range of topics. The second problem arises from our use of the word 'typical'. To date, systems have focused on what is normal – such as what to do when we eat in restaurants, how we make a flight reservation, or how we work out the plans of someone who is entering a railway station. What happens when the unexpected occurs, when something happens which is not typical? Humans can normally deal with the unexpected, the untypical, but current systems are at a total loss. This means that the main problem is not just to decide what sorts of knowledge have to be built into a natural language processing system but, more importantly, to understand how this knowledge is acquired in the first place, how it is organized in memory and how it is retrieved from memory and used as required.

Learning language

Language acquisition is an interdisciplinary research area which has expanded widely over the past few decades. Students of language acquisition are concerned with topics such as the development of linguistic systems – in phonology, syntax and lexical semantics – relationships between language and cognition, environmental influences on language learning, and the acquisition of communicative competence (see papers in Fletcher and Garman 1986 for a recent overview). The results of this research contribute to our understanding of how children use and acquire language and ultimately to what we know about the nature of the human mind. Recently, attempts have been made to model the language acquisition process computationally. We will report briefly on two significant pieces of work in this area.

Within Chomskyan linguistics the acquisition of syntactic knowledge is seen as a major topic of enquiry. Syntax is viewed as a formal and autonomous system which cannot be learned solely from the degenerate input which the child might happen to hear. Indeed, given that this input is insufficient and varies widely from child to child, how, it is asked, do children come to internalize the same systems of syntactic rules? Part of the answer, proposed by Chomsky (1965), is that children are endowed with an innate ability to structuralize language which is triggered off by interaction with the environment. Chomsky claims that those aspects of language which are universal do not have to be learned and in more recent versions of the theory reference is made *parameters* which are set as the child makes its first encounters with language – for example, that the word order in the language is SVO (subject-verb-object), SOV (subject-object-verb) or one of the several other possible combinations. Thus, the environment itself, by which is meant the normal linguistic interaction the child experiences in the early years of life, is necessary but not sufficient, and one of the major questions remaining unanswered is what is the precise nature of the interaction between the child's innate genetic endowment and the input from the environment? For ethical reasons, the interaction cannot be tested empirically; children cannot be deprived of normal input in order to control for its role in language acquisition. The computational modelling of this question is therefore particularly useful. Berwick (1985) has written a program which simulates language acquisition in this way. Among the issues explored in this model are the acquisition of lexical categories, phonological rule systems and phrase structure rules, and the ways in which semantics and syntax interact in language acquisition. The system addresses some of the central concerns of Chomskyan linguistics, such as the nature of parameter setting, and the syntactic rules which the system acquires are based on those incorporated in the deterministic parser developed by Marcus (1980) which was referred to briefly in chapter 3. The results obtained from Berwick's system are impressive; the system is able to learn most of the syntactic rules after a short exposure to well-formed input. Thus this program makes an important contribution to the Chomskyan theory of language acquisition. The most serious shortcoming of work within this theory, however, is that by focusing on the acquisition of syntactic knowledge it ignores the role of pragmatics and, in particular, the interaction between world knowledge and formal systems of language. Thus Berwick's program is a good example of how a computational model can be used to test a theory of language acquisition, but the theory itself is at best partial and so leaves many empirical questions unanswered.

The second piece of research involved the modelling of the acquisition of lexical comprehension and it was based on Schank's conceptual dependency theory (Selfridge 1982). This model, like Berwick's, was based on the notion that children bring to language learning a substantial amount of previous knowledge. However, whereas Berwick was referring to innate syntactic structures, Selfridge was referring to concepts and world knowledge which had been acquired during the first year of life and which interact with general learning abilities and inference abilities. Thus the question of what is innate is not raised in this model; instead Selfridge begins with empirical observations of a child, Joshua, at age one – the starting point for the model – and exposes his program to the kinds of experiences which Joshua had during the next year in order to see whether the program's knowledge of vocabulary would be similar to the child's at age two. At age one the child was knowledgeable about simple objects, events and relations while at age two he knew the names of most of the objects he was familiar with at age one and had some knowledge of sentence structure. Selfridge argues that acquisition of word meaning takes place when the child encounters a new word in context and associates the meaning of that word with that context. One such context was an event sequence familiar to the child. If the child heard an utterance within such a sequence, he could infer that the appropriate response was the next action in the sequence and, if his inference turned out to be correct, he would associate the meaning of the utterance he had heard with the action which he already understood. This would lead to the child learning the meanings of new words occuring in such utterances.

Selfridge proposes a set of inferences and rules to cover the child's experience of language in familiar contexts and the interested reader is referred to the detailed account in the original source. The findings of this research are interesting. First, it was found that the system was able to acquire word meanings starting from the same position as the child at age one and with exposure to the same kind of experiences. But second, it was found that the system made errors in the acquisition of word meanings similar to those made by children. Young children often acquire word meanings which are particularly restricted in their reference or which are over-extended – for example, they may use the word *ball* for all round objects or they may understand utterances containing *in* but misunderstand those containing *on*. As acquisition was tied to the context, the child – and the computer model – would often acquire context-specific aspects of word meanings, for example, that *bye-bye* was used only to say farewell to the particular person to whom it was first addressed. Later experience would indicate that this initial rule was too specific and that the meaning of the word had to be generalized. Thus as well as accounting for the acquisition of word meanings, the program also models the processes of acquisition in which learning is gradual and consists of the formation of hypotheses which are modified on the basis of subsequent experience.

Language and memory

Learning and memory go hand in hand. In the process of learning something we commit it to memory, but at the same time learning involves comparing new input with what is already stored in memory from previous experiences. Schank (1982) sees language as a memory-based process. Scripts were a useful high-level knowledge structure which supplied background information to enable inferences to be made during the processing of texts but they were not a model of how cognitive processes work. For one thing, programs like SAM did not learn anything new from the texts they processed, as their memory was static. What is required is a dynamic memory which is flexible and open-ended and which can be changed in the light of new information. A second point was that experimental studies revealed that people often confused actions from scripts which were similar (Bower, Black and Turner 1979). For example, when asked to recall stories they had read about visiting the doctor and visiting the dentist, subjects often confused the actions that had occurred in one story with those that had occurred in another. What this suggested to Schank was that memory for events was not stored in terms of a preset sequence of events but in terms of many different levels of specificity, some highly specific and some quite general. For example, specific events such as a visit to a particular dentist and the more salient and interesting parts of that visit would be remembered in Event Memory whereas the features which were common to several such visits would be stored in Generalized Event Memory. Information about visits to dentists would thus be stored here, but more general situational information such as our knowledge of waiting rooms and visits to a health professional's office would be stored under Situational Memory. All these sources of information are organized in Memory Organization Packets (MOPs) and we call on many such MOPs when processing any experience. For example, when we hear about a visit to a restaurant, we call on a script for restaurants but we might also need to call on a number of MOPs such as those for social situations, business contracts and service encounters.

One source of evidence which Schank uses to support his theory of memory comes from the phenomenon of reminding. Frequently, when we experience an event we are reminded of something which happened to us in the past. This is not necessarily directly related to the event we are presently experiencing; for example, when we see a noisy child disturbing all the other guests in a restaurant, we are not necessarily reminded of previous visits to restaurants but perhaps of a train journey on which a child caused embarrassment to its parents. In other words, certain events can be stored under a more general category such as *Difficult children* or *Embarrassing situations in public* and we can be reminded of them when we experience similar situations on other occasions. Note, however, that MOPs are highly general and are quite different from the preset sequences of events in scripts. Schank maintains that instances of reminding are informative in that they tell us how memory is organized as well as how we learn and make generalizations.

This brings us to the connections between learning and memory. Our understanding is based on what we already know and when we experience an event we make predictions about what is likely to occur in the course of that event. Sometimes our predictions will be incorrect and we revise our knowledge structures in the light of our mistakes. This is how learning occurs. When an experienced event differs from what we had expected, *expectation failure* can lead us to modify our original knowledge structures and this leads us to new generalizations. Our earlier examples from language acquisition are an illustration of this process. Selfridge's program would make an initial hypothesis about the meaning of a word based on its experience of that word in a particular context. When subsequent experience suggested that that meaning was too restricted, the program was able to modify its knowledge structures in the direction of a more general meaning.

This brief discussion of dynamic memory may seem to have taken us a long way from the issues involved in the use of language. If we accept, however, that what we know has a bearing on what we can say and on how we interpret what others say, then it is appropriate to ask how we come to know what we know and how this knowledge changes as a result of our experiences. There is an interesting corollary between what we said earlier concerning understanding and what Schank writes about memory. Understanding is a dynamic process which undergoes continual changes during the course of a conversation. For this reason there is no absolute interpretation of an utterance but rather we are left with what is negotiated and agreed between the participants in a dialogue. Understanding is imperfect and so is memory. As Schank (1980: 282) writes: People have imperfect memories because they are looking to make generalizations about experience that will serve as a source of useful predictions in understanding.

Thus understanding and memory are linked and, paradoxical though it might seem, these apparent imperfections could well be the clue to how we ought to proceed further in artificial intelligence. As Schank goes on to say:

I do not believe that there is any other alternative available to us in building intelligent machines other than modelling people. People's supposed imperfections are there for a reason. It may be possible that in the distant future we will build machines that improve upon what people can do; but machines will have to equal people first, *and I mean equal very very literally*.

This would seem to be a good point to turn our attention to some of the ways in which studies of the use of language by humans might inform future developments in artificial intelligence research.

Some directions for future research

Given that the modelling of human conversational competence provides useful information on which to base future research on articulate computers, what directions could this research take? There are several sources of information on human conversation which we will consider briefly. The first is the extensive literature on empirical studies of conversation conducted by psychologists, linguists, and discourse and conversation analysts. In conversation analysis, for example, many detailed studies have been made of how people open and close conversations, change topics, make repairs, respond to complaints, compliments and jokes, and such studies have drawn attention to the largely unnoticed, but extremely complex, interactional work which is involved in the smooth management of everyday conversation. Conversation analysts use a method of investigation which is mainly inductive; it involves looking for recurrent patterns across large samples of naturally occurring conversation and the resulting description is to be seen not just as a detailed analysis of conversational texts but, more importantly, as a model of the processes which conversational participants actually employ when understanding and producing conversation. This approach differs from that adopted in computational modelling in several ways. First, conversation analysts are rigorously empirical and any conversational process which is proposed has to be supported by evidence from the transcribed data. No reference is made to the intentions of speakers unless these can be verified explicitly from the text. In computational modelling, for example the speech-act based work on plan recognition, heavy emphasis is placed on inferences about the intents and beliefs of the conversational participants. Related to this is the point that the conversation analysts are concerned with conversation as a social-interactional accomplishment – with carrying out such things as bringing a conversation to a mutually agreed close – whereas computational work has been concerned more with the cognitive structures and processes of language users. Finally, because conversation analysts adopt an inductive approach to their data, they wish to avoid premature theory construction. As a result there is the danger that each new set of data will be treated as the grounds for a unique and detailed analysis in its own terms without reference to any guiding theoretical principles. Computational modelling, on the other hand, requires the formalization of analytic terms and processes in an explicit, computationally tractable form.

Despite these differences there is scope for greater co-operation between researchers in conversation who, although they come from a range of different disciplinary backgrounds, have much to offer each other. Conversation analysis would profit from a more explicit formalization of the rules and principles underlying conversational participation while workers in the computational modelling of conversation would be well advised to pay attention to the results of detailed, empirical analyses of conversation in order to avoid the danger of basing theories on unsupported intuitions about what constitutes a well-formed text, especially when these theories can only account for specially constructed or highly idealized data.

Most of the work which has been described in this book has been concerned with language in its written form, with user's input typed in at a keyboard and a system's responses printed on a TV screen or VDU. Future research must consider other modalities. One obvious contrast is between spoken and written forms of language. There are many formal differences between spoken and written language, some of which were discussed briefly in chapter 9 with reference to the so-called ill-formedness of conversational language, and obviously systems which adopt speech rather than writing as their medium will have to be able to cope with the characteristics of spoken language (see, for example, Chafe 1982 and Ochs 1979).

Modality differences can also refer to different interactional situations. As a basis for her analysis of task-oriented dialogues in which an expert instructed an apprentice in the assembly of an air compressor (see chapter 7), Grosz used the following conditions:

1 free dialogue in which expert and apprentice could see each other and in which they were free to interrupt each other, for example, to resolve misunderstandings.
2 free dialogue as above, except that the expert was not able to see what the apprentice was doing.
3 restricted interaction via computer terminals, which precluded interruptions. The apprentice was informed that the expert was a person simulating a computer system.

4 restricted interaction as in 3 except that the apprentice was told that the expert was a computer system whereas the expert was in fact a human simulating a computer system.

Grosz found that the different conditions produced different results. There were frequent interruptions in the first two conditions, as one would expect with fairly unrestricted naturally occurring speech. Many of these interruptions were occasioned by the expert and apprentice co-operating on completing utterances as well as on completing the task, as the following extract illustrates (Grosz 1978: 242).

(5)
A   now should I unscrew the nuts from the bolts?
E   no, the wire goes on top of that . . . on top of the nuts that are on there . . .
A   I see . . .
E   . . . and they're . . .
A   other nuts
E   . . . there are other nuts

Descriptions were affected by the different visibility conditions. Where vision was shared, it could be used in descriptions, as can be seen in the next extract which contrasts dramatically with the one following (Grosz 1978: 242).

(6)
(with vision)
E   you have a top piece with a knurled section that you take a hold of
A   what's a knurled section?
E   you've got your fingers on it

(7)
(without vision)
E   now underneath is what they call a cap assembly. It has a knurled face around it
A   what does knurled mean?
E   little lines running up and down on it so you can take a hold of it

In situations where visual information is not shared, much more complex descriptions have to be generated. Similar findings are reported by Cohen (1984) in a study of the differences between requests for the identification of referents in telephone and keyboard mode. Thus it will be important to consider modality differences when designing natural language systems as what is required under one condition can differ sharply from what is required under another.

Protocols of human-computer interaction provide a further source for future research by indicating the sorts of problems which arise in such interactions. For example, one study of question-answering systems showed that systems typically lacked the ability to infer and respond to the apparent yet unstated goals of their users and to interpret input from the user in the light of the preceding discourse (Cohen et al. 1982). The following is an example from a protocol in which a user was interacting with a natural language question-answering system which was used as an interface to a relational database of aircraft flight and maintenance records (Cohen et al. 1982: 247).

(8)
(Note: explanations of technical abbreviations which appeared in the original are given in brackets for ease of reading)
U   Which A7 (aircraft) had NORMU hours greater than 100?
    (NORMU = Not Operationally Ready due to Unscheduled Maintenance)

S	ACTDATE	SERIAL	PLANE TYPE
	304	4	AAF
	305	5	AAF
	305	9	AAF
	.	.	.
	.	.	.

U   No, how many NORMU hours greater than 100?
S   I could not understand the word no, will skip it
    ((COUNT BUSER) (SUM NORMUNS)) = (4,6444)
    (BUSER = unique identification number for an aircraft)
U   which four?
S   (S translates utterance to an incorrect query. User does not allow system to continue)
U   which 4 planes had NORMUS greater than 100 hours?
S   (program fails)

In this example, the system replies to the user's first question with a potentially satisfactory answer. However, the user's response indicates that he wanted a further column displaying the number of NORMU hours for each plane. The system is unable to interpret the user's *no*, which is a discourse marker indicating dissatisfaction with the previous response, followed by a modification of the original query. However, by disregarding *no*, the system treats the user's second question as a new and independent query and answers it accordingly. Moving on, the user asks *which four* (planes), based on the response that the system had just computed. However, the system has simply evaluated a function and printed out its result without keeping track of the fact that it has communicated some information about planes.

As can be seen, some of the problems which arose in this extract involve issues which were discussed in earlier chapters. In particular, the system lacks the ability to

1 Deduce the apparent, yet unstated goals of the user.
2 Interpret discourse markers such as *no, well* and *by the way.*
3 Interpret the user's queries in the light of the preceding discourse.

The analysis of protocols of human-computer interaction can thus highlight those areas in which natural language systems are still deficient.

A related approach involves protocols of users interacting with a simulated program – that is, one in which the system is replaced by a human respondent. In this case the simulation can point to those expectations which human users would bring to a more competent natural language interface. The following is an extract from an interaction between a human user and S-PLANES where a human played the role of the system (Tennant 1980).

(9)
U how many cases of FOD (foreign object damage) were experienced?
S that query would take about 20 minutes to compute it can be usefully limited by considering specific air-craft
U consider aircraft 27
S nil

This example shows how a potentially helpful system might work. The system indicates that it would be too expensive to compute an answer to the user's query and averts an ineffective and inefficient communicative exchange by suggesting how the user might achieve a response through a modification of the original query. In this way it is possible to highlight directions for future research by showing the sorts of responses which an ideal, co-operative system would be expected to give.

Finally there are two areas of research on human subjects which less obviously could play an important role in future systems research – language acquisition and language pathology. Language acquisition was discussed earlier in relation to the modelling of the acquisition of syntactic and lexical competence. As yet there are no computational models of the acquisition of conversational competence although this is a rapidly expanding area both in naturalistic studies of conversational development (McTear 1985) as well as in experimental studies of children's referential communication (Dickson 1981). There have also been a few studies which have shown that children make use of script-like knowledge structures in story recall tasks (Nelson and Gruendel 1979; McCartney and Nelson 1981). The acquisition of such knowledge structures awaits further investigation.

Language acquisition is a complex process which normally goes unnoticed. Some children, however, have difficulty in acquiring language and language pathology, which is an important research area in its own right, also has a potential contribution to make to the study of natural language processing, as an analysis of language breakdown can often shed interesting light on the nature of the system being acquired. Recent work on pragmatic disabilities – by which is meant disorders in the use of language – has suggested that one aspect of this syndrome is an inability to process incoming information in terms of the knowledge structures which have been described in earlier chapters. McTear (1985), for example, presents data from a child who was deficient in the ability to describe temporal and causal relations between everyday events and to make simple inferences which depend on a basic world knowledge. This child also had problems in making assessments about his listener's knowledge and in distinguishing what he himself knew from what he believed his listener to know. In some ways the performance of this child was like an inferior natural language program. A close analysis of pragmatic disorders such as these could provide useful information about what computers ought to know if they are to engage in meaningful conversation.

The articulate computer: fact or fiction?

This is the question with which we began this book. I hope I have been able to show that the notion of an articulate computer is not pure fantasy and indeed that considerable progress has been made in this important area of AI. Some directions for future research have also been discussed. It might be interesting to end on a more fanciful note by looking briefly at a fictional computer and comparing it with the systems we have encountered during the course of the book.

Science fiction abounds with computers that can talk, think, explain, reason and perform a wide range of human-like actions. One of the best known – and perhaps the prototype for the articulate computer of the future – is HAL 9000 in Arthur C. Clarke's novel *2001: A Space Odyssey*. HAL (Heuristically programmed Algorithmic computer) had the task of controlling a space mission from the moon to Jupiter and on to Saturn. As well as dealing with all the aspects of flight control such as life-support systems and intricate navigational manoeuvres, HAL could understand English and could reply in 'the perfect idiomatic English he had learned during the fleeting weeks of his electronic childhood'. But HAL could not just talk; he could think. Here is an extract from a conversation between HAL and Bowman, the flight commander:

(10)

'Do you know where the trouble is?' asked Bowman.

'It's intermittent and I can't localise it. But it appears to be in the AE 35 unit.'

'What procedure would you suggest?'

'The best thing would be to replace the unit with a spare, so that we can check it over.'

'O.K. – let us have the hard copy.'

Later, when Bowman loses his colleague in an 'accident', HAL displays human-like empathy.

(11)

'Too bad about Frank, isn't it?'

'Yes,' Bowman answered, after a long pause. 'It is.'

'I suppose you're pretty broken up about it?'

'What do you expect?'

HAL processed this answer for ages of computer-time; it was a full five seconds before he continued: 'He was an excellent crew member.'

Apart from this display of empathy, there are other signs of HAL's conversational abilities in this extract. Bowman asks 'what do you expect?' But this is not really a question in the sense of a request for information; the most appropriate response is in fact the display of affiliation with Bowman's grief which HAL makes. It goes well beyond the literal meanings of the actual words spoken and it is no wonder that this utterance involved extra processing on HAL's part.

When we compare the limited powers of conversation of the systems described in this book with HAL's sophisticated performance, we can see how much has yet to be accomplished in the computational modelling of conversational competence. One thing should be certain, however: when we consider some of what is involved in designing a system which can communicate in natural language and in a human-like way, we begin to appreciate the complexities of the processes we normally take for granted every time we take part in a conversation.

Further Reading

Language generation

There is a rapidly expanding literature on language generation. In addition to the sources cited in this chapter, see Mehan (1976) and Yazdani (1982) for work on story writing by computer, Matthiessen

(1983) for an approach to sentence generation based on systemic linguistics as well as related work by Mann (1984) on rhetorical structures and discourse generation. McDonald (1983) presents a system which aims to reflect human language production processes. See also Davey (1979) for a program which provides commentary on the progress of a game of noughts and crosses (tic-tac-toe).

References

Aitchison, J. 1978: *Linguistics*. Sevenoaks: Hodder and Stoughton.

Aitchison, J. 1983: *The articulate mammal: an introduction to psycholinguistics* London: Hutchinson.

Allen, J. 1983: Recognizing intentions from natural language utterances. In M. Brady and R. C. Berwick (eds), *Computational models of discourse.* Cambridge, Mass.: MIT Press.

Allen, J. and Perrault, C. R. 1980: Analysing intention in utterances. *Artificial Intelligence*, 15, 143–78.

Appelt, D. E. 1985: *Planning English Sentences*. Cambridge: Cambridge University Press.

Atkinson, J. M. and Heritage, J. (eds) 1984: *Structures of social action.* Cambridge: Cambridge University Press.

Barr, A. and Feigenbaum, E. A. 1981 *The handbook of artificial intelligence.* 3 vols. Los Altos, CA: William Kaufman.

Bates, M. 1978 The theory and practice of augmented transition network grammars. In L. Bolc (ed.) *Natural language communication with computers.* Berlin: Springer-Verlag.

Berwick, R. C. 1985: *The acquisition of syntactic knowledge*. Cambridge, Mass:. MIT Press.

Bobrow, D. G. 1968: Natural language input for a computer problem-solving system. In M. Minsky (ed.), *Semantic information processing.* Cambridge, Mass.: MIT Press.

Bobrow, D. G. and Collins, A. (eds), 1975: *Representation and understanding: studies in cognitive science.* New York: Academic Press.

Bobrow, D. G., Kaplan, R. M., Kay, M., Norman, D. A., Thompson, H. and Winograd, T. 1977: GUS, a frame-driven dialogue system. *Artificial Intelligence*, 8, 155–73.

Boden, M. 1977: *Artificial intelligence and natural man.* New York: Basic Books.

Bower, G. H., Black, J. B. and Turner, T. J. 1979: Scripts in text comprehension and memory. *Cognitive Psychology*, 1, 177–220.

Brady, M. and Berwick, R. C. (eds), 1983: *Computational models of discourse.* Cambridge, Mass.: MIT Press.

Brown, J. S. and Burton, R. R. 1975: Multiple representations of knowledge. In

D. G. Bobrow and A. Collins (eds), *Representation and understanding: studies in cognitive science*. New York: Academic Press.

Brown, J. S., Burton, R. R. and de Kleer, J. 1982: Pedagogical, natural language and knowledge engineering techniques in SOPHIE I, II and III. In D. Sleeman and J. S. Brown (eds), *Intelligent tutoring systems*. New York: Academic Press.

Brown, K. (1984): *Linguistics today*. London: Fontana.

Burton, R. R. 1976: *Semantic grammar: an engineering technique for constructing natural language understanding systems*. Technical report 3453, Bolt, Beranek and Newman.

Butler, C. S. 1985: *Computers in linguistics*. Oxford: Basil Blackwell.

Carberry, M. S. 1986: The use of inferred knowledge in understanding pragmatically ill-formed queries. In R. Reilly (ed.), *Communication failure in dialogue and discourse*. Amsterdam: North-Holland.

Carbonel, J. 1981: POLITICS. In R. C. Schank and C. K. Riesbeck (eds), *Inside computer understanding*. Hillsdale, NJ: Lawrence Erlbaum.

Carbonell, J. and Hayes, P. 1984: Coping with extragrammaticality. *Proceedings of Coling84*, Stanford, 437–43.

Chafe, W. 1982: Integration and involvement in speaking, writing, and oral literature. In D. Tannen (ed.), *Spoken and written language: exploring orality and literacy*. Norwood, N.J.: Ablex.

Charniak, E. and McDermott, D. 1985: *An introduction to artificial intelligence*. Reading, Mass.: Addison-Wesley.

Charniak, E. and Wilks, Y. (eds), 1976: *Computational semantics: an introduction to artificial intelligence and natural language comprehension*. Amsterdam: North-Holland.

Chomsky, N. 1965: *Aspects of the theory of syntax*. Cambridge, Mass.: MIT Press.

Clark, H. H. and Clark, E. V. 1977: *Psychology and language: an introduction to psycholinguistics*. New York: Harcourt Brace Jovanich.

Codd, E. 1974: Seven steps to rendezvous with the casual user. In J. Klimbie and K. Koffema (eds), *Data base management*. Amsterdam: North-Holland.

Cohen, P. 1984: The pragmatics of referring and the modality of conversation. *Computational Linguistics*, 10, 2, 97–146.

Cohen, P., Perrault, C. and Allen, J. 1982: Beyond question answering. In W. G. Lehnert and M. H. Ringle (eds), *Strategies for natural language processing*. Hillsdale, NJ: Lawrence Erlbaum.

Cole, P. and Morgan, J., (eds) 1975: *Syntax and semantics. Volume 3: Speech acts*. New York: Academic Press.

Coulthard, M. and Brazil, D. 1979: *Exchange structure*. University of Birmingham: Discourse analysis monographs no. 5.

Coulthard, M. 1985: *An introduction to discourse analysis*. London: Longman.

Crain, S. and Steedman, M. J. 1985: On not being led up the garden path: the use of context by the psychological parser. In D. Dowty, L. Kartunen and A. Zwicky (eds), *Natural language parsing*. Cambridge: Cambridge University Press.

Crystal, D. 1985: *Linguistics*. Harmondsworth: Penguin.

Cullingford, R. 1981: SAM. In R. C. Schank and C. K. Riesbeck (eds), *Inside computer understanding*. Hillsdale, NJ: Lawrence Erlbaum.

Davey, A. 1979: *Discourse production: a computer model of some aspects of a speaker*. Edinburgh: Edinburgh University Press.

Dickson, W. P. (ed.) 1981: *Children's oral communication skills*. New York: Academic Press.

Dowty, D., Kartunen, L. and Zwicky, A. (eds), 1985: *Natural language parsing*. Cambridge: Cambridge University Press.

Dresher, B. E. and Hornstein, N. 1976: On some supposed contributions of artificial intelligence to a scientific study of language. *Cognition*, 4, 321–98.

Dreyfus, H. L. 1972: *What computers can't do: a critique of artificial reasoning*. New York: Harper & Row.

Dyer, M. G. 1983: *In-depth understanding: a computer model of integrated processing for narrative comprehension*. Cambridge, Mass.: MIT Press.

Eastman, C. M. and McLean, D. S. 1981: On the need for parsing ill-formed input. *American Journal of Computational Linguistics*, 7, 4, 257.

Feigenbaum, E. A. and Feldman, J. (eds), 1963: *Computers and thought*. New York: McGraw-Hill.

Findler, N.V. (ed.) 1979: *Associative networks*. New York: Academic Press.

Fletcher, P. and Garman, M. (eds), 1986: *Language acquisition*. Cambridge: Cambridge University Press.

Frazier, L. and Fodor, J. D. 1978: The sausage machine: a new two-stage parsing model. *Cognition*, 6, 291–325.

Gaines, B. R. and Shaw, M. L. G. 1984: *The art of computer conversation*. Englewood Cliffs, NJ: Prentice-Hall International.

Garnham, A. 1985: *Psycholinguistics: central topics*. London: Methuen.

Garvey, C. 1979: Contingent queries and their development in discourse. In E. Ochs and B. Schieffelin (eds), *Developmental pragmatics*. New York: Academic Press.

Goodman, B. A. 1986: Repairing reference identification failures by relaxation. In R. Reilly (ed.) *Communication failure in dialogue and discourse*. Amsterdam: North-Holland.

Green, B. F., Wolf, A. W., Chomsky, C. and Laughery, K. R. 1963: BASEBALL: an automatic question-answerer. In E. A. Feigenbaum and J. Feldman (eds), *Computers and thought*. New York: McGraw-Hill.

Greene, J. 1986: *Language understanding: a cognitive approach*. Milton Keynes: Open University Press.

Grosz, B. 1978: Discourse. In D. Walker (ed.), *Understanding spoken language*. New York: Elsevier North-Holland.

Grosz, B. 1981: Focusing and description in natural language dialogue. In A. Joshi, B. Webber and I. Sag (eds), *Elements of discourse understanding*. Cambridge: Cambridge University Press.

Hammond, P. 1983: *Representation of DHSS regulations as a logic program*. Department of Computing report no. 82/26, Imperial College, London.

Harris, L. H. 1984: Natural language front-ends. In P.H. Winston and K. A. Prendergast (eds), *The AI business: commercial uses of artificial intelligence*. Cambridge, Mass.: MIT Press.

Hayes, P. and Reddy, D. 1983: Steps toward graceful interaction in spoken and written man-machine communication. *International Journal of Man-Machine Studies*, 19, 213–84.

Hendrix, G. G. 1977: LIFER: a natural language interface facility. *SIGART Newsletter*, 61.

Hoeppner, W., Morik, K. and Marburger, H. 1984: *Talking it over: the natural language dialogue system HAM-ANS*. University of Hamburg research unit for information science and artificial intelligence, report ANS-26.

Hudson, R. 1984: *Invitation to linguistics*. Oxford: Martin Robertson.

Joshi, A., Webber, B. and Sag, I. (eds), 1981: *Elements of discourse understanding*. Cambridge: Cambridge University Press.

Joshi, A., Webber, B. and Weischedel, R. M. 1984: Preventing false inferences. *Proceedings of Coling84*, Stanford, 134–8.

Kaplan, J. 1983: Cooperative responses from a portable natural language database query system. In M. Brady and R. C. Berwick (eds), *Computational models of discourse*. Cambridge, Mass.: MIT Press.

Kaplan, R. M. 1972: Augmented transition networks as psychological models of sentence comprehension. *Artificial Intelligence*, 3, 77–100.

King, M. 1983: Transformational parsing. In M. King (ed.), *Parsing natural language*. New York: Academic Press.

King, M. (ed.), *Parsing natural language*. New York: Academic Press.

Labov, W. and Fanshel, D. 1977: *Therapeutic discourse: psychotherapy as conversation*. New York: Academic Press.

Lehnert, W. G. 1980: Question answering in natural language processing. In L. Bolc (ed.), *Natural language question answering*. Munich: Hanser.

Lehnert, W. G. 1981: A computational theory of human question answering. In A. Joshi, B. Webber and I. Sag (eds), *Elements of discourse understanding*. Cambridge: Cambridge University Press.

Lehnert, W. G. and Ringle, M. H. (eds), 1982: *Strategies for natural language processing*. Hillsdale, NJ: Lawrence Erlbaum.

Levin, J. A. and Moore, J. A. 1977: Dialogue games: metacommunication structures for natural language. *Cognitive Science*, 1, 4, 395–420.

Levinson, S. C. 1983: *Pragmatics*. Cambridge: Cambridge University Press.

Litman, D. J. and Allen, J. 1984: A plan recognition model for clarification subdialogues. *Proceedings of Coling84*, Stanford, 302–11.

Lowerre, B. T. 1976: *The HARPY speech recognition system*. PhD thesis, Pittsburg: Department of Computer Science, Carnegie-Mellon University.

Mann, W. C. 1984: Discourse structures for text generation. *Proceedings of Coling84*, Stanford, 367–75.

Marcus, M. P. 1980: *A theory of syntactic recognition for natural language*. Cambridge, Mass.: MIT Press.

Matthiessen, C. M. 1983 Systemic grammar in computation: the Nigel case.

Proceedings of the first conference of the European chapter of the Association for Computational Linguistics, Pisa, 155–64.

McCartney, K. A. and Nelson, K. 1981: Children's use of scripts in story recall. *Discourse Processes*, 4, 59–70.

McCorduck, P. 1979: *Machines who think*. San Francisco: Freeman.

McCoy, K. F. 1986: Generating responses to property misconceptions using perspective. In R. Reilly (ed.) *Communication failure in dialogue and discourse*. Amsterdam: North-Holland.

McDonald, D. D. 1983: Natural language generation as a computational problem: an introduction. In M. Brady and R. C. Berwick (eds), *Computational models of discourse* Cambridge, Mass:. MIT Press.

McKeown, K. R. 1985: *Text generation: using discourse strategies and focus constraints to generate natural language texts*. Cambridge: Cambridge University Press.

McTear, M. 1985: *Children's conversation*. Oxford: Basil Blackwell.

Meehan, J. R. 1976: *The metanovel: writing stories by computer*. Research report 74, Yale University.

Michie, D. and Johnston, R. 1984: *The creative computer: machine intelligence and human knowledge*. Harmondsworth: Penguin.

Milne, R. W. 1982: Predicting garden-path sentences. *Cognitive Science*, 6, 249–73.

Minsky, M. (ed.) 1968: *Semantic information processing*. Cambridge, Mass.: MIT Press.

Minsky, M. 1975: A framework for representing knowledge. In D. G. Bobrow and A. Collins (eds), *Representative and understanding: studies in cognitive science*. New York: Academic Press.

Nelson, K. and Gruendel, J. M. 1979: At morning it's lunchtime: a scriptal view of children's dialogues. *Discourse Processes*, 2, 73–94.

Ochs, E. 1979: Planned and unplanned discourse. In T. Givon (ed.), *Syntax and semantics vol. 12: discourse and syntax*. New York: Academic Press.

O'Shea, T. and Eisenstadt, M. (eds), 1984: *Artificial intelligence: tools, techniques, and applications*. New York: Harper and Row.

Pereira, F. and Warren, D. 1980: Definite clause grammar for language analysis: a survey of the formalism and a comparison with augmented transition networks. *Artificial Intelligence*, 13, 231–78.

Petrick, S. P. 1973: Transformational analysis. In R. Rustin (ed.), *Natural language processing*. Engelwood Cliffs, NJ: Prentice-Hall.

Pollack, M. E. 1986: Some requirements for a model of the plan inference process in conversation. In R. Reilly (ed.) *Communication failure in dialogue and discourse*. Amsterdam: North-Holland.

Psathas, G. (ed.), 1979: *Everyday language: studies in ethnomethodology*. New York: Irvington.

Quillian, R. 1968: Semantic memory. In M. Minsky (ed.), *Semantic information processing*. Cambridge, Mass.: MIT Press.

Radford, A. 1981: *Transformational syntax*. Cambridge: Cambridge University Press.

Ramsay, A. 1986: Computer processing of natural language. In M. Yazdani (ed.), *Artificial intelligence: principles and applications*. London: Chapman and Hall.

Ramshaw, L. A. and Weischedel, R. M. 1984: Problem localization strategies for pragmatics processing in natural language front ends *Proceedings of Coling84*, Stanford, 139–43.

Raphael, B. 1968: SIR: a computer program for semantic information retrieval. In M. Minsky (ed.), *Semantic information processing*. Cambridge, Mass.: MIT Press.

Raphael, B. 1976: *The thinking computer*. San Francisco: Freeman.

Reichman, R. 1984: Extended person-machine interface. *Artificial Intelligence*, 22, 157–218.

Reichman, R. 1985: *Getting computers to talk like you and me: discourse context, focus, and semantics*. Cambridge, Mass.: MIT Press.

Reilly, R. 1986: *Communication failure in dialogue and discourse*. Amsterdam: North-Holland.

Rich, E. 1979: User modelling via stereotypes. *Cognitive Science*, 3, 329–54.

Rich, E. 1983: *Artificial intelligence*. New York: McGraw-Hill Inc.

Ringle, M. and Bruce, B. 1982: Conversation failure. In W. G. Lehnert and M. Ringle (eds), *Strategies for natural language processing*. Hillsdale, NJ: Lawrence Erlbaum Associates.

Ringle, M. and Lehnert, W. G. (eds), 1982: *Strategies for natural language processing*. Hillsdale, NJ: Lawrence Erlbaum Associates.

Ritchie, G. and Thompson, H. 1984: Natural language processing. In T. O'Shea and M. Eisenstadt (eds), 1984: *Artificial intelligence: tools, techniques, and applications*. New York: Harper and Row.

Robinson, E. 1981: The child's understanding of inadequate messages and communication failure: a problem of ignorance or egocentrism. In W. P. Dickson (ed.), *Children's oral communication skills*. New York: Academic Press.

Rosenberg, R. S. 1981: Approaching discourse computationally: a review. In L. Bolc (ed.), *Representation and processing of natural language*. Munich: Hanser.

Rumelhart, D. E. and Norman, D. A. 1983: *Representation in memory*. CHIP Technical report No. 116 San Diego: Center for Human Information Processing, University of California.

Rustin, R. (ed.) 1973: *Natural language processing*. Englewood Cliffs, NJ: Prentice-Hall.

Schank, R. C. 1972: Conceptual dependency: a theory of natural language understanding. *Cognitive Psychology*, 3, 4, 552–630.

Schank, R. C. 1973: Identification of conceptualizations underlying natural language. In R. C. Schank and K. M. Colby (eds), *Computer models of thought and language*. San Francisco: Freeman.

Schank, R. C. 1975: *Conceptual information processing*. Amsterdam: North-Holland.

Schank, R. C. 1980: Language and memory. *Cognitive Science*, 4, 243–84.

Schank, R. C. 1982: *Dynamic memory.* Cambridge: Cambridge University Press.

Schank, R. C. 1984: *The cognitive computer.* Reading, Mass.: Addison-Wesley.

Schank, R. C. and Abelson, R. F. 1977: *Scripts, plans, goals and understanding.* Hillsdale, NJ: Lawrence Erlbaum.

Schank, R. C. and Rieger, C. J. 1974: Inference and the computer understanding of natural language. *Artificial Intelligence,* 5, 373–412.

Schank, R. C. and Riesbeck, C. K. 1981: *Inside computer understanding.* Hillsdale, NJ: Lawrence Erlbaum.

Schegloff, E. A., Jefferson, G. and Sacks, H. 1977: The preference for self-correction in the organization of repair in conversation. *Language,* 53, 361–82.

Schegloff, E. A. and Sacks, H. 1973: Opening up closings. *Semiotics,* 8, 289–327.

Schenkein, J. (ed.) 1978: *Studies in the organization of conversational interaction.* New York: Academic Press.

Searle, J. R. 1980: Minds, brains and programs. *The Behavioral and Brain Sciences,* 1, 417–24.

Selfridge, M. 1982: Inference and learning in a computer model of the development of language comprehension in a young child. In W. G. Lehnert and M. H. Ringle (eds), *Strategies for natural language processing.* Hillsdale, NJ: Lawrence Erlbaum.

Shortliffe, E. H. 1976: *Computer-based medical consultations: MYCIN.* New York: American Elsevier.

Simmons, R. F. 1973: Semantic networks: their computation and their use for understanding English sentences. In R. C. Schank and K. M. Colby (eds), *Computer models of thought and language* San Francisco: Freeman & Co.

Simmons, R. F., Klein, S. and McConlogue, K. 1964: Indexing and dependency logic for answering English questions. *American Documentation,* 15, 196–202.

Simmons, R. F. and Slocum, J. 1972: Generating English discourse from semantic networks. *Communications of the ACM,* 15, 10, 891–905.

Sinclair, J. M. and Coulthard, M. 1975: *Towards an analysis of discourse: the English used by teachers and pupils.* Oxford: Oxford University Press.

Sparck Jones, K. and Wilks, Y. (eds), 1985: *Automatic natural language parsing.* Chichester: Ellis Horwood.

Stubbs, M. 1983: *Discourse analysis: the sociolinguistic analysis of natural language.* Oxford: Basil Blackwell.

Sudnow, D. (ed.) 1972: *Studies in social interaction.* New York: Academic Press.

Tennant, H. 1980: *Evaluation of natural language processors.* Technical report T–103, Coordinated Science Laboratory, University of Illinois.

Tennant, H. 1981: *Natural language processing.* New York: Petrocelli.

Thompson, B. H. 1980: Linguistic analysis of natural language communications with computers. *Proceedings of Coling80,* Tokyo, 190–210.

Turing, A. M. 1950: Computing machinery and intelligence. *Mind,* 59, 433–60.

Walker, D. (ed.), 1978: *Understanding spoken language.* New York: Elsevier North-Holland.

Wanner, E. 1980: The ATN and the sausage machine: which one is baloney? *Cognition* 8, 209–25.

Wanner, E. 1981: The parser's window. In T. Myers, J. Laver and J. Anderson (eds), *The cognitive representation of speech*. Amsterdam: North-Holland.

Weischedel. R. M. and Sondheimer, N. K. 1983: Meta-rules as a basis for processing ill-formed input. *American Journal of Computational Linguistics*, 9, 3/4, 161–77.

Weizenbaum, J. 1966: ELIZA – a computer program for the study of natural language communication between man and machine. *CACM*, 9, 36–45.

Weizenbaum, J. 1967: Contextual understanding by computers. *Communications of the ACM*, 10, 474–80.

Weizenbaum, J. 1984: *Computer power and human reason: from judgement to calculation*. Harmondsworth: Penguin.

Wilensky, R. 1981: PAM. In R. C. Schank and C. K. Riesbeck (eds), *Inside computer understanding*. Hillsdale, NJ: Lawrence Erlbaum.

Wilks, Y. 1985: Right attachment and preference semantics. *Proceedings of the second conference of the European chapter of the Association for Computational Linguistics*.

Winograd, T. 1972: *Understanding natural language*. New York: Academic Press.

Winograd, T. 1973: A procedural model of language understanding. In R. C. Schank and K. M. Colby (eds), *Computer models of thought and language*. San Francisco: Freeman.

Winograd, T. 1981: What does it mean to understand language? In D. A. Norman (ed.), *Perspectives on cognitive science*. Norwood, NJ: Ablex.

Winograd, T. 1983: *Language as a cognitive process. Vol. 1: Syntax*. Reading, Mass.: Addison-Wesley.

Winston, P. H. 1984: *Artificial intelligence*. Reading, Mass.: Addison-Wesley.

Winston, P. H. and Prendergast, K. A. (eds), 1984: *The AI business: the commercial uses of artificial intelligence*. Cambridge, Mass.: MIT Press.

Woods, W. A., Nash-Webber, B. L. and Kaplan, R. M. 1972 *The Lunar sciences natural language system final report*. BBN report 3438, Cambridge, Mass.: Bolt Beranek and Newman.

Yazdani, M. 1982: *Story writing by computer*. Research report R-106, University of Exeter.

Yazdani, M. (ed.), 1986: *Artificial intelligence: principles and applications*. London: Chapman and Hall.

Zampoli, A. (ed.) 1977: *Linguistics structures processing: computational linguistics and artificial intelligence*. New York: Elsevier North-Holland.

Author Index

Subject Index